Tradition and Subversion
in Renaissance Literature

Medieval & Renaissance Literary Studies

General Editor
Albert C. Labriola

Advisory Editor
Foster Provost

Editorial Board
Judith H. Anderson
Diana Treviño Benet
Donald Cheney
Ann Baynes Coiro
Mary T. Crane
Patrick Cullen
A. C. Hamilton
Margaret P. Hannay
A. Kent Hieatt
Michael Lieb
Thomas P. Roche Jr.
Mary Beth Rose
John T. Shawcross
John M. Steadman
Humphrey Tonkin
Susanne Woods

Tradition and Subversion in Renaissance Literature

Studies in Shakespeare, Spenser, Jonson, and Donne

Murray Roston

DUQUESNE
UNIVERSITY
PRESS

Copyright © 2007 Duquesne University Press
All rights reserved

Published in the United States of America by
DUQUESNE UNIVERSITY PRESS
600 Forbes Avenue
Pittsburgh, Pennsylvania 15282

No part of this book may be used or reproduced,
in any manner or form whatsoever,
without written permission from the publisher,
except in the case of short quotations
in critical articles or reviews.

Library of Congress Cataloging-in-Publication Data

Roston, Murray.
  Tradition and subversion in Renaissance literature : studies in Shakespeare, Spenser, Jonson, and Donne / Murray Roston.
       p. cm.—(Medieval & Renaissance literary studies)
  Summary: "Roston offers detailed and essentially new analyses of works by Shakespeare, Spenser, Jonson, and Donne, arguing that the seemingly contradictory presence of traditional and subversive elements in their major works actually creates the source of much of their literary achievement"—Provided by publisher.
  Includes bibliographical references and index.
  ISBN-13: 978-0-8207-0390-9 (alk. paper)
  ISBN-10: 0-8207-0390-7 (alk. paper)
      1. English literature—Early modern, 1500–1700—History and criticism. 2. Shakespeare, William, 1564–1616—Criticism and interpretation. 3. Spenser, Edmund, 1552?–1599—Criticism and interpretation. 4. Jonson, Ben, 1573?–1637—Criticism and interpretation. 5. Donne, John, 1572–1631—Criticism and interpretation. 6. Ambiguity in literature. 7. Intertextuality. 8. Renaissance—England. I. Title.
  PR421.R67 2007
  820.9'003—dc22
                             2006039039

∞ Printed on acid-free paper.

Contents

	Acknowledgments	vii
	Introduction	ix
One	Sacred and Secular in *The Merchant of Venice*	1
Two	Hamlet and the Stoic	39
Three	Spenser and the Pagan Gods	87
Four	*Volpone,* Comedy or Mordant Satire?	135
Five	Donne and the Meditative Tradition	171
	Epilogue	213
	Notes	219
	Selected Bibliography	241
	Index	249

Acknowledgments

Excerpts from this book have appeared in *Hamlet Studies*, the *Ben Jonson Journal*, and in *Sacred and Secular in Medieval and Early Modern Cultures: New Essays*, ed. Lawrence Besserman (Basingstoke: Palgrave, 2005). Portions of chapter 5, "Donne and the Meditative Tradition" are reprinted with permission granted by the University of Notre Dame, *Religion & Literature*, Volume 37, Issue 1 (Spring 2005). I am grateful to the editors and publishers of the above-mentioned works for permission to make use of the material here.

I would like to express my thanks to my colleague, A. R. Braunmuller, who commented on the Shakespeare section; to Susan Wadsworth-Booth for her editorial support; to the English Department at UCLA for the hospitality invariably extended to me on my frequent visits there. Lastly, as always, my deepest gratitude and affection to my wife, Faith—for everything.

Introduction

Postmodernist criticism, by acknowledging the arbitrary quality of language and the diacritical nature of sign or word, has led to the view that all literary works contain insoluble disparities entailing ultimately irreconcilable readings. The existence of such *aporia* compels us, we are told, to discard the concept of a work's autonomy. In a seminal definition of that view, J. Hillis Miller saw the co-presence in any text of host and parasite, of text and subtext, as producing for the critic an inevitable "undecidability," an impasse that in effect paralyzes literary analysis, creating a blank wall beyond which rational analysis cannot go:

> Far from being a chain which moves deeper and deeper into the text, closer and closer to it, the mode of criticism sometimes now called "deconstruction" which is analytic criticism as such, encounters always, if it is carried far enough, some mode of oscillation. In this oscillation two genuine insights into literature in general and into a given text in particular inhibit, subvert, and undercut one another. This inhibition makes it impossible for either insight to function as a firm resting place, the end point of analysis.[1]

It is a view repeated many times over, as in Barthes's statement that "writing ceaselessly posits meaning ceaselessly to evaporate it, carrying out a systematic exemption of meaning," or, as he expressed the concept elsewhere: "the meaning of a text can be nothing but the plurality of its Systems, its infinite (circular) 'transcribability': one system transcribes another, but reciprocally as well: with regard to the text, there is no 'primary,' 'natural,' 'national,' 'mother' critical language: from the outset, as it is created, the text is multilingual; there is no entrance language or exit language."[2]

In the flood of books that has followed, the negative implications of that approach have predominated, with only rare exceptions, one of which is especially notable. Mikhail M. Bakhtin's theory of the "dialogic imagination," while acknowledging the multiplicity of contradictory meanings within literary works, defines multiplicity not as a disqualification but as a positive value, singling out the novel as exemplifying in its finest form the thematic and linguistic tensions created by the varied and often antithetical viewpoints that the genre makes possible. The diverse speech-types, social class, and personal viewpoints of the fictional characters in a novel, as well as their contrasting interrelationships, by resisting the univocal effect of the narrator's authorial voice, produce what he terms "heteroglossia," a clash of viewpoints and stylistic forms that generates the vitality of the work.

Within the dissentient elements of the novel, Bakhtin perceives two primary forces, the "centripetal," which canonizes traditional linguistic and cultural patterns, and the "centrifugal," which subverts or challenges them:

> Every concrete utterance of a speaking subject serves as a point where centrifugal as well as centripetal forces are brought to bear. The processes of centralization and decentralization, of unification and disunification, intersect in the utterance; the utterance not only answers the requirements of its own language as an individualized embodiment

of a speech act, but it answers the requirements of heteroglossia as well; it is in fact an active participant in such speech diversity.

In the novel, the result is a dialogically agitated environment of alien words and alien value judgments, weaving in and out in complex interrelationships, merging with some, recoiling from others, and intersecting with further groups to shape the complex discourse of prose fiction. Such internal stratification, Bakhtin argues, is not to be found in other literary genres. Poetry, in his view, epitomizes the univocal, the poet being "utterly immersed" in his or her own language, making use of each word and expression according to its unmediated power to assign meaning. The epic, by valorizing the past, adopts a canonical rigidity locking out the possibility of open-endedness. Drama, especially tragedy, Bakhtin excludes on the grounds that it is centripetal, pulling the reader toward the dominant contemporary ideologue, its leading characters drawn from royalty or aristocracy, from figures in "high estate," and hence negating the possibility of variegated social interaction.[3]

The one troubling aspect of this stimulating theory is Bakhtin's limitation of it to the genre of the novel. The concept of heteroglossia is surely even more applicable to the theater than to the novel, since drama, lacking a narrator, is deprived of any authorial, univocal voice, and is hence restricted to conveying its ideas through the dialogical exchanges of the individual characters. Audience or critic, in attempting to discern the underlying message of a play, must resort tangentially to the comments of supposedly "choric" figures, sources whose function in that capacity may be open to doubt, so that the heteroglossia is even more marked there than in the novel. And the same applies to class; for if the leading characters in tragedy are indeed drawn from the upper social levels, it is frequently the lower-class characters—the porter in *Macbeth*, the gravediggers in *Hamlet*, the nonaristocratic Iago—that serve most effectively either to convey or to subvert the main theme, evidencing the existence in drama of that same sociological and linguistic variety as Bakhtin finds in the novel. To give one example, Shakespeare may have sympathized in general with the Elizabethan faith in the Chain of Being, in the order of the heavens, and in the close relationship between microcosm and macrocosm, evidenced in the fear so often expressed in his plays that the "late eclipses in the sun and moon portend no good to us." But the scorn that the bastard Edmund pours on his father's statement, rejecting it as the crassest superstition, is so powerfully presented that its negative effect must reverberate throughout the play, creating that same complexity of response that Bakhtin finds in the novel, a validation of emergent Renaissance skepticism that undercuts and challenges the predominant view of hierarchical, cosmic order:

> Edmund: ... we make guilty of our disasters the sun, the moon, and the stars; as if we were villains on necessity; fools by heavenly compulsion; knaves, thieves, and treachers by spherical pre-dominance; drunkards, liars, and adulterers by an enforc'd obedience of planetary influence; and all that we are evil in, by a divine thrusting on. An admirable evasion of whore-master man, to lay his goatish disposition to the charge of a star! My father compounded with my mother under the Dragon's Tail, and my nativity was under Ursa Major, so that it follows, I am rough and lecherous. Fut! I should have been that I am, had the maidenl'est star in the firmament twinkled on my bastardizing.[4]

The application of Bakhtin's theory to those literary genres that he excluded from it—poetry, drama, and epic—constitutes a challenge to the deconstructionists' view of *aporia*, suggesting that the conflict of text and subtext that they have come to regard as negating any possibility of coherent interpretation needs to be seen as a positive feature, a complexity of response, animating, profoundly enriching, and, at times, forming the motive force of each work. Such is the theme coordinating the following chapters, an exploration of the creative tension between centripetal and centrifugal factors, between tradition and subversion, in the variegated genres listed above, as well as from a further genre that might, because of its doctrinal affiliation, be thought exempt from such inner conflict, namely, religious prose. I have restricted my quotations from deconstructionists to the pronouncements of its founders and leading exponents, since they provide the most reliable definitions of that critical approach. Deconstruction has frequently been announced dead,[5] yet continues to inform all aspects of criticism, not least the teaching of literature in colleges and universities. It is both crucial and timely to reassess its conclusions.

ONE

Sacred and Secular in
The Merchant of Venice

The Merchant of Venice contains an extraordinary number of biblical allusions. It repeatedly echoes or cites passages from the Gospels, from Ecclesiasticus, from Corinthians, and from the Old Testament at large. To an Elizabethan audience, familiar with the Bible from regular readings both in church and in the family setting, those allusions would have created a complex of connective filaments and associations, both verbal and thematic, that affect cumulatively the overall message of the play. The scriptural element is not obtrusive, the drama being dramatically energized and variegated by such nonscriptural elements as Bassanio's journey to the magical world of Belmont, the clowning of Launcelot Gobbo, and the lively theme of misplaced rings with which it concludes. But the plethora of biblical allusions, however latent, signals the existence of a subdued yet pervasive concern with some religious theme. That subdued theme, marking the play's traditional or centripetal aspect, will be explored in the first half of the chapter, after which we shall turn to the subversive or centrifugal elements relevant to our present concerns.

Shakespeare was no pietist. The religious elements in his plays do not, in general, involve matters of doctrinal or sectarian dispute. They indicate only the author's allegiance to the broadest moral principles of Christianity, to the ideals of compassion, altruism, and forgiveness as represented by Cordelia, Edgar, or Desdemona. Even the plays dealing most prominently with those Christian virtues, such as *Measure for Measure,* lack the proliferation of biblical references and quotations that distinguish this play, which includes a dispute over the theological lessons to be derived from Jacob's method of increasing his flock, reiterated allusions to whited sepulchers, the parody of Isaac's blessing in Gobbo's encounter with his father,[1] and Shylock's premature assumption that Portia is a Daniel come to judgment. In that latter instance, only an audience familiar with the story of Susanna and the Elders in the Apocrypha would grasp the irony of Shylock regarding himself as an innocent Susanna about to be vindicated, while those witnessing the court proceedings identify him more accurately, together with his friend Tubal, with the corrupt elders of that story, perverting justice to serve their own ends.

In a justly admired article, Barbara Lewalski many years ago defined the underlying theme of the play as the victory of the New Law over the Old, the triumph of Christian ethics over Hebraic legalism.[2] Antonio, embodying the ideals of selflessness, generosity, and love, eminently fulfills in his generous loan to Bassanio the Gospel injunction: "Giue to euerie man that asketh of thee: . . . do good, and lend, looking for nothing in return, and your rewarde shalbe great" (Luke 6:30, 35).[3] In that context, Shylock, associated by his Jewish ancestry with the Old Testament, represents the antithesis of Christian benevolence.

Shylock, however, represents not the Old Testament itself—for that body of law was no less insistent upon the requirement to love one's neighbor as oneself, to provide interest-free loans to the needy, and to care for the widow and the orphan. Shylock embodies instead the code of the Pharisees as they are depicted with hostility in the New Testament, the rabbis viewed there as perverters of the covenant, as mere "scribes" insisting upon the letter of the law rather than the mercy implicit within it, to be revitalized by the New Law: "Wo be to you, Scribes and Pharises, hypocrites: for ye tithe mynt, & annyse, & cummyn, & leaue the weightier matters of the law, as iudgement, and mercy and fidelitie. These ought ye to haue done, and not to haue left the other" (Matt. 23:23).

The identification of the Pharisee with the sterner aspects of law, with the revenge principle of an eye for an eye and a tooth for a tooth, had been dictated in large part by a theological factor. Within the Old Testament, God, the sole ruler of the universe, had been not only the arbiter of justice and executor of vengeance but also the source of divine love and mercy. He was indeed a zealous God, "visiting the iniquitie of the fathers vpon the children, vpon the third generation and vpon the fourth of them that hate me," but he was at the same time a God of benevolence, "shewing mercie vnto thousandes to them that loue me, & keepe my commandements" (Exod. 20:5–6). But the transfer of the more amiable qualities of the divine to Jesus at the advent of Christianity left God the Father with only the harsher functions, the tasks of imposing Law and exacting retribution— attributes now represented by the Gospels as characterizing in their worst form the rabbis or Pharisees of the day who, of course, rejected the Trinity. There, the latter stand accused of bigotry, demanding the letter of the law in order to exact the maximum penalty from transgressors, rather than granting the forgiveness and love now seen as the distinguishing qualities of the new faith.

Lewalski's perception of the play as representing the victory of the New Law over the Old is explored in some detail as she traces many of the play's scriptural allusions to their source. But there is a problem in her reading of the play, which she herself admits. If Antonio embodies Christian virtue in the matter of the loan, he is, Lewalski points out, sadly lacking in a further and no less fundamental principle—the injunction to love one's enemies, as set forth in a passage in the Gospels that articulates the central contrast posed in this play, the love, altruism, and generosity of the new faith as against the grasping, selfish, and legalistic impulses of the old: "Ye haue heard that it hath bin said, Thou shalt loue thy neighbour, and hate your enemie. But I say vnto you, Loue your enemies: blesse them that curse you: doe good to them that hate you, and pray for them which hurt you, and persecute you" (Matt. 5:43–47). Antonio at the outset of the play, Lewalski remarks, lacks the basic virtue delineated here; for if he loves Bassanio, he reveals only contempt and hatred for his enemy, Shylock. He spurns him, calls him dog, voids his rheum upon him, and when charged with such persecution, declares stubbornly, "I am as like to call thee so again, / To spet on thee again, to spurn thee too" (1.3.130–31). That, Lewalski maintains, is a flaw, a grave moral blemish that he will need to correct by the end of the play, as when he waives the fine imposed on Shylock.

If Lewalski is right and Antonio does undergo a process of self-improvement, maturing and learning forgiveness in the course of the play, Shakespeare does not prepare us for that spiritual amelioration. No hint of remorse on Antonio's part is suggested to make such moral change credible. But there is a more serious problem in Lewalski's reading, this apparently minor element having, I believe, profound implications for an understanding of the play. The assumption that Antonio's harsh treatment of Shylock is un-Christian prevents Lewalski, as it has prevented later critics, from perceiving the major mythological underpinning of the drama. The Christian, it is true, is enjoined to turn the other cheek, to submit patiently to abuse, to love and forgive those who smite him or her; but there is one fundamental exception—

the Christian is to reach no such accommodation with the devil. On the contrary, Christians are to be ever on their guard, hostile to any approach and firm in their resistance to Satan. "Put on the whole armour of God," Paul warns, "that ye may be able to stand against the assaultes of the deuil" (Ephes. 6:11). Antonio's spurning of Shylock is thus in full accord with Jesus' rebuke, "Get thee behind me, Satan, thou art an offence vnto me" (Matt. 16:23), and echoes his rejection of Satan's temptations in the wilderness.

If Shylock is a devil figure, as I propose to argue, and Antonio is, accordingly, justified in spitting on his gabardine, Lewalski's perception of a failing in Antonio's character falls aside, leaving him serving in this play as a flawless embodiment of the Christian ideal. Once that point is made, the mythological subtext that Lewalski misses becomes apparent—the play being in the fullest sense not only a contrast between the New Testament and the Old but, in addition, a reenactment of the Crucifixion story located within the contemporary setting of Venice, where a Jew attempts to shed the blood of a Christ figure. Shakespeare's version has, of course, a happy ending, constituting what Freud calls "wish-fulfillment," Christ's death being replaced by the more congenial scene of a last-minute reversal of judgment. But the basic tale remains the same, together with the lessons intended to be derived from it, and the text repeatedly confirms the parallel. Antonio, before knowing of the clause that will be inserted in Shylock's contract, declares himself ready not only to lend Bassanio money but, like his New Testament counterpart, to offer his body for his friend's salvation, to sacrifice for Bassanio "my purse, *my person*, my extremest means." Later, when preparing for death, he echoes the words and images associated with Christ, opposing his "patience" to Shylock's fury, declaring himself "armed / To suffer, with a quietness of spirit, / The very tyranny and rage" of his persecutor (4.1.9–11) and describing himself, with patent allusion to the Lamb of God, as a "tainted wether of the flock / Meetest for death"

(4.1.114–15)—with "tainted" in its original sense of "tinged" or "marked out," and with no pejorative connotation.[4] If he is, as the text suggests, a Christ figure, to argue that he needs to improve, that he must learn to turn the other cheek, would imply a failing in Christ himself.

The recognition that Antonio represents Jesus illumines a facet of the play that has long proved puzzling to critics, the unexplained melancholy of Antonio in the first scene. Its importance could not be more marked, as it opens the play, Antonio declaring,

> In sooth, I know not why I am so sad;
> It wearies me, you say it wearies you;
> But how I caught it, found it, or came by it,
> What stuff 'tis made of, whereof it is born,
> I am to learn.

From his exchange with his friends Salerio and Solanio, the audience learns that his sadness derives neither from financial care nor from unrequited love; but no reason for the melancholy is proffered, either here or elsewhere in the play. L. L. Schücking, finding it puzzlingly extraneous to the play, suggests that it is a relic from an earlier version, while others think it must arise from Antonio's sadness at Bassanio's imminent departure (although the audience as yet knows nothing of that parting and would thus fail to perceive the reason).[5] Once, however, he is seen in terms of a Christ figure, the reason becomes evident. Alone among the leading male characters, he must, like his celibate model, be gravely segregated from romantic love and humorous byplay.[6] In the midst of Gobbo's clowning, the comic exchange of the rings, and the love affairs being pursued around him, Antonio remains solemn and aloof, as befits his shadowy role: "I hold the world but as the world, Gratiano, / A stage, where every man must play a part, / And mine a sad one" (1.1.77–79).

Since it has become customary in our own day to view Shylock sympathetically as the wronged member of an oppressed minority, it may be necessary to spend a moment on that point before turning to our main theme. Transferring the villainy in this play to the Christians has become customary in contemporary criticism—Leslie Fiedler describes Portia as expressing "in a ritual of Jew-baiting not only her own anti-Semitism, but that of all the other characters in the play," while many have described the entire play as "crudely antisemitic," an attitude resulting in a tendency to side with Shylock.[7] However, the sympathetic reading of Shylock's character as victim or scapegoat—understandable as it may be in a post-Holocaust era, in a generation that has, we hope, learned to deplore racism—ignores or downplays the fact not only that the text identifies him repeatedly as a devil but that his own daughter Jessica, clearly one of the heroines as evidenced in the charming love-scene towards the end, regards him with similar aversion, expressing her thankfulness that, though she be a daughter to his blood, she is not to his manners (2.3.17–19). She symbolizes, as Harold Fisch notes, the Christian belief in the conversion of the Jews that was to precede the coming of the Messiah, and in fulfilling that symbolic role she is contrasted with the perversity of her father. In that, Jessica parallels Marlowe's Abigail who, in *The Jew of Malta*, similarly rejects her father's faith by entering a convent.[8] Any attempt in a modern staging of the play to avoid anti-Semitic implications by presenting Shylock sympathetically is, however admirable in its intent, not only a violation of the text but also a misunderstanding of the play. My purpose here, however, is not to solve the problem involved in staging the play for a modern audience without causing offense, but to explore the message of the play as it would have been received by the Elizabethan audience for which it was intended.

An element of theatrical history underscores the contrast. An Elizabethan audience, familiar with the mystery cycles, would have immediately identified Gobbo as the comic vice who traditionally accompanied his master, the devil, that recognition carrying obvious implications for the character of Shylock himself.[9] Lest anyone miss the point, as Gobbo is about to leave his master's service, Jessica declares that Shylock's house is hell, "and thou, a merry devil, / Didst rob it of some taste of tediousness." Time after time, Shylock himself is named a devil in the play, whether as a devil citing Scripture for his purpose or, in Gobbo's garbled phrase, as "the very devil incarnation." Moreover, no modern attempt to soften his character can mute the horror of the scene in which he maliciously sharpens the knife upon his shoe in preparation for excising the pound of flesh, an action prompting Gratiano's choric protest:

> Not on thy sole, but on thy soul, harsh Jew,
> Thou mak'st thy knife keen; but no metal can,
> No, not the hangman's axe, bear half the keenness
> Of thy sharp envy.   (4.1.123–26)

The duke is surely expressing the audience's view when he describes Shylock, insisting on his pound of flesh, as, "A stony adversary, an inhuman wretch, / Uncapable of pity, void and empty / From any dram of mercy" (4.1.4–6).

Sympathetic readings of Shylock's character have, of course, based themselves upon the famed "Hath not a Jew" speech, expressing the Jew's resentment of the treatment meted out to him as the member of a despised minority, and the charge that his tormentors fail to regard him as human. But Shakespeare characteristically allows such moments of insight or commiseration even to the most villainous of his characters without detracting from the audience's ultimate sense of their turpitude. Richard III, in his opening soliloquy, expresses his justified grievance against heaven for having made him a hunchback, a physical deformity depriving him of the accoutrements requisite for romance or career advancement:

> I, that am not shap'd for sportive tricks,
> Nor made to court an amorous looking-glass;
> I, that am rudely stamp'd, and want love's majesty

To strut before a wanton ambling nymph,
I, that am curtail'd of this fair proportion,
Cheated of feature by dissembling nature,
Deform'd, unfinish'd, sent before my time
Into this breathing world, scarce half made up.

Such misfortune entitles him, Richard claims, to use every means to circumvent the handicap. But as he proceeds on his evil path, the crimes he commits leave no room for further compassion. So Shylock's complaint does seem momentarily warranted, evoking a temporary degree of empathy; but in a drama contrasting Christian forgiveness with Old Testament reprisal, the chilling conclusion of his speech would scarcely have won respect from an Elizabethan audience: "and if you wrong us, shall we not revenge?" Another passage in the play often seen as arousing some degree of compassion, the depiction of Shylock running through the streets crying desperately, "My daughter! O my ducats," does not record Shylock's words. They are Solanio's mocking parody of Shylock, the latter at no time behaving so incoherently upon the stage.

Shylock, in this reenactment of the Crucifixion, is not only a counterpart to the devil, as he is repeatedly identified by the Christian characters, but serves also in the role of Judas Iscariot who, in medieval drama, had been merged with the devil. That merger was based on Jesus' remark to his disciples, "Haue not I chosen you twelue, and one of you is a deuill?" (John 6:70), as well as the statement: "Then entred Satan into Iudas, who was called Iscariot" (Luke 22:3). The red wig and red beard traditionally worn on the stage by Shylock underscored the equation, as those were the accoutrements distinguishing Judas in numerous depictions from the fourteenth century onward, such as *The Last Supper* by Master Bertram and two anonymous *Betrayal* scenes in Aachen and Nuremburg.[10] Moreover, the association of the name Judas with "Jew" has heightened the equation through generations. Lest anyone should miss the association, Shakespeare includes a patent reference for his audiences. After Shylock's condemnation in court for the attempted murder of a Christ figure, Gratiano gleefully offers him a rope to hang himself—recalling the suicide of Judas as recorded in the Gospels. Such parallels between the Crucifixion and Shylock's infamous contract are pursued throughout the play, the centrality of the shedding of a drop of blood on which the court reversal is based, hinting both at the Eucharist and the Holy Grail.

The ramifications of this underpinning are extensive. Recurring throughout the play's imagery as well as its plot are allusions to one of the basic conflicts between the Christian and the Pharisee, namely the former's claim that God "hath made vs able ministers of the Newe testament, not of the letter, but of the Spirite: for the letter killeth, but the Spirite giueth life" (2 Cor. 3:6). If the Pharisee, scrutinizing each jot and tittle of the text, was obsessed with the outward form or letter of the law, the Christians aimed at restoring and fulfilling the inner truths that, they claimed, had been suppressed in that process. The time had come, Christians argued, for the true Jew (by which was meant the new Christian due to supersede the previous heirs of the covenant) to rescue the spiritual import of the Scriptures that had been forgotten or discarded by the legalists: "For hee is not a Iewe, which is one outwarde: neither is that circumcision, which is outward in the flesh: But he is a Iewe which is one within, and the circumcision is of the heart, in the spirite not in the letter, whose praise is not of men, but of God" (Rom. 2:28–29). Hence Shylock's insistence on the precise wording of the contract, his reliance on the "jot and tittle" so derided in the New Testament. The sole response he offers to Portia's humane query, whether he has provided a surgeon to stop Antonio's wound, is to scrutinize the text for written evidence: "Is it so nominated in the bond? . . . I cannot find it, 'tis not in the bond" (4.1.259–62). Hence also Shakespeare's preference for the word "bond" rather than "contract," with its connotation of constraining or binding the victim by the written word in contrast to the Christian demand for liberality. Thus,

Shylock demands from the gaoler a closer confinement of Antonio, insisting with nauseating repetition:

> I'll have my bond. I will not hear thee speak;
> I'll have my bond; and therefore speak no more.
> I'll not be made a soft and dull-ey'd fool,
> To shake the head, relent, and sigh, and yield,
> To Christian intercessors. Follow not;
> I'll have no speaking; I will have my bond. (3.3.12–17)

That contrast between the Pharisaic insistence on the letter and the Christian preference for the spirit is subtly echoed in the seemingly irrelevant casket scene. Although it formed no part of *Il Pecorone* and was in all likelihood derived from an entirely different source, namely the *Gesta Romanorum*, as usual Shakespeare did not merely import it but made it intrinsic to the plot. Bassanio's deliberation before his choice highlights the distinction between outer and inner worth, between letter and spirit, and he specifically relates that distinction to the twin spheres of law and religion in which false interpreters of texts obscure its spirit:

> So may the outward shows be least themselves—
> The world is still deceiv'd with ornament.
> In law, what plea so tainted and corrupt
> But, being season'd with a gracious voice,
> Obscures the show of evil? In religion,
> What damned error but some sober brow
> Will bless it, and approve it with a text. (3.2.73–79)

In law, Shylock has twisted the wording of the contract to suit his needs, transforming a "merry bond" into a vicious trap. In religion, like the Pharisee he represents, he has distorted the scriptural text to justify vengeance in place of love. He is, as Antonio describes him in that same contrast of outer and inner worth, a villain with a smiling cheek, a goodly apple rotten at the heart (1.3.100–101).

The New Testament had, in fact, offered a further image for such duplicity, an image recurring in this play: "Wo be to you, Scribes and Pharises, hypocrites: for ye are like vnto whited tombes, which appeare beautifull outward, but are within full of dead mens bones, and all filthines" (Matt. 23:27). It is echoed in the scroll that Morocco discovers inside the golden casket: "Many a man his life hath sold / But my outside to behold. / Gilded tombs do worms infold" (2.7.67–69), the casket itself containing a carrion Death's head.

One aspect of the play would seem to militate against this disparagement of the letter of the law; for Portia at the climax of the trial scene does resort to scrutinizing the precise wording of the contract in order to frustrate Shylock's plan, observing that it contains no permission to extract a drop of blood. But there is no contradiction. Jesus had stated explicitly, "Think not that I am come to destroy the Lawe, or the Prophets. I am not come to destroy them, but to fulfill them," adding, "For truely I say vnto you, Till heauen, and earth perish, one iote or one title of the Law shall not scape, till all things be fulfilled" (Matt. 5:17–18). His aim was not to nullify the Law but to restore the spirit of the Law that had, he believed, been suppressed by the rabbinic legalists. And that is exactly what Portia effects here. The law, even the secular law of Venice, she repeatedly declares, must be upheld. Bassanio may beseech her, "Wrest once the law to your authority; / To do a great right do a little wrong" (4.1.213–14), but Portia insists on the law's validity, just as Antonio himself does in rejecting Solanio's belief that the Duke will bend the law in this exceptional instance:

> The Duke cannot deny the course of law;
> For the commodity that strangers have
> With us in Venice, if it be denied,
> Will much impeach the justice of the state.   (3.3.26–31)

Thus Portia, exemplifying the principle laid down in the Gospels, extracts from the letter of the law, from the same jot or tittle of the text so misused by the Pharisees, the quality of mercy that had been obscured in Shylock's reading of the contract.

With the rescue triumphantly effected, the contrast between the Christian and Pharisaical principles is now demonstrated in action. Critics have frequently referred to the harsh treatment of Shylock at the play's conclusion, Hermann Sinsheimer complaining that the cruelty of the Christians "smashes the representative of Jewry with the hammer weight of legality."[11] But that is a stricture not borne out by the text. Portia may insist that Shylock will have all justice, that he shall have nothing but the penalty; but that is only before the dramatic turnabout, as she attempts to intimidate him in the hope that he will yet withdraw his demands. The moment, however, that he is convicted, the Christians demonstrate their commitment to mercy. The duke, distinguishing between the New and the Old Law, declares, "That thou shalt see the difference of our spirit / I pardon thee thy life before thou ask it," and he proceeds, in addition, to reduce the confiscation of property to half on condition that Shylock show remorse. Portia then turns to Shylock's intended victim, the one most likely to demand the harshest sentencing, with the query, "What mercy can you render him?" Antonio's response is at once to waive all claim to Shylock's fine.[12] If the forced conversion is distasteful to a modern audience, it marked for the Elizabethan the granting to Shylock of his sole chance of heavenly redemption, that aspect prepared for in the amusing exchange between Gobbo and Jessica concerning her chances of salvation. There, Gobbo can only offer her the "bastard" hope that she will prove not to be her father's daughter, to which Jessica replies that she will be saved by her husband, who has made her a Christian (3.5.17).

The play, then, is steeped in theological debate, revealing Shakespeare's preoccupation here with the most traditional of Christian precepts. Disparate as the comic scenes may appear, they reflect and reinforce the play's central message, the concluding caper with the rings, for example, relying for its humor upon this theme of letter and spirit, outer and inner value. A wedding ring, by its circular form and the intrinsic value of its metal, is a symbol of unending love and fidelity. The oath imposed by Portia and Nerissa forbidding their lovers to part with the rings has, as she and the audience know full well, been violated by them only in the literal sense. They have parted with the material object, but have remained true to the spirit of their pledge. When Gratiano dismisses the quarrel as concerning only,

> a hoop of gold, a paltry ring
> That she did give me, whose posy was
> For all the world like cutler's poetry
> Upon a knife, "Love me, and leave me not," (5.1.147–50)

he regards the word "me" in the inscription as referring to the external symbol of their troth, the ring itself, while the pretended anger of both Nerissa and Portia focuses upon the inner significance, the conjugal loyalty it symbolizes. And the same principle, by extension, underlies the humor in Portia's threat to sleep with the chimerical doctor, the word "jewel," while ostensibly referring to the ring, slyly connoting the "treasure" of maidenhood she had been preserving for Bassanio, a reference reinforced by the biblical undertone of the subsequent "know":

> Let not that doctor e'er come near my house,
> Since he hath got the jewel that I loved,
> And that which you did swear to keep for me,
> I will become as liberal as you,
> I'll not deny him any thing I have,
> No, not my body, nor my husband's bed.
> Know him I shall, I am well sure of it. (5.1.223–29)

The scene is thus not extraneous, but intrinsically related to this biblical distinction between letter and spirit that underlies the play at large.

ès

We may seem to have moved far away from the problem of *aporia*, but it was essential to establish those aspects of the play that were "centripetal," reinforcing the traditional teachings of Christianity. It is now time to turn to the subversive elements. Why did Shakespeare, who is elsewhere so loath to engage in the details of Christian doctrine, choose so theological a subject? Much has been written on the play's focus upon usury, on the assumption that the unsavory depiction of Shylock reflected Shakespeare's condemnation of the practice.[13] Numerous protests were being voiced at that time as moneylenders began to employ subterfuges and chicanery to circumvent the 10 percent limitation on interest imposed in 1571, and they extorted considerable sums for the service. The complaint arose "that instead of charitable dealing, and the use of alms (for lending is a spice thereof), hardness of heart hath now gotten place, and greedy gain is chiefly followed, and horrible extortion commonly used?"[14] Lenders began linking loans to fluctuations in foreign currency as a method of avoiding the legal restriction, or used land transactions to disguise the loan. As Tawney records, when Lord Shrewsbury approached a leading moneylender, Sir Horatio Pallavicino, for a loan of £3,000, the arrangement to which the unfortunate Lord was forced to agree in return for that sum was to convey to Sir Horatio a parcel of land that was in fact worth £7,000, more than double the sum loaned and, in addition, to pay all legal and other expenses, the land to be forfeited in its entirety in the event that the mortgage was not paid off within three months. How profitable these subterfuges proved is evidenced by a report submitted to Lord Burghley in 1597 (about the time this play was written), charging that a certain William Beecher had amassed the sum of £40,000, an immense sum in that period, by such circumvention of the law.

Yet the relevance of all this to the play is, in the final analysis, minimal, since there is firm evidence that Shakespeare was far from being opposed to the practice of usury as such. Within the play, Antonio may proudly insist that he neither lends nor borrows on interest, but he is ready enough to waive that rule to aid his friend, while Bassanio, the beneficiary and the hero of the romance, not only has no hesitation in accepting the offer but also eagerly embraces it. There is, moreover, significant evidence nearer to home, as we know that Shakespeare's family customarily lent out money at 7.5 percent interest, and that Shakespeare himself willingly indulged in such activity. Richard Quiney, in a letter to Sturley in 1598 responding to the latter's enquiry concerning the need for a loan, informed him that Mr. William Shakespeare could probably provide the funds needed on "indifferent conditions."[15] If, therefore, Shylock represents the worst form of moneylending, the demanding of excessive interest and the harsh pursuance of defaulters, activities that are deplored in the play, Shakespeare did not seem unduly concerned about the practice of usury itself, either in his personal life or in his depiction of the Christian characters in the play.

I would like to suggest that there was a more cogent reason for Shakespeare's choice of this theme—his attempt to reach an accommodation between the precepts of his religion and the demands of the new Renaissance economy, not merely as abstract elements but in direct relation to his own concern at this time with enlarging his financial assets, of which the lending out of money formed only one part.

Although discussions of the theme of usury in this play focus upon the taking of interest, in fact medieval Christianity had employed the term "usury" in a much wider sense, including within that category the basic concept of trade itself. With its principle of *contemptus mundi* and its advocacy of the monastic life, no room had been left for doubt concerning the Church's attitude to the acquisition of worldly possessions, "usury" being seen to include any form of profit-making. The definitive canonical work of the Middle Ages, the *Concordia Discordantium Canonum* compiled by the twelfth century Benedictine monk Gratian, had condemned unequivocally the function of middleman or merchant. A craftsman, he pointed out, was justified in requesting payment for the labor he had invested in constructing a stool out of pieces of wood and was therefore entitled to charge a sum over and above the value of the wood itself; but a merchant buying the completed item from him and selling it at a higher price without improving it was, he declared, a mere profiteer. That man, Gratian declared, "is of the buyers and sellers who are cast out from God's temple." As regards usury in its more specific form, the Council of Vienne, meeting in 1312, recorded its dismay on learning of the existence of certain communities which, in defiance of human and divine law, sanctioned interest, compelling debtors to fulfill usurious contracts. It proclaimed accordingly that all rulers and magistrates knowingly maintaining such laws were to incur the penalty of excommunication, and demanded that such legislation be revoked within three months of the decision. Moreover, to put an end to the frequent camouflaging of such transactions, it ordered ecclesiastical authorities to insist that all moneylenders submit their accounts for examination. Any person obstinately maintaining that usury is not a sin was to be punished as a heretic, and inquisitors were commanded to proceed against them.[16]

This was not, we should recall, merely a medieval view but, as Gratian's reference to the casting out of the moneychangers in the Temple confirms, was rooted in the New Testament's condemnation of all forms of acquisitiveness. Discarding possessions and shunning wealth formed a cornerstone of Gospel teaching, Jesus instructing his disciples, "go, sell that thou hast, & giue it to the poore," adding in a famous phrase, "Verely I say vnto you, that a rich man shall hardly enter into the kingdome of heauen" (Matt. 19:21–23). The growth of trade in the Middle Ages had compelled the Church to modify its stand, permitting what was termed "just profit," that is, a minimal profit sufficient to enable the trader to earn a livelihood; but anything beyond that was, it warned, avarice and hence sinful.

The command in Deuteronomy 23:19–20, while permitting interest-bearing loans to Gentiles, warns, "Thou shalt not giue to vsurie to thy brother." In the fourth century, this verse was interpreted by Jerome, in the new world of universal Christian brotherhood, as a prohibition binding on all members of the Church.[17] This view persisted through the centuries and was confirmed by the Second Lateran Council of 1139, which went so far as to deny Christian burial to all unrepentant usurers. Under the pressure of changing times, the Church did make certain allowances in 1425, when it permitted public loans such as rent contracts (*census utrimque redimibilis*), a concession of which it made full use for its own advantage. As is well known, it was the prohibition imposed on Christians that led to the use of the Jews as a means of supplying the community's needs in that regard, with the added "advantage" that, once a sizable amount of wealth had been accumulated by the Jewish moneylenders, they could be stripped of it and expelled from the country.

What concerns us more closely in connection with this play is the conflict that existed between the condemnation of usury on the one hand—not only of usury in the narrower sense but also of all commercial activity—and, on the other, the demands of Renaissance trade, a conflict accentuated by the rise of Protestantism. In Italy, the growth of trade and banking had coincided with a period when the Catholic Church worked closely with leading bankers, and the Medici family was amassing its immense fortune with full ecclesiastical approval. Pope Leo X was himself a Medici, the son of Lorenzo the Magnificent, that family connection stilling any potential opposition. In Catholic France, Jacques Coeur, who owned banking houses in every city in France and whose merchant ships crisscrossed the Mediterranean, had obtained from his personal friend, Pope Nicholas V, formal permission to trade with the Moslems of Egypt and the Levant, once again because such activity would help fill the coffers of the Church. Bathed in such riches, the Church did not merely ignore the contradictions between the pursuit of wealth and the injunctions of the New Testament but encouraged such activities. In fact, during the fourteenth and fifteenth centuries the monasteries, employing the subterfuge of the rent contracts mentioned above, became the major moneylenders in most European countries, either competing with the Jews or employing them as intermediaries to lessen their sense of responsibility for the transactions, although they remained rigorously in control, personally overseeing each contract. As religious institutions they were, like the papal emissaries collecting *chevisances*, to some degree protected from criticism by their calling, in a manner that the lay merchant was not.[18]

The rise of the Reformation ensured the emergence of a new sensitivity within Protestant countries, not least because the Wittenberg protest had in large part been initiated by opposition to the growing opulence of Rome. That concern, coupled with the new focus upon the text of the Old Testament, whose prohibitions were now seen to be still valid unless specifically revoked in the New, ensured a reassessment of the problem of usury. One of Luther's leading supporters, the fiery preacher Jakob Strauss, initiated in Eisenach in 1523 a savage campaign directed against usurious contracts. The use of the *casus* by the monasteries aroused the ire of Luther, who saw it as a major source of the Church's economic oppression of the poor.[19] In 1540, he declared categorically that all forms of usury were sinful; and if he and other Protestant leaders, such as Melancthon and Bucer, eventually made limited modifications to that ruling, those modifications constituted reluctant concessions to the economic crisis of the time, attempts to relieve the suffering of the indigent rather than an encouragement of commerce itself. Calvin's more lenient approach to the subject, important as it was in granting some legitimacy to mercantile activity, divided the Protestant camp, becoming a frequent object of attack and dissent among his peers. And in the course of these disputes it is important to stress that usury was still seen as including all mercantile activity, as is evidenced in two highly publicized incidents. In Rudolstadt (1564) and Regensburg (1587), preachers reverted to the earlier rulings, denying communion not only to the moneylender but also to the merchant on the grounds that both were comparable to thieves or murderers in flouting the scriptural prohibition of usury.[20]

Those tensions and conflicts not only found their counterpart in Protestant England but also reached their most acute form there at the time Shakespeare composed *The Merchant of Venice*. In response to urgent business demands, interest had, in 1545, been briefly legalized under Henry VIII, but the law proved so offensive to Christian sensitivities that the ruling was formally abrogated a few years later, in 1552, under Edward. The repeal, however, proved impossible to maintain, as usury was intrinsic to commerce. And here was the crux of the problem underlying the play. Merchants planning new undertakings needed substantial loans in order to stock their stores or warehouses; owners of coal mines and initiators of factories in the munitions industry needed to make considerable investment in equipment and to cover the salaries of their workers until profits could be realized. The preamble to the subsequent law of 1571 regretfully admitted that the repeal of the 1545 law had proved ineffective, usury having "much more exceedingly abounded, to the utter undoing of many gentlemen, merchants, occupiers, and other, and to the importable hurt of the commonwealth." The new law, aimed at rectifying the situation, was ingeniously contrived to conciliate potential opposition by ensuring that its wording would in no way formally permit the taking of interest. It reiterated the condemnation and the legal penalties but provided an escape clause that the merchant could use if he so wished. While again prohibiting interest above 10 percent and making it, as in the repealed law of 1545, criminally punishable both by imprisonment and by a heavy fine, it added an innovative ruling. Lower interest, that is, below 10 percent, was no longer automatically punishable but legally forfeitable, the borrower being empowered to take court action, if he wished, in order to have the interest canceled. The law thus reaffirmed in the strongest terms the criminality of all interest, including that below 10 percent—"forasmuch as all usury being forbidden by the law of God is sin and detestable"—but it placed upon the borrower the responsibility for challenging the lower interest, since no court action would be taken against the usurer *unless* a formal complaint had been lodged. In fact, no instance of such recourse to the courts has been recorded during that period.

As the careful wording of the new law indicated, the stigma remained, with interest-taking still condemned as sinful. The loophole was, indeed, fiercely attacked by traditionalists such as Miles Mosse, whose *Arraignment and Conviction of Usury* of 1595 continued to insist that usury, including that below 10 percent, was "manifestly forbidden by the Word of God." If financiers tended to dismiss such attacks as emanating from religionists unfamiliar with the requirements of commercial dealings and therefore unqualified to intervene, they could scarcely employ that argument when Thomas Wilson published his *A Discourse on Usury* in 1572, since he was a person of considerable eminence in the financial world, extraordinarily well versed in commercial affairs. As Master of Requests, he had been responsible for trying numerous mercantile cases and negotiating major business transactions; yet his treatise constituted a fierce attack on all forms of usury. The Scriptures, he reminded his readers, specifically state: "thou shalt not lend out thy money for gain, to take anything for the loan of it, and yet we do all these things, as though there were neither scripture that forbade us, nor heaven for us to desire, nor hell to eschew; nor god to honor nor devil to dread. And this last horrible offense, which I count greater, or as great, as any of the rest, is so common amongst us, that we have no sense to take it for sin, but count it lawful bargaining."[21] It is a transgression, Wilson added, of a further commandment in the decalogue, since the usurer, hoping to obtain an "overplus" on the loan, was coveting his neighbor's goods. Moreover—and here too we come close to the theme of our play—he specifically equated usury with commerce. There was little discernible difference, he pointed out, between a usurer lending the sum of £500 in order to receive £600 for it a few months later and a profiteer purchasing land for £500 and selling it for £600. Moneylenders, in fact, came to exploit that similarity for their own purposes, frequently circumventing the law by disguising their transactions. The borrower would "sell" some trivial object to the lender in exchange for the money loaned, undertaking to repurchase it later at a price including the prohibited interest.

What emerges, therefore, is that a disturbing awareness of the biblical condemnation of usury remained and, no less important, that commerce continued to be castigated as a form of profiteering closely allied to usury. When the popular preacher Daniel Price delivered a sermon at Paul's Cross in 1607 dedicated to the London Company of Merchants and intended as a justification of mercantile activity, he began with the admission that Erasmus had condemned traders as accounting "nothing good or holy, but only the lucre of money," adding the further concession that Jerome had called them "the thieves of the world." His defense of trade he then based on passages drawn from the Old Testament, not the New. King Solomon, he pointed out, had brought great wealth to his country through commerce, and Price proceeded to cite as evidence of divine blessing the verse from Psalm 107: "They that go down to the seas in ships and merchandise in great waters, these men see the works of the Lord." The text he chose for this sermon, which did come from the Gospels (Matt. 13:45–46), offered somewhat dubious support, since it compared the finding of the kingdom of heaven to a good merchant's discovery of a pearl of great value, and his prompt selling of all he possessed in order to purchase it. He seems not to have noticed that the main point of the Christian parable was the merchant's renunciation of the pursuit of wealth in favor of the spiritual life. But this very attempt on the preacher's part to console the merchant company indicates the sense of guilt that affected the profession, its awareness that there was something un-Christian in such activity and that their standing in the eyes of their contemporaries was not of the best.[22] John Wheeler, secretary of the Merchant Adventurers' Company, in issuing in 1601 his *Treatise of Commerce* in an attempt to counter the widespread hostility to the profession, justified trade not on religious grounds, since the evidence was so strongly against it, but on the advantages it brought to the kingdom. A prince, he suggests, can use merchants "to the great benefit, and good of his state, either for foreign intelligence or exploration, or for the opening of an entry and passage unto unknown and fair distant parts, or for the furnishing of money, and other provisions in time of wars, and death." A devotional manual surviving from this period, Immanuel Bourne's *The Godly Mans Guide*, addressed especially to "Merchants and Tradesmen," strives once again to counter the disrepute with which commerce was regarded in his day, recalling that it had in earlier periods been held in esteem. But, like Wheeler, he confines his defense to the by-products of commerce rather than the activity itself:

> as Merchandise hath beene auncient, euen in the dayes of Noah (as Josephus affirmes) so it hath beene glorious in former Ages; By this we haue gotten acquaintance with forreigne Nations, and the Kingdome of Christ hath beene enlarged; By this we haue leagues of amitie, contracted with people of diuers Languages: By this we have gotten knowledge, and experience in seuerall Sciences. Yea, some Merchants haue beene builders of great and famous Cities (as *Plutarke* in *Solon* reporteth). And not to trauell like a Merchant beyond the Sea, if we make a search neerer home, how many religious Merchants and Tradesmen, haue been Benefactors to the Vniuersities, for the maintenance of learning and Pietie.[23]

Most people, however, continued well into Shakespeare's day to treat the profession with disdain, the merchant in Elizabethan popular literature being, as Laura Stevenson notes, regularly classified together with the usurer as a personification or "type" of greed.[24] Philip Stubbes, who approvingly quotes Cato's definition of usury as a kind of murder, adds, "And good reason, for he that killeth a man, riddeth him out of his paines at once, but he that taketh Vsury, is long in Butchering his pacient, causing him by little and little to languish, and sucking out his vitall blood, neuer leaueth him so long as he feeleth any life in him or any more gaines comming from him. The Vsurer killeth not one, but many, both husband, wife, children, seruants famelie, and all not sparing anie."[25] The merchant, classed together with the usurer, is condemned not only for his greed but also for his double-dealing, as William Perkins writes in 1612: "In the calling of the Merchant and trades-man, there is false weights, and false measures, divers weights and divers measures; ingrossing, mingling, changing, setting a glosse on wares by powdering, startching, blowing, darke shops, glozing, smoothing, lying, swearing, and all manner of bad dealing."[26]

In England, the expansion of commercial activity reached its peak in the late 1580s, shortly before the writing of *The Merchant of Venice*. When Elizabeth succeeded to the throne, the country had been close to bankruptcy, but under the direction of her gifted financier, Sir Thomas Gresham, founder of the Royal Exchange, its commercial expansion advanced impressively, England eventually replacing Antwerp as the financial center of Europe. It was at that period that numerous mercantile projects were undertaken. The founding of the Muscovy Company to develop trade with Russia proved so successful that by 1588 100 vessels a year were sailing to and from the Baltic. The defeat of the Spanish Armada in 1588 opened the way for trade in oriental silk and spices with the Orient, leading to the establishment of the East India Company. In 1593, the queen gave her personal authorization to the amalgamating of two merchant groups into the Levant Company, devoted to the expansion of England's commerce with the Mediterranean countries, while the voyages of exploration emanating from England were motivated primarily by the desire to find new areas for trade, with John Hawkins sailing in 1562 for Africa,

Martin Frobisher setting out in the 1570s for northern Canada, and Sir Francis Drake circumnavigating the globe in search of the great southern continent, Terra Australis. The new trading companies and the voyages of exploration demanded financial investment and speculation, for which the obtaining of substantial loans on interest was a prerequisite. As an English observer of the scene remarked, "the chief merchandise now is clear and plain usury."[27] But if that period of expansion has so often been viewed in history books as a glorious moment in England's development, it was by no means so generously regarded by contemporaries, the merchants still being viewed with scorn. Jonson's Volpone, in justifying the plan he had devised for divesting legacy hunters of their money, declared with pride the superiority of such activity to the contemptible professions of commerce, moneymaking, and usury:

> I use no trade, no venture;
> ... expose no ships
> To threat'nings of the furrow-faced sea;
> I turn no monies in the public bank,
> Nor usure private.

Accordingly, there was a compelling need for the Christian who participated in these new mercantile activities to find some method of validating the financial enterprise and the acquisitive impulse that stimulated it; to attempt, that is, to remove the stigma still attached to them.

One last point before returning to the play. The theory adduced by Max Weber and extended later by R. H. Tawney that attributed the burgeoning of Western economy and the encouragement of the garnering of wealth to the emergence of Protestantism might seem to militate against this disdain for commerce among Protestants. That is, in part, true. Although early Protestants such as Luther had continued to condemn the pursuit of wealth in terms no less denunciatory than their medieval forebears, there entered gradually into the Protestant consciousness, with its sympathy for the Old Testament, a recognition that if the biblical Abraham had been blessed by God with flocks, herds, and material possessions, there could be nothing basically evil in the acquisition of wealth, provided, of course, it be obtained honestly. Thus, Richard Sibbes declared in 1637, "worldly things are good in themselves, and given to sweeten our passage to Heaven . . . this world and the things thereof are all good, and were all made of God, for the benefit of his creatures."[28] The individual Protestant may still be urged to dissociate from those who aimed at "vaine pompe" or conspicuous consumption, but a modicum of financial independence was encouraged, since "they that apply themselves to labour for their livings do eat their own bread and are profitable to others; whereas those stately idle persons are driven to put their feet under other men's tables, and their hands into other men's dishes."[29] But a by-product of this approval was the advancement of the Protestant work ethic in a manner not easily distinguishable from acquisitiveness. Richard Bernard's *Ruth's Recompense* deduces from the account of Boaz in the biblical story that wealth could enhance the piety of its possessor:

> Riches well used bring grace in estimation before men, for they inable men to shew forth godlinesse, & to passe on their time with more comfort, and to countenance and defend their poore Christian brethren in well-doing. Therefore if grace and goods goe together, thou hast great cause to blesse God: for it is a most happy estate, to bee rich towards the world, and to God too, to bee rich body and soule: But although this is a very rare estate, yet we see that they may meete together: and therefore we may not thinke that he which is rich, can not be religious. True it is, that it is hard for a rich man to enter the Kingdome of heaven; but it is not impossible.

Hence, the Quakers came to occupy a leading position in the banking concerns of early America, where their judicious knowledge of investment, combined with unequivocal honesty in their dealings, won the trust of their clients.

The dating of this change is relevant, for, whatever hints may have come earlier, the Protestant validation of commerce was, as Tawney confirms, a phenomenon that emerged only in the mid-seventeenth century.[30] During the Elizabethan era, Protestantism was firmly opposed to the attaining of wealth. William Harrison, for example, in 1570 urged an end to foreign imports and a return to the simplicity of earlier days when each village was self-sufficient, producing all of its needs. Protestants, he maintained, should eschew luxuries, and should earn only enough to provide for their basic needs, seeking no more "than was necessary for the competent maintenauns of themselves."[31] As Charles and Katherine George note, the so-called "spirit of capitalism" attributed to the Protestants "simply did not exist in England until the 1640s."[32] With Protestant approval of commercial activity as yet unavailable, Shakespeare needed to find some other way of coping with the conflict between the Christian disapproval of financial gain and the Renaissance endorsement of mercantile self-enrichment. He needed, in effect, to create in the contemporary imagination a separation of the traditional identification of merchant and usurer, a dichotomy that would cleanse the merchant of that association and, we may assume, ease Shakespeare's own conscience in acquiring wealth and in lending money on interest.

It was in *The Merchant of Venice* that Shakespeare made the attempt, by presenting the two, the merchant and the usurer, not merely as separate entities but as polarized figures, mutually antagonistic, contemptuous of each other's activities and deriding each other's moral principles. But in contrasting the two professions, he took a further and remarkably daring step. By merging the merchant with the figure of Christ, by implication he validated commercial enterprise as fully compatible with Christian principles. To the devil he transferred those aspects that had given it a bad name, assigning to Shylock the sins of avarice and deviousness while dignifying the merchant as noble, generous, and high-principled.

With the merchant exonerated, the principle of acquiring wealth (provided it be honestly attained) is not only condoned in the play but comes to dominate it, viewed throughout as a fully commendable activity. Bassanio, in search of financial enrichment, proudly compares himself—and with no hint of embarrassment—to Jason in his heroic quest for the golden fleece. There is an unabashed hint of his priorities in his statement to Antonio describing the proposed quest: "In Belmont is a lady richly left," to which he adds only as an afterthought, "*And* she is fair." His frank admission of his purpose in journeying to Belmont in search of a wealthy wife not only evokes no disapproval from his friend but also meets with full encouragement. Nor are they alone in this approval of wealth, Lorenzo confiding to Gratiano his pleasure at Jessica's promise of the gold and jewels she will bring with her as her dowry.

One notes, too, the significant change in the magical territory that Shakespeare often contrasts with the city in these early romances. The "green world" of those plays, the wood at midsummer night and the forest of Arden that provide relief from the harsh legalism of the city, is here replaced by a very different idealized setting, also magical with regard to its casket theme but no longer part of the natural world. Instead it is a golden city, a Belmont flowing with untold wealth. Portia, hearing that Shylock is owed 3,000 ducats, cries, "What, no more? / Pay him six thousand . . . / Double six thousand and then treble that." Karoline Szatek has condemned Belmont as being, in the worst sense, commercially oriented, that its "capitalist ethos and commercial practices far outmeasure" those of Venice; but the evidence she adduces contradicts her thesis. Portia's sweet response to Bassanio's victory, that she wishes herself for his sake "a thousand times more fair, ten thousand times more rich," is scarcely Venetian merchandising but the generosity of one who wishes only to give. And equally unpersuasive is Szatek's interpretation of the casket device as an entrepreneurial strategy for selling a daughter at the highest price "in an open market of prosperous suitors," when Bassanio, clearly the intended winner, is financially the poorest of them all.[33] Belmont, one may add, epitomizes the generosity and trust exemplified by the Christian characters in the play, as when Portia hands over the management of her mansion to a Lorenzo whom she has only just met, requiring no guarantee other than his being a friend of "her lord."

How, we may ask, does Shakespeare justify his innovative merger of Christ with the professional merchant; how does he validate—for himself, as well as for his audience—the contemporary acquisitive impulse despite its patent inconsistency with Christian teaching? The question is especially relevant if we bear in mind that Shakespeare was engaged at this time in augmenting his own financial assets, investing in projects intended to ensure his future prosperity. During the year he wrote this play, Shakespeare was negotiating the purchase of one of the largest houses in Stratford. A few years later, he obtained title to 107 acres of arable land, and made his shrewdest move in 1605 when he purchased a half-interest in the leasing of tithes for Stratford, Bishopton, and Welcombe, an acquisition that provided him henceforth with a substantial annual income.[34] It would seem that his personal discomfort at this time concerning the conflict between religious ideals and Renaissance acquisitiveness was a major factor in stimulating him to work out in this play a method of coping with the problem.

The technique he employed is fascinating, its ramifications spreading throughout the action. Antonio, as we learn from the opening scene, has valuable merchandise on the seas, investments described in glowing terms as argosies sailing like "signiors and rich burghers on the flood," the petty traffickers seeming to curtsey to them and do them reverence. His friends Solanio and Salerio, were they in Antonio's position, would worry lest the ships founder, but Antonio is calm and unperturbed. The reason becomes apparent in the course of the play, for Shakespeare presents the merchant's commercial enterprises not as stemming from avarice in the way Elizabethan drama had previously depicted such activity, but as acts of Christian faith, evidence of an abiding trust in God. In contrast to Shylock, who demands security, insisting on guaranteeing his investments through signed contracts and sureties on a principle he defines as "Fast bind, fast find," Antonio's tradings are consistently described, both by him and his friends, as "hazards" or "ventures." Shylock, as his name implies, insists on locking the house each time he leaves, just as he locks up or secures each contract, the words "bind" and "bond" reiterated throughout the play in connection with his business affairs. Antonio, however, is presented as open handed, entrusting his ships and his merchandise to the will of heaven, committing them, as it were, into the hands of a benevolent deity who, if he so wishes, will return them to him laden with profit; if not, the Christian merchant will accept with due patience the divine will. By that process any implication of greed or acquisitiveness is dispelled, commercial enterprise being presented thereby as a pious act. Informed later in the play that his ships have miscarried, Antonio responds with quiet fortitude and sufferance, free from complaint or reproach, assuring Bassanio that all debts between them are to be regarded as annulled.

The two words "venture" and "hazard," which define this new approach, recur throughout the play, always, on Antonio's part, with the implication of a laudatory trust in the divine. In the opening scene, replying to the lengthy speeches of Solanio and Salerio expressing the anxiety they would experience were their own property at such risk, Antonio assures them that he is free from worry, since it is not a ship he trusts but heaven: "I thank my fortune for it," he assures them. Similarly, the analogy Bassanio employs in requesting a second loan from Antonio is his practice of venturing, of allowing fortune to direct a second arrow to find the first, "by adventuring both, I oft found both." Shakespeare, in adopting the term, may have been influenced by Miles Mosse's *Arraignement*, which, in a central passage, defines usury as a form of investment *lacking* any element of risk because of the contractual coverage that guaranteed a profitable return. The activity forbidden by God is, he states, "a lending for gaine, by compact, not adventuring the principall. Or more plainly thus. Usurie is, when a man not adventuring the goodes which hee lendeth covenanteth to receive againe more then he lendeth."[35] By implication, merchants who adventure their goods without the guarantee of a contract or covenant do not fall within this forbidden category. It is possible also that Shakespeare borrowed the term from the Merchant Adventurers, a chartered company founded to encourage trade with the Netherlands, which was particularly active at this time. But whatever the source, it was a term due to play a major part in the development of his plot.

Shakespeare's conception of trade as a form of trust in the divine sheds light on the otherwise problematic dispute between Antonio and Shylock, namely their contrasting interpretations of Jacob's contract with Laban. Shylock cites the biblical account as offering evidence that the Scriptures approve of usury; yet, as many critics note, there is in Jacob's project no hint of usury as such, Jacob neither lending nor borrowing on interest. J. R. Brown, puzzled by the scene, states in his Arden edition that no reference to the biblical story exists in any sixteenth century book on usury. Joan Holmer discovers that there was in fact one such mention, in Mosse's *Arraignment*, but it is quoted there not as an instance of usury but simply as an example of the harshness with which evil men often treat those in their power. Mosse himself remarks that he had suffered cruelly from the moneylenders, "as Laban dealt with Iacob, when he saw how God had blessed him, their countenance hath not been towards me," adding at the conclusion of the treatise, "let them feare, that as God took the goods of couetous Laban, and gaue them to holy Iacob: so he will take riches which they haue vnlawfully gathered, from them, and from their house, and from their children: and will bestow them vpon others, who shall shew themselues better imployers and disposers of his blessinges." The relevance of the Laban story within this play remains, therefore, unexplained.[36]

Jacob had, it will be recalled, reached an agreement with Laban that only such lambs as were born striped or spotted would accrue to him—an agreement readily accepted by Laban since such births are rare in nature. However, before the eyes of the pregnant ewes Jacob placed striped sticks to encourage them to produce the type of offspring that would, by this arrangement, fall to his lot. Shylock admits in his opening comment that the story does not deal directly with interest. He cites it instead as a scripturally approved device for ensuring or guaranteeing Jacob's profits, and hence authenticating his own insistence on binding the borrower by law as a means of covering all eventualities. That, he concludes, is the way to thrive. Antonio hotly disputes that reading, seeing the story as validating a totally different conception of commerce: "This was a venture, sir, that Jacob serv'd for; / A thing not in his power to bring to pass, / But sway'd and fashion'd by the hand of heaven" (1.3.91–93). Like the merchant, Antonio implies, Jacob establishes the terms of the venture; but its outcome he leaves in God's hands. That contrast in attitude parallels an earlier instance, where Shylock scorns Antonio's form of trade. The latter's merchandising consists, he scornfully comments, of "ventures he hath squand'red abroad"—squandered because they are left vulnerable to chance: "there be land rats and water rats, water thieves and land thieves—I mean pirates—and then there is the peril of waters, winds, and rocks" (1.3.20ff). In that same scene, the distinction between the two views is highlighted by a single word. Shylock, in considering (or pretending to consider) the loan, murmurs half to himself that "Antonio is a good man"—good in the sense of a financially reliable investment, while Bassanio, interpreting the word as a questioning of Antonio's moral rectitude, indignantly responds, "Have you heard any imputation to the contrary?" The Christian's primary concern is with moral behavior, Shylock's with collateral and guarantees.

If there exists no contradiction between Antonio's function as the embodiment of selfless Christian charity and his willingness to increase his wealth, Bassanio elicits a more ambiguous response. Not only is his courtship of Portia motivated by a desire for monetary gain but, as he informs us early in the play, he is by nature an unconscionable spendthrift whose prodigality has plunged him into debt. He falls, therefore, considerably short of Antonio as a model of Christian comportment. Were that all, his role as the leading male lover would inevitably contradict or, at the very least, detract from the fundamental message of the play. But Shakespeare takes care to counter that aspect of Bassanio's behavior within the casket scene, where he is allowed to redeem himself and to parallel there the noble principles of Antonio. Portia prepares us for that scene by employing the two key words as she lovingly urges him to postpone the decision and protract their courtship:

> I pray you tarry, pause a day or two
> Before you hazard . . .
> I would detain you here some month or two
> Before you venture for me.   (3.2.1–4)

And venture he does in the fullest sense. Suppressing the Jason-like tendencies that motivate him elsewhere in his pursuit of gold, he rejects the attractions of the first casket. With echoes of the whited sepulchre, he compares the golden exterior to false golden curls, "the dowry of a second head— / The skull that bred them in the sepulchre." The silver casket he spurns too, in accordance with Christian disdain for riches, money being merely "that common drudge twixt man and man." Instead he risks everything on the least promising casket, the one that bears the notable legend, "Who chooseth me must give and hazard all he hath." The reason that he offers for his final choice is, moreover, couched in markedly religious terms, echoing the

Christian principle of compassion for the poor and the humble of this world: "but thou, thou meagre lead, / Which rather threaten'st than dost promise aught, / Thy paleness moves me more than eloquence" (3.2.104–06). At the very moment of obtaining Portia's wealth, he thus counteracts the acquisitiveness he has displayed in Venice, employing images that, as with Antonio, lend a religious coloring to his action, endowing it with a noble hue.

A moment later, one might imagine that he has eschewed this principle of venturing. Dazed by his success, he declares to Portia that he is in doubt "whether what I see be true, / Until confirmed, signed, ratified by you." Are signed contracts therefore in order? Has Bassanio resorted to Shylock's mode of commerce, requiring a legal guarantee before proceeding? His remark, it transpires, is a lover's jest, a parody of Shylock's approach, the confirmation he requires being not a legal document but the kiss from Portia that will ratify their troth, certifying that his success was, after all, no dream. And, sure enough, no contract or signed ratification between them is recorded.

The central trial scene now follows, and the closing comedy of the rings. But just before the final scene a brief exchange plays on the word "bound" to highlight the central contrast—the difference between the legal bond employed by Shylock and the spiritual bond of affection and gratitude characterizing the Christians. Bassanio, introducing his friend Antonio to Portia, asks her to "Give welcome to my friend. / This is the man, this is Antonio, / To whom I am so infinitely bound" (5.1.133–35), to which Portia replies, "You should in all sense be much bound to him, / For as I hear he was much bound for you" (136–37). That reminder of the contrasting bonds, Christian gratitude and Pharisaic contracts, reaches its apogee when Antonio, a little later, reminds the audience of the function he had fulfilled earlier in the play, thereby completing the circle. Having witnessed Portia's berating of Bassanio for his supposed infidelity, he once again offers himself as guarantor. This time, however, he proffers not his body as security for Bassanio but his soul, an offer involving no legal compact, only mutual trust and goodwill:

> I once did lend my body for his wealth,
> Which, but for him that had your husband's ring
> Had quite miscarried. I dare be bound again,
> My soul upon the forfeit, that your lord
> Will never more break faith advisedly.   (5.1.249–53)

"Then you shall be his surety," cries Portia, that term confirming the parallel to and contrast with the earlier bond.

To summarize this aspect, therefore: by presenting us with a Shylock embodying the worst excesses of financial avarice and by identifying him at the same time as an amalgam of the repulsive figures of the devil, of Judas, and of the New Testament Pharisee, Shakespeare succeeds in sanctioning by contrast the activities of the Renaissance trader. The presentation of Antonio as a Christ figure serves to dignify the status of the merchant, portraying him as selfless, generous, and dedicated to noble precepts. But even more effective is the imaging of commercial enterprise as a form of trust in the divine, a process that absolves the trader from any imputation of cupidity. In contrast to Marlowe's *The Jew of Malta*, believed by many to have prompted Shakespeare's play, the Jew here is not the central character. Shakespeare chose not to follow Marlowe's lead by calling his play *The Jew of Venice*.[37] Shylock serves in a distinctly subordinate capacity, as a foil highlighting the virtues of the protagonist. Transferring the focus to the Renaissance entrepreneur, Antonio, the dramatist entitled it more appropriately, *The Merchant of Venice*, using that hybrid figure as a means of conflating Christian and commercial ethics.

There is, thus, a remarkable conflation of opposites in this drama. On the one hand, and most obviously, the play confirms the Christian condemnation of usury as sin, with Shylock symbolizing the evils of such practice. But on the other hand, and working against that principle, is a redefining of the prohibition, a defense of mercantile activity intended to refute the church's long-time inclusion of it within the category of that sin. The two views, traditional and subversive, would appear incompatible, mutually irreconcilable readings such as have so intrigued deconstructionists. Paul De Man argues that in such oppositional interpretations, "the one reading is precisely the error denounced by the other and has to be undone by it," the result being, in his view, a critical deadlock.[38] Jacques Derrida too proclaims that such conflicts of text and subtext in effect frustrate the possibility of a coherent reading, admitting that the result is nihilistic:

> Perhaps you will think that I am leading you toward a purely aporetic conclusion . . . that there is no such thing as a literary essence or a specifically literary domain strictly identifiable as such; or, indeed, that this name of literature perhaps is destined to remain improper, with no criteria, or assured concept or reference, so that "literature" has something to do with the drama of naming, the law of the name and the name of the law. You would doubtless not be wrong.[39]

Yet the conflict of text and subtext in this drama results not in an impasse. On the contrary, it provides a perfect example of one of the central principles articulated in the drama itself, namely the restoring of the true spirit of the law to misconstrued interpretation. The purpose of the scriptural ban on interest had been intended, as the scriptural text makes explicit, to protect the poor against exploitation. Thus, the lender is required to return to the needy each evening the blanket that has been surrendered as guarantee for the loan, since it is the sole covering to keep the indigent warm at night:

> If thou lende money to my people, that is, to the poore with thee, thou shalt not bee as an vsurer vnto him: yee shall not oppresse him with vsurie. If thou tak thy neighbours rayment to pledge, thou shalt restore it vnto him before the sunne

go downe: For that is his couering only, and this is his garment for his skin: wherin shal he sleepe? therefore when he crieth vnto mee, I will heare him: for I am mercifull. (Exod. 22:25–27)

The cry that heaven wished to prevent was the plea emanating from the indigent and the defenseless; it was not aimed against a merchant requesting a loan for purposes of commercial investment. In this play, the original intention of the passage is restored. The sin of extortion or oppression is assigned to the villainous Shylock, whom Antonio spurns. But excluded from the scriptural prohibition here is the commercial activity so long condemned by the church—now presented not only as permissible but also as a commendable act of Christian piety. By restoring the spirit to the long-established misapplication of biblical law, the drama creates not an impasse but a dialogical heterogeneity, a playing off of text against subtext, of spirit against letter, of the traditional condemnation of commerce against an innovative validation of it, to produce a fully coherent reading.

TWO

Hamlet and the Stoic

T. S. Eliot disliked *Hamlet*, describing it disparagingly as "the Mona Lisa of literature." He claimed that it was an inscrutable work, disquieting because of the impossibility of ever identifying with precision the source of Hamlet's emotional disturbance. The plethora of causes adduced, he pointed out, are generally projections onto the play of the critic's personal sensibilities with no unanimity achieved, Goethe transforming Hamlet into a Werther, and Coleridge into a Romantic poet.[1] However, there may be in Eliot's comparison of the play to the *Mona Lisa* a more positive element than he had in mind. The two works reflect within their different media a transformation that was occurring in Renaissance concepts of human character, a transformation in large part responsible for the artistic eminence of both. By introducing the innovative technique of *sfumato*, a "smokiness" or delicate shading, especially at the corners of the mouth, eyes, and nostrils, Leonardo da Vinci bestowed upon his figures a subtlety and mystery lacking in earlier portraits. Like all such innovations, the technique introduced was not fortuitous but motivated by a contemporary need, a desire to convey in visual form his generation's growing awareness of the complexity of the individual implicit in humanism. Artistic focus was no longer on external appearances—an attention to clothing, facial features, or outer appurtenances as reliable indications of character and social standing, as in Chaucer's *Canterbury Tales* or in the distinction between nobility and their servants in the depiction of *August* by the Limbourg brothers. Instead, art and literature now aimed at conveying the recondite, unfathomable elements of the individual's inner being, the enigmatic qualities concealed within. Mona Lisa fascinates us by the ambiguity of her smile, by the impossibility of determining whether it denotes pleasure or sadness or, indeed, whether she is smiling at all. Titian's *Young Englishman*, set against a somber background, gazes not at us, but past us, in a manner suggesting that he is meditating some indefinable problem, some concern that we, the viewers, will never be privileged to know.

So it is in drama. In contrast to the flat characters of mid-sixteenth-century plays—such as the almost indistinguishable Ferrex and Porrex in Sackville and Norton's *Gorboduc*—Shakespeare's leading figures in his more mature phase are marked by their complexity and introspection. As Granville-Barker points out, the change can be perceived in Shakespeare's development as a dramatist; the resolute figure of Henry V so clearly foregrounded in the play of that name has, in *Hamlet*, moved into the background, where his name is now Fortinbras, and our focus is transferred to the far more intriguing character of one deeply conscious of the problematic condition of man, a condition of which Fortinbras is utterly oblivious.[2]

Shakespeare, it seems, was fully conscious of the cultural shift in sensibility to which he was giving expression, as a seemingly minor scene in this play confirms. Hamlet, aware of the crass disloyalty of his two supposed friends, thrusts a recorder into the hands of a reluctant Guildenstern and urges him to play on it. Guildenstern replies that he cannot, that he knows nothing of its stops, at which point Hamlet angrily retorts:

> Why, look you now, how unworthy a thing you make of me! You would play upon me, you would seem to know my stops, you would pluck out the heart of my mystery, you would sound me from my lowest note to the top of my compass; and there is much music, excellent voice, in this little organ, yet cannot you make it speak. "Sblood, do you think I'm easier to be play'd on than a pipe?" (3.2.362-70)

He cherishes here the mystery of his inner being, jealously guarding it against the intrusive attempts of others to reveal its riddling intricacies.

Yet despite the close parallel between Da Vinci's innovation and Shakespeare's new conception of the human character, there remains a substantial difference between its representation within the contrasting media. A painted portrait, restricted to a fixed moment in time, cannot attempt to relate the story, cannot elaborate the reasons for Mona Lisa's pensiveness. For the painter, it is sufficient to convey her mood by means of a tantalizing half-smile, but the same cannot hold for a full-length play. The search for the cause of Hamlet's inner disturbance and of the procrastination it produced cannot be shrugged off, subtle though it may be. It would be simple enough to assume in deconstructionist terms the existence here of an unresolvable inconsistency that exempts the critic from any need to explain. But as James Calderwood has so ably argued, although this play begins with *aporia*, seemingly dedicated to its own deconstruction by virtue of its employment of negation and erasure, its stress on silence and secrecy, its self-conscious creation of divisions and junctures, and its metadramatic denial of its own illusions, yet it moves, he points out, from deconstruction to reconstruction.[3] The silence and secrecy end, the revenge is fulfilled, and order is restored in the kingdom. The need, therefore, to define the nature of Hamlet's dilemma remains paramount.

The problem is that the explanations hitherto offered are disturbingly unsatisfactory. J. Dover Wilson believes Hamlet's frustrations arise from the loss of the throne, even though Hamlet makes no mention of that supposed deprivation until as late as act 5, and then only in the casual comment that Claudius has "Popp'd in between th' election and my hopes"; Francis Fergusson sees him in exclusively ritualistic terms as searching for the "imposthume" corrupting the kingdom; Ernest Jones follows Freud in attributing Hamlet's problem to an Oedipal complex—a theory persuasively argued until one recalls that in the play Hamlet expresses only affection and admiration for the father he supposedly hates. Jacques Lacan, only too predictably, sees Hamlet's crisis in phallic terms, the result of a castration phobia; while Janet Adelman, in a feminist reading, views him as threatened by a maternal figure who problematizes the distinction between his two "fathers."[4] But I will concentrate here upon two of the most widely held theories.

A. C. Bradley's claim that Gertrude's remarriage lies at the core of Hamlet's agitation cannot be refuted. Hamlet repeatedly identifies that event as the cause of his distress, sometimes pensively, often in wild and whirling words:

> So excellent a king, that was to this
> Hyperion to a satyr; so loving to my mother
> That he might not beteem the winds of heaven
> Visit her face too roughly. Heaven and earth!
> Must I remember? (1.2.138–43)

It is important to stress that Bradley focuses upon Hamlet's disgust with his mother for having remarried so soon and to so inferior a person. After dismissing various theories concerning the cause of Hamlet's depression, he declares, "It was the moral shock of the sudden ghastly disclosure of his mother's true nature, falling on him when his heart was aching with love, and his body doubtless was weakened by sorrow." But there is a serious problem with that theory. If the play has throughout the ages produced so electrifying an effect upon audiences, not least because it deals with matters of great moment to all, dislike of a mother's remarriage would scarcely seem sufficiently profound or sufficiently universal a theme to have fascinated generations of viewers. It would not leave us with the sense that we have witnessed a struggle with one of the most fundamental questions of human existence. We shall, however, need to return later to Bradley's theory. If, on the other hand, as Wilson Knight, C. S. Lewis, and others have argued, the play is concerned primarily with death and decay, a theme that is indeed a subject of intimate concern to us all, what relevance does that have to the remarriage that Hamlet repeatedly claims is driving him almost to madness?[5]

It was in this play that Shakespeare defined the function of drama as twofold—to hold the mirror up to nature, and at the same time to show "the very age and body of the time its form and pressure." The first aim is universal, depicting those elements in human nature that hold true for all generations, Hamlet confronting from that viewpoint problems that are relevant to us all and at all times. The second indicates, as for all great art, the dramatist's desire to discern and express, often in advance of his peers, cultural shifts in sensibility emerging in his own age, the form and "pressure" or impress of his time, such contemporary viewpoints often altering from decade to decade so that themes and assumptions informing his *Antony and Cleopatra* differ fundamentally from those animating *Hamlet*. In that context, Hamlet's preoccupation with mortality constitutes the universal aspect of the play, an anxiety germane to every generation. But the specific angle from which that problem was approached lent it an appositeness, a contemporary relevance that held a special significance for the audiences of Shakespeare's day.

The source of that immediacy is to be found—at least in its more general form—in the unbounded admiration Hamlet expresses for Horatio. Dover Wilson states a contrary view, declaring that Horatio is not really a character, merely "a piece of dramatic structure" serving to witness the Ghost's appearance and to function as the hero's confidant.[6] But that is surely belied by the speech in which Hamlet expresses his deep admiration not just for his friend but also for the Stoic philosophy his friend represents, praise prefaced by the prince's disclaimer lest the audience imagine the existence of an ulterior motive in a drama which, as Jan Kott perceives, is elsewhere permeated by deception, pretense, and duplicity.[7] As Hamlet declares, he has no reason to flatter, for he can hope for no advancement from his companion, and we are therefore disposed to take his remarks very seriously.

The basis of Hamlet's admiration is, of course, Horatio's *ataraxia*, his friend's immunity to the vagaries of fate and to the stirrings of passion.

> Since my dear soul was mistress of her choice
> And could of men distinguish her election
> Sh' hath seal'd thee for herself, for thou hast been
> As one in suff'ring all that suffers nothing,
> A man that Fortune's buffets and rewards
> Hast ta'en with equal thanks; and blest are those
> Whose blood and judgment are so well co-meddled,
> That they are not a pipe for Fortune's finger
> To sound what stop she please. Give me that man
> That is not passion's slave, and I will wear him
> In my heart's core, ay, in my heart of heart,
> As I do thee.   (3.2.63–74)

But, if Hamlet is so profoundly drawn to that philosophy, what element, either in his own nature or in the creed itself, prevents him from adopting it? What obstacle is there to his resisting with equal fortitude the passions to which, throughout the play, he so readily succumbs? To assume with Coleridge that he is fundamentally incapable of mastering his emotions, that, unlike Horatio, he is innately romantic, is to ignore the retrospective glimpses we are offered of Hamlet prior to his father's death, before the dark melancholy descended upon him. As the expectancy and rose of the fair state nostalgically recalled by Ophelia, a prince endowed with the courtier's, soldier's, scholar's eye, tongue, and sword, that earlier Hamlet bears no trace of morbid spiritual paralysis. Singled out for special praise is the "noble and most sovereign reason" he then possessed, enabling him to exercise the same rational self-control as his admired friend. Moreover, the obstacle to his adoption of the Stoic code, the problem that plunges him into deep meditation and near despair, emerges in this play not as a failing but as a quality that ultimately elevates him above Horatio who, like Fortinbras, lacks the sensibility that makes Hamlet so fascinating a figure. As Aristotle had noted and as Shakespeare confirms in Hamlet's speech on the "mole" of nature that often corrupts men, the *hamartia* or blemish in tragic heroes need not be a moral failing. It may be the result of nature's livery or fortune's star wherein they are not guilty; and in Hamlet the "mole of nature" that ultimately destroys him would seem, from the way he stands head and shoulders above his compeers in the play, to be a virtue redounding to his credit, making us admire him profoundly in the midst of his seeming failures.

What lies behind Hamlet's speech to Horatio? Stoicism understandably exercised an enormous attraction for the Renaissance, as it had in the early periods of Christianity. Saint Jerome admired aspects of it, Saint Augustine praised the younger Cato's moral independence, while Boethius in his *Consolation of Philosophy* lauded, as did Hamlet, the Stoic's refusal to succumb to joy or grief in reaction to the oscillations of fate: "A wise man ought not to take it ill, every time he is brought into conflict with fortune, just as it would not be fitting for a brave man to be vexed every time the sound of war crashed out. . . . And this is indeed why virtue is so called, because relying on its own powers, it is not overcome by adversity."[8]

For the Renaissance, however, reacting against the medieval concept of man doomed by original sin, subject to divine wrath, and granted only the slimmest chance of salvation in the world to come, it held an especial appeal, offering the possibility of a sorely needed dignity and self-respect. In its earlier form, Stoicism had been primarily concerned with ethics, the ideal of the Stoic sage being the person who is ruled by reason, displaying firmness, constancy, and self-sufficiency in his or her daily life, and by such "apathy" attaining to tranquility and peace of mind. But for somewhat fortuitous reasons, the last phase of Stoicism, as represented in the works of Seneca and Cicero, exerted the profoundest effect on the Renaissance, since the writings of the early and middle stoa had survived only in fragments, while those of a subsequent phase, the *Discourses* and *Manual* of Epictetus and the *Meditations* of Marcus Aurelius, had been written in Greek, a language unavailable to most readers.

The Roman form of Stoicism, as presented in the writings to which the Elizabethans had easier access, had emerged during the reign of that ruthless, mentally disturbed, and totally unpredictable emperor, Nero, when fate seemed to his subjects utterly devoid of justice. Stoicism provided for his unfortunate subjects a way not only of living but of dying, their admired models being Socrates, who willingly drank the hemlock even though offered a way of escape, and Cato, who died by his own hand after his defeat by Caesar. Suicide in that version became the bedrock of the Stoic's superiority to fate. For, however painful the fate destined him by the gods, that recourse could provide both a cessation from pain and a dignified form of withdrawal from this world. By his refusal to rejoice in success or to grieve at misfortune, by declining to be a slave to passion, and by taking his own life when life no longer seemed worth living, the Stoic deprived the gods of victory. Even in the earliest phase, when the founders of Stoicism were primarily concerned with ethics, they had advocated suicide in the event that life became unbearable, Epictetus advising: "Above all, remember that the door stands open. Do not be more fearful than children. But, just as when they are tired of the game they cry, 'I will play no more,' so too when you are in a similar situation, cry, 'I will play no more' and depart. . . . For you must remember this and hold it fast, that the door stands open."⁹ In Seneca's writings, however, that way of escape had become transformed into a fundamental principle. When beset by suffering or misfortune, Seneca advised,

> endure with fortitude. In this you may outstrip God. . . . Scorn poverty; no one lives as poor as he was born. Scorn pain; it will either be relieved or relieve you. Scorn death, which either ends you or transfers you. Scorn Fortune; I have given her no weapon with which she may strike your soul. Above all, I have taken pains that nothing should keep you here against your will; the way out lies open. If you do not choose to fight, you may escape. Therefore of all things that I have deemed necessary for you, I have made nothing easier than dying.[10]

At a time of adversity, the Stoic was calmly to weigh the advantages and disadvantages of continued living and, if the scales tipped toward the disadvantages, should end his life, that act being an assertion of human freedom, a noble and admirable deed.

The effectiveness of that doctrine, however, the basis of its main attraction, lay in a further tenet of the philosophy which is of special relevance to the play, namely the Stoics' conception of death itself. In their view, the soul or *psyche* was conceived as part of the *pneuma*, or life force, the latter composed of air and fire, held in tension, and forming the vital element of the cosmos. After death, the *psyche* might hold together for a short time before being reabsorbed into the universal *pneuma*, but even during that limited period of survival it did not retain its particularity.[11] There was, therefore, no afterlife in the Christian sense, death constituting an end of the self in any semblance of its previous form. It was a negation of the individual, the appeal of death for the Stoic deriving from that very aspect, since it offered a cessation of all tribulation, an inviolability to the depredations of fate. Earlier Stoics, such as Chrysippus, had been somewhat vague on that point,[12] but Seneca was

firm in his view that death was oblivion and extinction—
"*mors est non esse*":

> Death is non-existence, and I know already what that means. What was before me will happen again after me. If there is any suffering in this state, there must have been such suffering also in the past, before we entered the light of day. As a matter of fact, however, we felt no discomfort then. And I ask you, would you not say that one was the greatest of fools who believed that a lamp was worse off when it was extinguished than before it was lighted?[13]

As Marcus Aurelius declared in his *Meditations* 5.13, we are all due one day to be refashioned by a process of transformation into some portion of the universe, which in its turn will again be changed into yet another part, and so onward to infinity, since "such is the process by which we were brought into existence, and thus were our parents before us." Seneca, in Epistle 102, describes the process more poetically. The soul, he declares, abides in the body only as long as it is fettered there, after which its homeland is "the whole space that encircles the height and breadth of the firmament, the whole rounded dome within which lie land and sea, within which the upper air that sunders the human from the divine also unites them.... That day which you fear as being the end of all things, is the birthday of your eternity." That latter phrase was due in the eighteenth century to be seized upon by Christian Stoics as indicating Seneca's belief in an afterlife, a postmortal eternity, and was adopted as a means of integrating the two concepts; but it is clear from the context that Seneca was speaking of eternity only in terms of the soul's integration into the everlasting *pneuma* of the universe, its existence as a separate entity being terminated.

For the Elizabethan, that aspect of Stoicism was regarded as the cornerstone of the Stoic's superiority to fate. Edward Agass's 1576 translation into English of Du Plessis-Mornay's *Excellent Discours de la vie et de la mort*, which had included generous excerpts from Seneca's writings, was significantly entitled by Agass, *The Defence of Death*, with the reference to life omitted. Cicero's *De finibus*, which, together with his *Tusculean Disputations* (translated into English by John Dolman in 1561), provided access to many Stoic ideas, stated unambiguously as a basis of Stoicism that, "When a man's circumstances contain a preponderance of things in accordance with nature, it is appropriate for him to remain alive; when he possesses or sees in prospect a majority of the contrary things, it is appropriate for him to depart from life."[14] In addition to Socrates and Cato, the Elizabethans knew well that numerous Stoics such as Zeno, Cleanthes, and Brutus had ended their lives by suicide, and Shakespeare, a year or so before *Hamlet*, depicted Brutus's suicide in *Julius Caesar*.

During Nero's reign, when Stoicism was at its height, hundreds of Romans chose that path, including Seneca himself. Informed of the emperor's displeasure, Seneca at once returned home, cut his wrists, and ended his life, thereby following the advice he had offered to all who found themselves encountering vexations that disturbed their tranquility: "Dying early or late is of no relevance, dying well or ill is."[15] The solution to life's problems, he states elsewhere, always lies ready at hand: "In whatever direction you may turn your eyes, there lies the means to end your woes. See you that precipice? Down that is the way to liberty. See you that sea, that river, that well? There sits liberty at the bottom. See you that tree, stunted, blighted and barren? Yet from its branches hangs liberty. See you that throat of yours, your gullet, your heart? They are ways of escape from servitude."[16] One should think of life, he suggests, "in terms of quality, not quantity."

Seneca's prose works were not translated into English until Thomas Lodge's version of 1614, but his philosophical ideas had been widely disseminated during the sixteenth century. Erasmus's edition of Seneca's moral treatises in 1515 proved so popular that Calvin found it necessary in one of his earlier works to produce a commentary on the *De Clementia* in order to warn readers of the distinctions between Stoic fideism and Christianity, a theme he continued to confront in the *Institutes*. Cicero, as has been noted, provided a further source for Seneca's writings, while Jasper Heywood's widely read translation of the plays in 1581 stimulated interest in the philosophical prose works too. But the Elizabethan's knowledge of Stoicism was considerably augmented by the rediscovery at this time of Tacitus's *Annals* with its grim account of Nero's reign and its recording of the numerous senators and military commanders who, on falling into disfavor with the emperor, rather than submit to his whims, chose to end their own lives in what the historian termed the "mode of death then in fashion." Paetus Thrasea's demise is described as follows:

> When he heard the Senate's decision, he led Helvidius and Demetrius into a chamber, and having laid bare the arteries of each arm, he let the blood flow freely, and, as he sprinkled it on the ground, he called the quaestor to his side and said, "We pour out a libation to Jupiter the Deliverer. Behold, young man, and may the gods avert the omen, but you have been born into times in which it is well to fortify the spirit with examples of courage."

The importation of Tacitus's work into England was initiated and fostered at court, Sir Philip Sidney being the inaugurator. After corresponding with Lipsius, the continental editor of the Latin edition, through an intermediary he urged Henry Savile, the Latin Secretary to the queen, to translate the work into English, that version appearing with a dedication to Elizabeth in 1591. According to Ben Jonson, the preface to the translation was written by the Earl of Essex. It stimulated wide interest, a second edition being issued in 1598; and it was probably from that translation that Shakespeare learned in more detail of the Roman fashion, introducing it into his *Julius Caesar*, composed in the following year, as a threefold conclusion to the play.[17]

The significance of Stoic suicide for the Elizabethan has not been sufficiently acknowledged. Gordon Braden's classic study of Senecan tragedy devotes a lengthy chapter to the influence of Stoicism on the Renaissance, discussing in some detail the self-control and resistance to adversity embodied in the philosophy; but it makes no mention of suicide, even though, in Seneca's writings, the indifference to fate was so dependent upon that recourse.[18] That aspect was prominent in the Renaissance, as evidenced by the fanciful connection of Seneca's name at that time with the phrase *se necans* ("killing oneself"). Spenser could assume that readers of *The Faerie Queene* would recognize the source when the villain Despaire blandly cites Seneca's argument as exoneration for his having driven Sir Terwin to plunge a "rustie knife" into his entrails:

> What if some litle paine the passage haue,
> That makes fraile flesh to feare the bitter waue?
> Is not short paine well borne, that brings long ease,
> And layes the soule to sleepe in quiet graue?
> Sleepe after toyle, port after stormie seas,
> Ease after warre.   (1.9.40–45)

That aspect would seem central not only to Hamlet's most famous soliloquy, but to the underlying theme of the entire play. The obstacle preventing him from adopting the tenets of Stoic philosophy is the biblical prohibition exemplified in Hamlet's cry, "O . . . that the Everlasting had not fix'd / His canon 'gainst self-slaughter!" (1.2.131–32). The prohibition prevents him from adopting the form of escape to which he was so profoundly attracted but to which, for religious reasons, he was hesitant to subscribe.

The conflict lies at the heart of the play, expressed in its central monologue. The initial option—"to be"—to live on, represents the cardinal Christian virtue of endurance, to suffer the slings and arrows of outrageous fortune. The second option—"not to be"—is the act of Stoic suicide, taking arms against a sea of troubles to achieve a cessation of all further torment, and by opposing "end" them. Hiram Haydn, who was indeed aware of the importance of Stoicism in this play but only in terms of its self-control, unfortunately reversed the reading, seeing the opening of the speech as marking Stoic *ataraxia*, suffering the slings and arrows, and the second, the taking of arms, as representing the revenge demanded by the moral code of his time. As Haydn puts it, "The first alternative is the patience and endurance of the Stoic who suffers with equanimity all that fortune brings, strong in his inner serenity. The second is the position of honor, which seeks a just revenge."[19] But the text of the speech does not support this reading; for the arms that Hamlet considers taking up are not, we learn, the sword or rapier but, as we are informed a few lines later, the "bare bodkin" whereby he could effect *his own* quietus, the dagger that constituted the favored means of suicide for the hundreds of Stoics who chose that path. Indeed, the image of the bodkin is probably an echo of Seneca's assurance to his fellow Stoics that "a prick makes you free of cares."[20] The first option suggested in the speech—to *suffer* the slings and arrows—applies therefore not to Stoicism but to the cardinal Christian counsel of sufferance, as in Paul's advice to accept the edicts of heaven and show "patience and faith in all your persecutions and tribulations that ye endure" (2 Thess. 1:4), contrasted here with the suicide so attractively embedded in Stoicism, the taking of arms against a sea of troubles in order to "end" them.

Eleanor Prosser states that the speech has nothing to do with suicide, though it is surely significant that she never mentions the bare bodkin that could his quietus make. She deduces instead that Hamlet's paralysis derives from his belief that fulfilling the Ghost's demand for vengeance contradicts a basic tenet of his faith, the Christian demand for forgiveness. But the evidence Prosser adduces cannot erase the known fact—that the Elizabethan wore his sword by his side ready to unsheathe it at the slightest provocation, determined to avenge affronts untroubled by any contradiction between the defense of his honor and the Christian injunction to suffer insults meekly. Shakespeare clearly objects, as in *Romeo and Juliet*, to pointless family feuds, the chain reaction whereby the avenger of a murder now becomes the object of revenge; yet even in that play, Romeo, despite his enormous reluctance to attack a kinsman of Juliet's, sees no alternative but to fight when insulted by Paris. Similarly, Macduff in *Macbeth*, on learning of the murder of his wife and children, experiences no moral hesitation in crying:

> Cut short all intermission. Front to front
> Bring thou this fiend of Scotland and myself;
> Within my sword's length set him; if he 'scape,
> Heaven forgive him too!   (4.3.232–35)[21]

Nor is there any hint of disapproval in the text, the play concluding with his triumphant killing of Macbeth. William Segar's *Booke of Honor and Armes* (1590) recognized the existence of a contradiction between the religious injunction and Elizabethan practice, admitting, "True it is, that the Christian law wills men to be of so perfect patience, as not only to endure injurious words, but also quietly to suffer every force and violence"; but that, he maintained, was not the ethos of his own day in matters of honor. Moreover, even in the teachings of the Church itself, Christ's rejection of the *lex talionis* was seen as applying to private individuals, not to a magistrate or prince who was, by virtue of his office, duty-bound to execute justice. Hamlet's recognition that heaven had appointed him, as prince and heir, to act as its "scourge and minister" echoes Aquinas's similar definition of this distinction, based on Romans 13:4: "He who takes vengeance on the wicked in keeping with his rank and position does not usurp what belongs to God, but makes use of the power granted him by God. For it is written of the earthly prince that 'he is God's minister, an avenger to execute wrath upon him that doeth evil.'"[22] How much more did this principle of the prince's duty to execute justice apply to avenging a regicide. Hamlet is, by rank, position, and family relationship, the individual on whom that duty unquestionably devolved.[23]

We return, then, to the reading of the opening lines of Hamlet's speech as contrasting the Christian "sufferance" of misfortune with the Stoic action of obtaining quietus for one's self with a bare bodkin. The two doctrines of Christianity and Stoicism were in Shakespeare's day diametrically opposed, for the concept of Christian Stoicism, the blending of the two systems due to be embraced by many of Addison's generation, had not yet come into vogue. Justus Lipsius was indeed attempting at this time to perform for Stoicism what Pico della Mirandola had succeeded in performing so much earlier for Platonism, to reconcile it with Christianity and to create a hybrid form, Neo-Stoicism, in which the secular or pagan version could be made acceptable to his contemporaries. His *De constantia* of 1584 and his *Politica* of 1589, both widely known and admired throughout Europe,[24] suggest, for a generation having witnessed the bloodshed of the sack of Antwerp in 1576 and the burning of Leuven in 1578, that Stoic constancy or patience in the face of adversity could be effectively combined with Christian devotion to produce a laudable submission to divine will. But there is no mention in either of those treatises of the recourse to suicide that formed, for the Renaissance, so central a part of Seneca's philosophy. When Lipsius did deal with that aspect, in his *Manuductio* (1604), he abruptly brushed it aside as incompatible with Christianity—"I do not give my vote to the Stoics on this matter"—since he was fully aware of the serious contradiction on that point between Stoic philosophy and the religious faith with which he was attempting to reconcile it.[25] He did, in fact, compose a treatise in favor of suicide, entitled *Thraseas*, but he destroyed it out of fear of the reaction it might provoke, an action that again suggests his realization that it could not be made compatible with the Christian faith. For Hamlet, therefore, Stoicism in its Senecan form, which at that time included suicide as a fundamental part of its program, was the antipole to Christianity, a recourse to the bare bodkin being, as he fully realized, a sin that no philosophizing could justify.

In Hamlet's depressed mood, then, the Stoic conception of death as release, as total cessation, made suicide so wonderfully tempting, offering an escape from the wearisome world into a void. It represents for him a *consummation* devoutly to be wished, but only on the condition that it is indeed a consummation, an ending to existence—"to die, to sleep, / No more." The phrasing here echoes Cicero's definition of the Stoic view of death as a dreamless sleep greatly to be desired—as it appeared in the translation by John Dolman that Shakespeare may have used: "my sense shall be extyncte, and my death resemble sleepe, whyche often wythout anye trouble of dreames, doth brynge a man most quiete reste."[26] Its allure lay in the assurance that all sense experience would be extinct, that the individual would cease to exist as such.

Yet in Hamlet's thoughts, the temptation of oblivion offered by Stoicism is suddenly and ominously offset as he envisions the dread possibility that, instead of the blankness of dreamless sleep, there may be an awakening into the Christian afterlife, with the dire penalties accorded there to suicide, fears that had not existed for the pre-Christian era of Seneca:

> To die, to sleep—
> To sleep, perchance to dream—ay, there's the rub,
> For in that sleep of death what dreams may come
> When we have shuffled off this mortal coil,
> Must give us pause; there's the respect
> That makes calamity of so long life.   (3.1.63–68)

It is the fear of such awakening that puzzles him, making him bear the ills he has rather than risk the damnation accorded to such a sin.

There is, in fact, notable support for this reading in the version of the speech preserved in quarto 1, the so-called "Bad Quarto," that version being even more specific in its reference to the afterlife, to the Day of Judgment, and to the rewards and penalties awaiting the soul. Whether that quarto was an early version by Shakespeare or a pirated reconstruction jotted down from memory for a rival company, it indicates what the speech conveyed to an Elizabethan, that the dreams Hamlet fears are indeed those associated with the Christian conception of postmortal existence and the reckoning due to take place on the Day of Judgment:

> For in that dreame of death, when wee awake,
> And borne before an euerlasting Iudge,
> From whence no passenger euer retur'nd,
> The vndiscouered country, at whose sight
> The happy smile, and the accursed damn'd.
> But for this, the ioyfull hope of this,
> Whol'd beare the scornes and flattery of the world.

Robert Watson suggests that faith in an afterlife was not universal in this period, since many religious works of the day, such as William Leigh's *The Christians Watch; or, An Heavenly Instruction* (1605) attacked those rejecting it, those who believed that after death "the Spirit vanisheth as the soft ayre" and "we shal bee hearafter as though wee had never been." The existence of such belief might seem, therefore, to have been sufficiently widespread to evoke such attacks. Some critics, however, have argued to the contrary, that Renaissance attacks on atheists do not prove their existence, that the theologians were demonizing an invented Otherness that would allow them to formulate more vigorously their own religious views.[27] But whichever view happens to be correct, there can be no doubt that mortalism was a heresy and that Hamlet was fully aware that denial of the afterlife could not accord with Christian faith.

As has long been noted, there is, in fact, no passage in Scriptures confirming Hamlet's statement that the Everlasting had set his canon against self-slaughter; but if the prohibition did not have scriptural sanction, in Shakespeare's day there was a consensus, both in Catholic and Protestant circles, that suicide was a sin fully deserving of damnation, indeed believed by some to be an act even more execrable than murder. Throughout the sixteenth and seventeenth centuries, it was rigorously condemned, perpetrators being tried posthumously by a coroner's jury for what was regarded as a heinous "offence against God, against the king, and against Nature."[28] Their moveable goods, including household items, tools, and money, were confiscated, even the leases they held on land were forfeited to the crown, so that their dependents were often reduced to pauperism. The night following the inquest, in a macabre ceremony, the body was cast naked into a pit dug at a crossroads, and a wooden stake hammered through the body before the grave was filled in. No prayers were recited and no minister attended.[29] As Puck chillingly remarks of past suicides,

> ghosts, wand'ring here and there,
> Troop home to churchyards. Damned spirits all,
> That in cross-ways and floods have burial,
> Already to their wormy beds are gone.
> For fear lest day should look their shames upon,
> They willfully themselves exile from light,
> And must for aye consort with black-brow'd Night.
> (3.2.381–87)

The burial ceremony was both a ritual exorcism and an example intended to discourage others.

John Donne's *Biathanatos* is often quoted as counterevidence, as a contemporary authorization of suicide, but the view is unfounded. Donne admits the attraction it holds for him, the method he visualizes suggesting a Stoic source— "whensoever any affliction assailes me, mee thinks I have the keyes of my prison in mine own hand, and no remedy presents it selfe so soone to my heart, as mine own sword." However, his conclusion in that treatise is to warn against any presumption that it is permissible: "I abstained purposely from extending this discourse to particular rules, or instances, both because I dare not professe my self a Maister in so curious a science, and because the limits are obscure, and steepy, and slippery, and narrow, and every errour deadly, except where a competent dilligence being fore-used, a mistaking in our conscience may provide an excuse." It is, he suggests, an act permissible only when performed in the service of God, such as Samson's toppling of the temple onto the heads of his enemies even though he knew that the collapse would cause his own death, in fact specifically praying, "Let mee lose my life with the Philistims."[30] Saint Augustine, in *The City of God*, took a firmer stand, disqualifying suicide that might be construed as being in God's service, ruling, for example, that the women who, during the capture of Rome in 410, slew themselves in order to avoid being raped were wrong to do so since rape would only have affected their bodies, not their souls.[31] But interesting as these aspects may be in assessing general attitudes to suicide, they are irrelevant to our present topic as Hamlet's contemplated suicide has in it no hint of martyrdom or divine justification.

The Faerie Queene provides evidence of prevalent views. Una, representing the true Church, reacts in horror as she snatches the dagger from the despairing Knight:

> Which when as *Vna* saw, through euery vaine
> The crudled cold ran to her well of life,
> As in a swowne: but soone reliu'd againe,
> Out of his hand she snatcht the cursed knife,
> And threw it to the ground, enraged rife.   (1.9.51–55)

and she castigates him as a "fraile, feeble, fleshly wight" for entertaining even for a moment such devilish and un-Christian thoughts. Marlowe's Faust, in the tradition that suicide was a form of temptation by the devil, hears in a moment of despair a voice informing him that he is damned. Before him appears an array of guns, knives, swords, poison, halters, and steel as the means to slay himself, and only the intervention of the Old Man prevents him from taking his life. Michel de Montaigne, for all his admiration of the ancient Stoics, concludes that there is "more constancie in using the chaine that holds us than in breaking the same; and more triall of stedfastnesse in Regulus than in Cato." Of the latter's suicide, Montaigne finds it difficult to imagine that it was motivated by rational Stoic *apathia:* "when

I see him die, tearing and mangling his entrails, I cannot simply content my selfe to beleeve that at that time he had his soule wholly exempted from all trouble or free from vexation: cannot imagine he did only maintaine himself in this march or course which the rule of the Stoike sect had ordained unto him, setled, without alteration or emotion, and impassible."[32] On the Continent, Pierre Charon, who combined his priesthood with an admiration of Stoicism, in his *De la Sagesse* (1601) advocated suicide on the condition that it resulted from mature reflection, but his book scandalized the clergy and was placed on the Catholic Index. In *Religio Medici,* Sir Thomas Browne attacked the Stoic doctrine "that can allow a man to be his owne *Assassine,* and so highly extoll the end and suicide of *Cato;* this is indeed not to feare death, but yet to bee afraid of life. It is a brave act of valour to contemne death; but where life is more terrible than death, it is then the truest valour to dare to live: and herein Religion hath taught us a noble example; for all the valiant acts of *Curtius, Scaevola,* or *Codrus,* do not parallel, or match, that one of *Job.*"[33] That last contrast, between the Stoics and Job, summarizes the crux of Hamlet's problem as expressed in his soliloquy, the choice between suicide and the Christian advocacy of sufferance.

If the above examples indicate how widespread was the philosophical interest in Stoic suicide during this period, there was, in the experience of one of Shakespeare's contemporaries, a real-life parallel to Hamlet's dilemma. Anthony Stafford, embittered by the dishonor to the family name incurred when his brother was publicly executed for sodomy, was driven seriously to consider suicide. He decided finally to reject Seneca's advice, explaining in *Niobe Dissolv'd into a Nilus* (1611) that his Christian principles forbade him from taking that course. Rhetorically, he addressed the spirit of Seneca: "Pardon me, therfore, thou deep Dictator of diuine morality, that I assent not to thy forenamed sentence; seeing it dissents from the word of God, & controules his commandement, who saith, *Thou shalt not kill.* Whom? Not thy selfe; not another. Which authoritie I am enforced to take vp."[34]

Of Shakespeare's own view there can be little doubt. Throughout the Roman plays he espouses the Stoic standpoint, presenting suicide as an admirable act. Apart from Brutus, the "noblest Roman of them all," who runs on his sword, Antony, dying in the same manner, proudly declares he is "a Roman by a Roman / Valiantly vanquish'd"; and even the Egyptian Cleopatra chooses to follow her lover's lead by doing what is brave, what is noble, determining to die "after the high Roman fashion." In non-Roman plays set in an essentially Christian world, however, the reverse is true. Romeo does not kill himself in order to achieve an honorable and noble end, a nullification of existence, but in despair, horrified by what awaits him:

> *Romeo.* Thou detestable maw, thou womb of death,
> Gorg'd with the dearest morsel of the earth,
> Thus I enforce thy rotten jaws to open,
> And in despite I'll cram thee with more food. (5.3.45–48)

Othello has no alternative, knowing as he does that death awaits him if he stays for trial. In *Macbeth,* a choric figure describes with contempt the suicide of Lady Macbeth, the "fiend-like queen / Who, as 'tis thought, by self and violent hands / Took off her life" (5.9.35–37). But the fullest indication of Shakespeare's view in the context of his non-Roman plays occurs in *King Lear,* which, despite its seemingly pagan setting and repeated references to "the gods," is permeated with the concepts of Christian selflessness and compassion, with Cordelia, Edgar, and Kent exemplifying those ideals. There, Edgar's device of the imaginary cliff from which Gloucester intends to throw himself to his death is designed to counter the Roman view, to impress upon his father the need to submit to the will of heaven, to suffer or "endure" misfortune, to eschew suicide and to wait patiently for the allotted time of decease. Chorically, he approves of Gloucester's eventual submission, his decision to discard all thought of self-slaughter and humbly await his destined end:

> *Glou.* You ever-gentle gods, take my breath from me,
> Let not my worser spirit tempt me again
> To die before you please!
> *Edg.* Well pray you, father. (4.6.217–20)

When the rescuing army is routed and Gloucester again considers, if not suicide then at least a passive self-exposure to death, Edgar is there once again to urge the Christian principle of sufferance, of submission to divine will, to which he receives Gloucester's assent:

> *Edg.* What, in ill thoughts again? Men must endure
> Their going hence, even as their coming hither,
> Ripeness is all. . . .
> *Glou.* And that's true too. (4.2.9–12)

In *Hamlet*, Shakespeare is at pains to affirm the Christian condemnation of suicide as being an iniquitous act, using Ophelia's death as a means of underscoring the point. Her demise, as we have learned both from the affecting scene of her madness and from Gertrude's melancholy account of her death, is clearly no suicide. She slips into the stream unawares, singing mindlessly until the weight of her wet clothes drags her to her death. Even had it been deliberate, the Church of England's stand on suicide by the mentally deranged was unequivocally merciful—it declared repeatedly, from the Reformation onward, that such persons were to be granted full Christian burial, a decision formally codified in the Anglican *Constitutions* of 1603. With that ruling familiar to every Elizabethan, the scene of the priest's harsh refusal to grant her obsequies emerges as entirely baseless—except insofar as it was Shakespeare's intent to highlight the reverse situation, the gravity of deliberate self-slaughter by those of sound mind. The debate, moreover, is introduced twice, as if Shakespeare were determined to emphasize the point. If the comic scenes in Shakespeare's tragedies offer in distorted form the themes fundamental to each play, it is surely significant that the opening of the famed gravedigger scene consists of a discussion, in comic pseudo-legal terms, of this very topic, the uncompromising attitude of the Church toward those deliberately ending their lives:

> *1 Clown.* Is she to be buried in Christian burial when she willfully seeks her own salvation?
> *2 Clown.* I tell thee she is, therefore make her grave straight. The crowner hath sate on her, and finds it Christian burial.
> *1 Clown.* How can that be, unless she drown'd herself in her own defense?
> *2 Clown.* Why, 'tis found so.
> *1 Clown.* It must be *se offendendo*; it cannot be else. For here lies the point: if I drown myself wittingly, it argues an act; and an act hath three branches—it is to act, to do, and to perform; argal, she drown'd herself wittingly.
> *2 Clown.* Nay, but hear you, goodman delver—
> *1 Clown.* Give me leave. Here lies the water; good. Here stands the man; good. If the man go to this water and drown himself, it is, will he, nill he, he goes, mark you that. But if the water come to him and drown him, he drowns not himself; argal, he that is not guilty of his own death shortens not his own life.
> *2 Clown.* But is this law?
> *1 Clown.* Ay, marry, is't—crowner's quest law.
> *2 Clown.* Will you ha' the truth an't? If this had not been a gentlewoman, she should have been buried out a' Christian burial. (5.1.1–25)

A little later, as the funeral cortège enters, the priest, angrily rejecting Laertes's demand for further funeral rites, insists, as had the gravedigger, that were it not for royal command she should "in ground unsanctified have lodg'd / Till the last trumpet," with shards, flints, and pebbles cast on her grave. A requiem sung in her honor would, he adds, have profaned the peaceable dead.

Roland Frye, who has studied closely the ecclesiastical rulings on suicide and the treatment afforded in instances recorded during this period, remains puzzled. He can find no explanation for the priest's attitude in this scene. There was, he points out, no theological justification in the Catholic, the Anglican, or the Reformed churches that would have sanctioned the canceling of obsequies for an insane suicide. Moreover, there was no legal basis whereby a priest could set aside the verdict of a coroner, so that the issuing of a royal command, which the priest claims has overruled his clerical objection, was entirely unnecessary. Frye therefore can find no reason for the inclusion of the scene.[35] But its inclusion is justified when one perceives Shakespeare's desire to draw his audience's attention to the reverse situation, to the dire consequences for those committing suicide while in full possession of their mental faculties, and hence to the implications of that threat for Hamlet himself.

Hamlet's misgivings, his fear of the undiscovered country from whose bourne no traveler returns, is, as he specifically states, the sole obstacle to the longed-for quietus offered by Stoicism, a fear intensified by his realization of the fate awaiting a Christian suicide should he himself choose that path. The importance Hamlet attaches to the afterlife in this passage contradicts Stephen Greenblatt's firm statement that "Shakespeare seems to have had little or no interest in the kind of posthumous existence that the cult of Purgatory and prayers for the dead had helped to foster."[36] What else is Hamlet's concern but, as he informs us in the clearest possible terms, the fear of the "dreams" that may emerge in the sleep of death, his fear of the country from whose bourne no traveler returns? It is that "conscience" or, in the Elizabethan usage of that term, our consciousness of postmortal existence that makes cowards of us all, and that prevents him from performing the courageous act of ending his life in the manner so enticing to him in this dark mood of world-weariness.[37] That awareness of the world to come is echoed, moreover, in his hesitation to kill Claudius on finding him at prayer in the chapel, his determination to catch him about some act that has no relish of salvation in it, so that "his soul may be as damned and black / As hell, whereto it goes" (3.3.94–95).

It is time to return to the central speech of the play and its implications for the drama as a whole. For, in searching for the cause of Hamlet's procrastination, we should listen to his own statement, that it is his fear of punishment for suicide that alone compels him to continue to bear the whips and scorns of time, that prevents him from ending his life, in the Stoic fashion, with a bare bodkin:

> Who would fardels bear,
> To grunt and sweat under a weary life,
> But that the dread of something after death—
> The undiscover'd country, from whose bourn
> No traveller returns, puzzles the will,
> And makes us rather bear those ills we have
> Than fly to others that we know not of?
> Thus conscience does make cowards of us all,
> And thus the native hue of resolution
> Is sicklied o'er with the pale cast of thought,
> And enterprises of great pitch and moment
> With this regard their currents turn awry
> And lose the name of action. (3.1.75–98)

It is the dread of something after death that "sicklie[s] o'er" the native hue of resolution, that puzzles the will, that plunges him into thought instead of action, that prevents him from fulfilling the enterprise of great pitch and moment to which he has been called.

His predicament is, however, more complex, since his meditation on the justification for ending his life does not address the reasons prompting him to do so. But the speech forms the lead-in to that most central question. As the king had remarked earlier with considerable justice, before Hamlet has any idea that his father was murdered, a father's death should not in itself induce the kind of inconsolable melancholy into which Hamlet has been plunged; nor, one may add, should the remarriage of his mother produce such profound morbidity.[38] There must be beyond those two factors some greater cause of despondency, more comprehensive in its significance and thereby of intimate concern to his audiences, both contemporary and subsequent.

The cause is, I believe, intimately concerned with an essentially new attitude toward death emerging near the end of the High Renaissance. While Wilson Knight is right in seeing Hamlet's obsession with mortality and putrefaction as the core of the play, he sees it not as a concern of universal significance for humankind but as an anomaly, as part of Hamlet's sickness of the soul, a disease of his wit creating in him a spiritual atrophy.[39] The horror of seeing himself doomed to decay has disintegrated his mind, leading him into a madness that makes him rail at Ophelia and upbraid his mother—although what connection his fixation on death has with upbraiding his mother and railing at Ophelia is left unstated. That connection and, indeed, the larger significance of his obsession with putrefaction must surely be seen as central to the play itself and the prelude to his contemplation of self-slaughter.

An integral part of the emergence from medievalism and the Renaissance's new concept of the dignity of the individual was its validation of the pursuit of eternal fame, the conviction that within the grasp of each human being was the potential for achieving noble and lasting reputation. In the medieval world, the Christian emphasis upon humility, with its categorizing of pride as a cardinal sin, had prevented such aspirations. But that interdiction gradually lost its force, supplanted by a new sense of the individual's ability, after attaining glory, to live on in human memory and thereby survive the grave. Pico's essay on the dignity of man claims that the pursuit of philosophy is justified by the honor and glory it provides. In Shakespeare's writings too, the composition of a sonnet is now seen as preserving throughout generations the fame of both poet and subject, outlasting mortality itself:

> Nor shall death brag thou wand'rest in his shade,
> When in eternal lines to time thou grow'st,
> So long as men can breathe or eyes can see,
> So long lives this, and this gives life to thee.

Even within the heart of the Catholic Church, despite its formal cultivation of humility, that aspiration took firm hold, with Pope Julius II commissioning the construction of a gargantuan tomb intended to preserve his memory, a tomb in which Michelangelo's massive figure of *Moses* was to form only a minor element. Where Masaccio's *Holy Trinity* had depicted, below the holy scene, a decaying corpse with the minatory legend, "What you are, I once was; what I am, you will become," the new view gradually replaced that medieval warning of decay, Ghiberti proudly inserting into the magnificent doors he designed for the Florentine baptistery a bust of himself, recording for posterity the artist who created them, while in no less famous a work, the portrait of Arnolfini and his wife, there appears on the wall the grandiose statement: "Jan Van Eyck was here."

Herein lay Hamlet's fundamental predicament. The splendor of Renaissance man, now able in Neoplatonic terms to reach up to heaven and imbibe elements of the divine, had animated such ambitiously imaginative projects as the attempt by Marlowe's Tamburlaine to conquer the world and achieve a reputation enduring through subsequent generations—aiming to "become immortal like the gods" (1.2.201). Before Agincourt, Shakespeare's Henry V exhorts his troops with the stirring vision:

> This day is call'd the feast of Crispian:
> He that outlives this day, and comes safe home,
> Will stand a tip-toe when this day is nam'd,
> And rouse him at the name of Crispian. . . .
> This story shall the good man teach his son;
> And Crispin Crispian shall ne'er go by,
> From this day to the ending of the world,
> But we in it shall be remembered.

By the end of the sixteenth century, however, a reaction had set in to this conviction of immortality. Doubts were beginning to arise, a dissatisfaction with that concept, producing the more disturbed, often agonized perspective of mannerist painting and of metaphysical verse that was to follow. Previously, at the height of the Renaissance, a skull appended to a portrait—such as the anonymous painting of Sir Thomas Gresham in the National Portrait Gallery, or that of an *English Gentleman* by Remigius Hogenberg in the library of the University of Pennsylvania—left the sitter untroubled by its presence. Death formed a natural part of life. Hans Holbein's painting *The Ambassadors* offers a frontal view representing the splendid achievements of the Renaissance, two distinguished personages in their gorgeous robes surrounded by the symbols of human achievement, including an astrolabe, navigational instruments, and items representing music, literature, and theology, while slashed across the foreground is a *memento mori*, a skull reminding us of the end of life. But neither figure reveals any concern, and the two views of life are physically divorced in the painting, the skull only recognizable as such by being gazed at from the side, through a hole in the frame, a view in which the main scene is blurred. There is no sense of horror involved. Death formed a natural part of life. As Hal casually reminds Falstaff on going gallantly into battle, "Why, thou owest God a death."

However, as a reaction set in, death began to seem a negation of all achievement. Donne was haunted by visions of the putrefaction of the body, by the sense that mortality vitiates everything attained in this world. For him, the sole remaining hope was belief in an afterlife, in a resurrection that would retrospectively inform life with meaning. Without that, the decay of the body, he declares somberly, would mark a negation of all. The dust of both aristocrat and plebeian will, he declares, be

> mingled with the dust of every high way, and of every dunghill, and swallowed in every puddle and pond. . . . This is the most inglorious and contemptible *vilification*, the most deadly and peremptory *nullification* of man, that we can consider. . . . This death of *incineration* and dispersion, is, to naturall *reason*, the most *irrecoverable death* of all, and yet *Domini Domini sunt exitus mortis*, unto God the Lord

belong the issues of death, and by *recompacting* this *dust* into the *same body,* and *reinanimating* the *same body* with the *same soule,* hee shall in a blessed and glorious *resurrection* give mee such an *issue from* this *death,* as shal never passe into any other death, but establish me into a life that shall last as long as the *Lord of life* himselfe.⁴⁰

The validity of existence is thus transferred from the hope of lasting fame in this world to the hope of existence in the next. If, as in the Stoicism that had at first seemed so attractive, there is no survival after death, then death is indeed a total nullification of man.

Hamlet, living during the period of that transition, is caught inextricably between the Renaissance and the Mannerist views. On the one hand, he perceives the divine potentiality of man, whose spirit, infinite in faculties is, in its apprehension, like a god. Yet his thoughts are fraught with qualms at the possibility of a tragic countermanding of that view if, deprived of a soul, nothing is to be left of man but the stench of a decaying corpse, a quintessence of dust: "What a piece of work is a man, how noble in reason, how infinite in faculties, in form and moving, how express and admirable, in action how like an angel, in apprehension how like a god! the beauty of the world; the paragon of animals; and yet to me what is this quintessence of dust?" (2.2.303–08). Ernest Jones remarks that the death of Shakespeare's father in 1601, the year of the play's first recorded performance, may have plunged the dramatist into thoughts of his own mortality, but that is unlikely to have been the cause, as the play seems to have existed in some form prior to that date.⁴¹ In 1598, Gabriel Harvey wrote in his copy of Thomas Speght's edition of the works of Chaucer: "The younger sort take much delight in Shakespeare's Venus and Adonis, but his Lucrece and his tragedy of Hamlet Prince of Denmarke have it in them to please the wiser sort."⁴² It is more likely that Shakespeare was responding to this cultural shift of his time, the new concern with death as seeming to disqualify all life's achievements. The skull Hamlet contemplates may technically be Yorick's, a fellow of "infinite" jest; but it is, of course, his own skull on which his thoughts focus, making his gorge rise at the thought that everything he cherishes, including eternal honor, may end in the stench of decaying flesh. That his concern is not merely with death as such but with the nullification of postmortal fame is evidenced by the historical figure to which his mind instinctively turns at that moment, a person whose name had become synonymous with greatness, a supreme example of human achievement and, it might be thought, of undying fame:

> *Ham.* Dost thou think Alexander look'd a' this fashion i' th' earth?
> *Hor.* E'en so.
> *Ham.* And smelt so? pah! (5.1.197–199)

Repeatedly Hamlet traces in his imagination the journey of such illustrious men to their gruesome and absurd end as stoppers to a bunghole, or traveling through the stomachs of worm and fish to conclude their existence in the guts of a beggar.[43]

For Hamlet the odor of mortal putrefaction bears enormous significance, becoming an obsession. Polonius has become a meal for worms, not where he eats but where he is eaten. The directions Hamlet offers the courtiers as they rush off at his hint of the body's whereabouts is accompanied with the parting quip that, if they cannot find him at once, they will soon "nose" him as they ascend the stairs. Here, indeed, is a foretaste of the obsession with "vermiculation" that was to play so central a role in Donne's sermons, the dread realization that fame and honor in this world do not survive the grave. And it points forward no less to Donne's perception that death equalizes not merely because it comes to all, but because it obliterates all distinction between the nobility and the lowborn:

> The dust of great persons graves is speechlesse too, it sayes nothing, it distinguishes nothing. As soon the dust of a

wretch whom thou wouldest not, as of a Prince whom thou couldest not look upon, will trouble thine eyes, if the winde blow it thither; and when a whirle-winde hath blowne the dust of the Church-yard into the Church, and the man sweeps out the dust of the Church into the Church-yard, who will undertake to sift those dusts again, and to pronounce, This is the Patrician, this is the noble flowre, and this the yeomanly, this the Plebeian bran.[44]

For Hamlet, it is not only the process of vermiculation that forms the basis of his spiritual torment—questioning obsessively how long a man will lie in the earth before he will rot. That concern is but a symptom of a deeper problem, namely, what little time it takes for the reputation of a man, however glorious, even a ruler who once intimidated the world, to fade into oblivion:

> Imperious Caesar, dead and turn'd to clay,
> Might stop a hole to keep the wind away.
> O that that earth which kept the world in awe
> Should patch a wall t' expel the winter's flaw! (5.1.213–16)

Such thoughts leave his Stoic friend totally unmoved, Horatio responding casually, "Twere to consider too curiously, to consider so." Wilson Knight's dismissal of Horatio as being, after the initial scene with the Ghost, a queer shadowy creature who rarely gets beyond such obsequious responses as, "E'en so, my lord," misses the dramatic effect of that Stoical indifference to death, an insouciance that throughout the play highlights by contrast the intensity of Hamlet's misgivings.[45]

If we place this concern against the background of the era, it becomes apparent how great a shift in conception this play displays. As Stephen Greenblatt notes in his study of Sir Walter Ralegh, deaths upon the scaffold had been treated by High Renaissance victims as dramatic scenes to be remembered with reverence by future generations.[46] The victims made every effort to ensure that their fame would survive the tomb. When Mary Queen of Scots' outer black gown was removed at the moment before her execution, she was revealed to be wearing defiantly beneath it a robe of crimson silk, the traditional garb of the Catholic martyr. Ralegh expressed his gratitude that "God, of his infinite Goodness . . . hath sent me to Die in the sight of so Honourable an Assembly, and not in Darkness," and he proceeded to play to the crowd, joking to his friends, refusing the offer of a blindfold, and boldly commanding the hesitant executioner to strike. Such theatricality implied a conviction that such scenes would redound to their future fame, an assumption contrasting vividly with Hamlet's growing conviction that fame was a mere chimera.

The occasional flippancy in Hamlet's comments about death, such as he "will stay till you come" or "seek him i' th' other place yourself," cannot conceal the angst that prompts them, the light-heartedness and pungent humor of such sallies serving not only to insult the king under the protection of the prince's supposed insanity but more importantly to provide for himself a safety valve for the pressures building within. Whether his madness is real or pretended is to some extent a pointless question—Harry Levin has discussed the terms that might define his condition, what was called on the Continent "English spleen," or by modern psychologists "melancholy adust"[47]—and there was, of course, the precedent of Hieronimo in Thomas Kyd's *Spanish Tragedy*. Whatever the source, however, and whatever the technical name affixed to his "wit's disease," the antic disposition that Hamlet puts on performs a far more subtle function than mere disguise for his plan of revenge. In the same way as those becoming tipsy at a party often play-act, pretending to be more seriously drunk in order to conceal their condition from others as well as to avoid confronting it themselves, so Hamlet, brought to the brink of nervous collapse by his crisis, instinctively assumes the guise of madness, of nervous breakdown, a semblance allowing him to blur the border between conscious pretense and moments of actual distraction. The pretense serves also, as it does for the tipsy reveler, to safeguard his privacy, to protect his inner self from the prying eyes of those about him.

It is time, perhaps, to return to Bradley's comment that Hamlet's madness derives, as he himself so frequently states, from his mother's hasty remarriage. As Bradley puts it (and the wording is especially important), it is the "ghastly discovery of her true nature," his disappointment at her appalling choice that maddens him. She had

> married Hamlet's uncle, a man utterly contemptible and loathsome in his eyes; married him in what to Hamlet was incestuous wedlock; married him not for any reason of state, nor even out of old family affection, but in such a way that her son was forced to see in her action not only an astounding shallowness of feeling but an eruption of coarse sensuality, "rank and gross," speeding post-haste to its horrible delight. Is it possible to conceive an experience more desolating to a man such as we have seen Hamlet to be; and is its result anything but perfectly natural? It brings bewildered horror, then loathing, then despair of human nature.[48]

Bradley is not wrong in seeing that event as the ultimate cause of Hamlet's anguish, but he has, I believe, viewed it from the wrong angle. For Hamlet, in contemplating the event, is focusing not on his mother's choice. It is not *her* character that has disgusted him but the implications her action has for his father. It is, in brief, the dreadful realization that her hasty remarriage, her swift forgetting of the memory of his father, seems to prove that nothing survives the grave even for a modicum of time:

> *Ham.* What should a man do but be merry, for look you how cheerfully my mother looks, and my father died within's two hours.
> *Oph.* Nay 'tis twice two months, my lord.
> *Ham.* So long? Nay then let the devil wear black, for I'll have a suit of sables. O heavens, die two months ago, and not forgotten yet? Then there's hope a great man's memory may outlive his life half a year. (3.3.125–32)

His fury derives from the time factor, the brief period that has elapsed before his father was forgotten, that aspect of time recurring maddeningly throughout his opening soliloquy, delivered before he knows of the murder:

> But two months dead, nay, not so much, not two . . .
> Must I remember? Why, she should hang on him
> As if increase of appetite had grown
> By what it fed on, and yet, within a month—
> Let me not think on't! . . .
> A little month . . .
> O God, a beast that wants discourse of reason
> Would have mourn'd longer. (1.2.138–51)

In the bedroom scene, he feverishly reminds his mother of the husband she has so readily forgotten, thrusting his father's portrait at her in order to recall to her the features she had once loved and that had so swiftly dimmed into oblivion:

> See what a grace was seated on this brow:
> Hyperion's curls, the front of Jove himself,
> An eye like Mars, to threaten and command,
> A station like the herald Mercury
> New lighted on a heaven-kissing hill,
> A combination and a form indeed,
> Where every god did seem to set his seal
> To give the world assurance of a man.
> This was your husband. (3.4.55–63)

No fame, it seems, not even the remembrance of devoted love, outlasts death. The funeral baked meats, as he wryly remarks to Horatio, did but coldly furnish forth the marriage tables.

Marjorie Garber, in her deconstructionist reading of the play, draws attention to the prominence of remembering, listing the numerous occurrences of the term throughout the play. But she interprets its significance in line with the Hegelian terms for memory, *Erinnerung* and *Gedchtnis*, as Paul De Man defines them. She develops, therefore, in part relying upon Derrida, a distinction between Hamlet's recollection of the past and his need to inscribe, to set down the Ghost's commands on his tables or tablets.[49] But the centrality of forgetting and memory in the play seems to me less abstruse, residing in this haunting fear that the memory of the dead evaporates at the graveside, incapable of surviving death.

For Hamlet, the implications of this contemporary problem extend beyond philosophical speculation; they paralyze action itself. If nothing exists beyond the grave and all life's attainments sink into oblivion at death, what value is there in settling scores in this world, in avenging crimes, and effecting justice? As was noted earlier, in the "To be, or not to be" speech he states specifically that, plunged into contemplation of the implications of death, his ability to act is paralyzed, the enterprise to which he refers there clearly including the duty of avenging his father's death.

Hamlet's tragedy is one of timing, his summons to act as scourge and minister reaching him at the very moment when the validity of the task has itself come into question. The "earlier" Hamlet, as he was before his father's death, the glass of fashion, the observed of all observers, epitomizing the finest ideals of the High Renaissance, would, we may assume, have had no hesitation in undertaking the task—hence his constant amazement at his own delay, when he castigates himself as coward and pigeon-livered for failing to fat the region kites with the murderer's offal as honor demands. But the pursuit of honor has itself come into question. Hence, Shakespeare's insertion of the scene in which Hamlet observes Fortinbras marching to Poland to attain the fame and glory of victory, fame that now appears to Hamlet to be an absurd and empty achievement. The "imposthume" that inward breaks and shows no cause without—the oft-quoted image characterizing Hamlet's sense of disease and decay—is invoked precisely at that point, as he perceives the madness of 20,000 men going to their graves for some paltry piece of ground, for no more than "a fantasy and trick of fame," to bring glory to a prince,

> Whose spirit with divine ambition puff'd
> Makes mouths at the invisible event,
> Exposing what is mortal and unsure
> To all that fortune, death, and danger dare,
> Even for an eggshell. Rightly to be great
> Is not to stir without great argument,
> But greatly to find quarrel in a straw
> When honour's at the stake. (4.4.49–56)

Honor is an illusion, eternal fame a chimera. If the sight of Fortinbras imperturbably pursuing martial glory goads Hamlet into swearing yet again that he, who has so much greater motives, whose own honor is at stake, will now act, implicit throughout that speech is his disturbing consciousness of the counterargument, the pointlessness of ambition in a world where renown is doomed to wither in the tomb together with the putrefying flesh.

Hamlet's melancholy, his sense of being his father's sole mourner, had, then, preceded his meeting with the Ghost, had preceded the knowledge of his father's murder. Amid the gorgeously robed celebrants in the opening scene at court, one lone figure sits in sable garb, provocatively reminding them of the debt owed to the memory of the dead. His thoughts dwell constantly on his late father. He sees him in his mind's eye even before Horatio informs him of the Ghost's appearance. Hamlet's fateful meeting with his father's spirit may have imposed upon him an unanticipated task of revenge, but in one respect it offered not a new demand, but the endorsement of an already present determination. The Ghost's repeated command not to forget, not to allow his father's memory to rot on Lethe's wharf, is one that he takes up with wild determination. Hence the impassioned, hyperbolic oaths that follow that injunction, revealing the sensitive point it has struck in his disturbed soul:

> Remember thee!
> Ay, thou poor ghost, whiles memory holds a seat
> In this distracted globe. Remember thee!

> Yea, from the table of my memory
> I'll wipe away all trivial fond records,
> All saws of books, all forms, all pressures past
> That youth and observation copied there,
> And thy commandement all alone shall live
> Within the book and volume of my brain,
> Unmix'd with baser matter.   (1.5.95–104)

Hamlet seizes upon the Ghost's final words, "Adieu, adieu! Remember me," as the command to direct all his future actions, conforming as it does to the somber thoughts that had already induced his melancholy.

Memory is thus the key concept of the play. Ophelia, mourning her lost father, offers rosemary for remembrance, adding the plea, "Pray you, love, remember," words that suggest retrospectively her empathy with Hamlet, an impression of her basic kinship with him tragically thwarted by events. All nature seems to her to be grieving for her father's decease, the violets withering away at his passing. But the reverse holds true for her less sensitive brother, the foil to Hamlet. Laertes's primary impetus for revenge is neither filial affection nor respect for his father's memory but the preservation of his own honor, the fear that failing to kill his father's murderer would brand *him* a bastard, detracting from his reputation:

> *Laertes*: That drop of blood that's calm proclaims me bastard,
> Cries cuckold to my father, brands the harlot
> Even here between the chaste unsmirched brows
> Of my true mother.   (4.5.118–21)

What infuriates Laertes is the dishonor to the family name involved in the hugger-mugger of the burial—an obscure funeral with no "trophy, sword, nor hatchment o'er his bones, / No noble rite nor formal ostentation." The thoughts of the afterlife that disturb Hamlet so profoundly hold no terrors for Laertes. He is ready to cut Hamlet's throat in the church, scorning all fears of heavenly retribution for desecrating the sanctuary offered by an altar. And his sentiments are the same in contemplating the killing of the heir to the throne. Both worlds, this world and the next, he spurns in his pursuit of honor:

> To hell, allegiance! vows, to the blackest devil!
> Conscience and grace, to the profoundest pit!
> I dare damnation. To this point I stand,
> That both the world, I give to negligence,
> Let come what comes. (4.5.132–36)

If the function of a dramatic foil is to highlight by contrast the qualities of the main character, the disparity here lies not only in the more obvious element of Laertes's impetuosity but also in the reasons motivating it, namely, his contempt for the next world and his total insensitivity to the philosophical problem afflicting Hamlet.

That problem, involving as it does Hamlet's doubts concerning the Christian afterlife and the attraction of a Stoic cessation after death, might be thought contradicted by the appearance of the Ghost returning from beyond the grave. Absolute certainty concerning the existence of an afterlife would free him from his dilemma, removing the possibility of Stoic suicide. Not only does the Ghost appear to Hamlet and to the audience in visible form but also he supplies a harrowing account of the penalties in Purgatory imposed upon him for his past misdemeanors:

> Doom'd for a certain term to walk the night,
> And for the day confin'd to fast in fires,
> Till the foul crimes done in my days of nature
> Are burnt and purg'd away. (1.5.10–13)

That would seem to provide sufficient evidence for Hamlet to cast aside his Stoic tendencies and, on this proof of the existence of heaven and hell, to adopt the Christian path. But Shakespeare is careful to inform us on more than one occasion that Hamlet remains unsure of the Ghost's authenticity, uncertain whether what he has seen was a spirit of health or a goblin damned. Noel Tailleped's *Treatise of*

Ghosts (1588) had declared that evil spirits search diligently for persons "already of a melancholic or Saturnian humor, who on account of some great loss, or haply because he deems his honour tarnished" will be especially susceptible to the subtle fetches and foul tricks employed by the spirit to drag him to hell, and a lengthy examination of Protestant and Catholic views has led some to believe that the Ghost in *Hamlet* is indeed evil. But that conclusion is unconvincing. It is true that Hamlet addresses the Ghost at his first meeting as a being of "questionable" shape, but the phrase is ambiguous. It is possible that he means the Ghost's nature is open to doubt, but more likely the word is used in its more literal sense, namely, that the Ghost appears available for questioning, for the series of passionate enquiries that follow:

> O, answer me?
> Let me not burst in ignorance, but tell
> Why thy canoniz'd bones, hearsed in death,
> Have burst their cerements; why the sepulchre. (1.3.45–48)

Immediately after that meeting, Hamlet firmly declares his conviction: "Touching this vision here, / It is an honest ghost, that let me tell you" (1.5.137–38). Were Hamlet seriously to question its authenticity, he would not have sworn so unequivocally in the first meeting to accept the task imposed upon him. So much for his basic conviction. On the other hand, there can be no ambiguity concerning the doubt he expresses later:

> The spirit that I have seen
> May be a dev'l; and the dev'l hath power
> T' assume a pleasing shape, yea, and perhaps,
> Out of my weakness and my melancholy,
> As he is very potent with such spirits,
> Abuses me to damn me. (2.2.627–32)

If, as many critics have noted, this hint of the Ghost's possibly devilish origin seems countered by the seriousness with which Hamlet and the audience have come to regard it, we may ask why Shakespeare should have introduced into the play any questioning of its validity. The answer would appear to lie just here. The presence of the Ghost as the motivating force for revenge was an essential ingredient of the plot, but Hamlet's momentary mistrust of its authenticity ensures that neither its appearance nor its account of Purgatory constitute for Hamlet any final proof of the existence of the afterlife. That doubt not only provides a further reason for deferring action but also leaves room for Hamlet's hesitant speculations concerning postmortal existence.[50]

Indeed, the contrast between Hamlet's view of the Ghost and that of the audience occupies a central place in the drama. Whether or not we believe in ghosts outside the theater, we as audience are presented at the opening with a scene leaving little doubt either of its actuality or of its veracity. It appears on the stage witnessed by two stolid guards, its presence soon corroborated by an otherwise skeptical Horatio. And any suspicion that it is evil in source is surely dispelled when its account of the murder receives the fullest corroboration both in the king's agitated response to the *Mousetrap* and in his confession in the chapel. With those endorsements, we are in a position to watch, as in all great tragedy, Hamlet's struggle to attain a truth already known to us—that, despite his doubts, there is indeed a Christian afterlife, that all does not end with the grave, and that consequently there is, after all, validity in the quest for renown and reputation. But while that message may reach us, it is exposed at the same time to questioning, as reflected in Hamlet's own doubts, creating once again a tension between the traditional Renaissance view and the emergent cultural configuration soon to dominate the Jacobean era, misgivings whether the pursuit of eternal fame is ultimately valid.

The problem Hamlet confronts is never resolved by him. He seems shortly before his death to have become more resigned to mortality, a little less troubled by its implications:

"There's a special providence in the fall of a sparrow. If it be now, 'tis not to come, if it be not to come, it will be now; if it be not now, yet it will come: the readiness is all" (5.2.220–22). On the other hand, he kills Claudius not because he has found an answer but because, as with Polonius's death and his own leap from the pirate ship, the situation in which he finds himself demands immediate action, leaving him no time to sink into thought and lose himself in speculation about life and death.

For the audience, however, an answer is suggested. As in tragedy at large, if the hero dies before fully grasping the answer to his predicament, he has pointed the way for us to apprehend it, to perceive it before he himself does. Hamlet at the last moment offers that indication when he resists the appeal of Stoicism in his final scene. Aware of his approaching end, with his last remaining strength he wrests the poisoned cup from the grasp of Horatio, opposing his friend's determination to act the antique Roman rather than the Dane.

Hamlet's plea, "Absent thee from felicity awhile," is more subtle than a mere plea for postponing suicide. On the one hand, the word "felicity" was the term applied in Stoicism to the freedom from pain and worry achieved by the cessation of existence at death. Hamlet thus acknowledges and respects Horatio's belief while begging him to postpone awhile the desired end. Yet beyond that plea for deferral is something more profound, marking the culmination of the process we have been following. Hamlet's main desire at this final moment is for some modicum of remembrance after his death. Let there be, at least from his friend, a period of mourning, an absence of felicity or joy to indicate that he has not been totally forgotten in the manner that his mother and the court had so swiftly forgotten the old Hamlet. His last concern is, significantly, for the preservation of his good name, the memory he will leave behind him:

O God, Horatio, what a wounded name,
Things standing thus unknown, shall I leave behind me!

> If thou didst ever hold me in thy heart,
> Absent thee from felicity a while,
> And in this harsh world draw thy breath in pain
> To tell my story.   (5.2.344–49)

The final tribute by Fortinbras implies the traditional view, that decay and putrefaction are not all that remain, that there is, after all, a splendor and universal respect that will live on in the minds of men:

> Let four captains
> Bear Hamlet like a soldier to the stage,
> For he was likely, had he been put on,
> To have prov'd most royal; and for his passage
> The soldiers' music and the rites of war
> Speak loudly for him.   (5.2.395–400)

James Calderwood is correct in noting that the events of the play end in resolution—the silence and secrecy are ended, Hamlet's father is avenged, and order has been restored to the kingdom. But the resolution is only partial. Fortinbras is not of Hamlet's stature—we have learned in the course of the play to suspect his standards, that he belongs to the school devoted to fame, and is impervious to the concerns that torment Hamlet. The kingdom, although cleansed of its imposthume, will lack the profundity and philosophical resonance that animated the drama. More important, the somber questions that had beset Hamlet remain unanswered; for he killed Claudius not because he had solved his dilemma but in the impetuosity of the moment. In terms of the new dispensation of Jacobean gloom and mistrust that Hamlet represents and to some extent inaugurated, we may wonder whether, if he had been "put on" and ascended the throne, he would ever have solved his problems; whether indeed the problems were solvable. This is the "mystery" of the play paralleling the unfathomability of the *Mona Lisa*.

And with that word "unfathomability" one returns to the question of *aporia*, whether this unsolved mystery disqualifies the validity of the text. In arguing their case, deconstructionists have consistently deplored the attempt of previous critics—by which was meant the so-called New Critics—to produce "univocal" readings of texts, arguing instead that there should be a plethora of interpretations. Geoffrey Hartman argues that this demand for multiple readings found significant support in Freudian psychology. In *The Interpretation of Dreams*, Freud maintains that analysis produces "a series of linguistic relays that could lead anywhere—depending on the system of rails and who is doing the switching. The dream is like a sentence that cannot find closure." It provides, therefore, an "extreme indeterminacy," as Hartman puts it, wherein "Ambiguities, overdetermined meanings, and strange linkages are more obvious than the coherent design they seem to contain."[51] The argument sound persuasive, until one recalls two factors—first, that the purpose of Freudian analysis was the contrary. In recognizing that suppressed fears or ideas surface in distorted form, that a dislike of Jones may appear, by associated sound pattern, as a dream of bones, his purpose was not to elaborate multiple interpretations but to identify the specific source of the ambiguity or displacement in order that, once it had been identified, the patient could be relieved of the associated symptoms of distress. In other words, the aim of the psychoanalyst's investigation was not to reveal a plethora of "linguistic relays that can lead anywhere" but to establish coherence from the seemingly disparate, to locate the link between the phobia and its metamorphosed manifestation.

Second, Freudian psychology did in that process reveal the existence of dualities and ambiguities such as had not been previously recognized, and that aspect has considerable bearing on the present discussion. The word "univocal," which was to become for deconstructionists the standard term for disparaging their predecessors' approach, with its implication that criticism until then had consisted of a Protean attempt to fit the text into a single unified frame, ignores the main contribution of the New Critics to literary analysis. Their primary innovation had been to reveal for the first time the efficacy of double entendres, wordplay, and connotations that make for the complexity of literary works. The ambiguity of language was an aspect that had until then, when recognized, been deplored as a literary failing. Samuel Johnson had condemned Shakespeare's punning in no uncertain terms. A quibble, as he called it, "is sure to engulf him in the mire. It has some malignant power over his mind, and its fascinations are irresistible," adding that it was the fatal Cleopatra for which Shakespeare lost the world and was content to lose it.[52]

In fact, the New Critics' perception of double entendres derived directly from Freud himself. Robert Graves first came into contact with the new psychological theories while undergoing analysis by W. H. Rivers, a disciple of Freud who was treating him for shell shock. And it was Graves's study of the multiple meanings in Shakespeare's sonnets, a study published together with Laura Riding, that inspired William Empson to produce his seminal *Seven Types of Ambiguity*, a work that became the spring-board for such essays as Cleanth Brooks's "The Language of Paradox." Even the term "ambivalence," which was to become a hallmark of such criticism, owes its introduction into English usage to Freud, who adopted it to describe the phenomenon of love-hate relationships, the puzzling concurrence of sadism and affection. For Virginia Woolf, Freud's term was a revelation, explaining to her the peculiar duality of her emotional experiences: "It was only the other day when I read Freud for the first time that I discovered that this violently disturbing conflict of love and hate is a common feeling and is called ambivalence." One need scarcely comment on the use D. H. Lawrence made of that love-hate relationship as a major theme in his novels. In brief, by 1936 I. A. Richards could state: "the old Rhetoric treated ambiguity as a fault in language, and hoped to confine or eliminate it; the new Rhetoric sees it as an inevitable consequence of the power of language and as an indispensable means of most of our important utterances."[53]

To claim, therefore, that the traditional critical approach was "univocal" and that a knowledge of Freud could reveal hitherto unperceived ambiguities in literature is to misconstrue the approach of the New Critics. The essential difference between their approach and that of the deconstructionists was not between multiple and univocal readings but in the response of the two schools to multiplicity. The New Critics perceived it as creating an enriching duality, an interweaving of ideas and connotations—as in Donne's use of "die" to evoke both death and sexual orgasm, revealing in "Wee die and rise the same" a covert allusion to the Crucifixion, an allusion seemingly antithetical to the sexual reading but contributing ultimately to the poem's main thesis, the lovers' "canonisation" by love; while the deconstructionists saw the multiplicity as a barrier to any coherent interpretation. Ultimately, the readings of the New Critics were univocal in the sense that they integrated the disparate meanings. But for deconstructionists to apply the term "univocal" as if their predecessors had failed to discern the multiple levels of meaning uncovered under the aegis of Freud is to do them a grave injustice.

It is to the more positive of those two approaches that the "mystery" of Hamlet should be related—the awareness of a coherent duality enriching the play's significance. Shocked at the celerity with which his father has been forgotten, Hamlet is caught between two contrary philosophies—the attractions offered by Stoicism, the "consummation devoutly to be wished," and the traditional Christian view of the penalties awaiting the suicide in the afterlife. His native resolution becomes "sicklied o'er with the pale cast of thought" and, until his conflict is resolved, he remains incapable of acting as a scourge and minister of justice. The conflict is never resolved, his act of revenge being undertaken impetuously, not predeterminedly. The purpose of the play, however, was not to provide a neat answer to the dilemma, but to present the conflict itself, the ambiguity of the human condition, with its central figure poised undecided between the Elizabethan and the Jacobean worlds, longing to achieve fame yet doubtful of its durability, yearning for death yet fearful of the consequences—a dilemma that has held true for humanity throughout subsequent generations, justifying its perennial fascination.

THREE

Spenser and the Pagan Gods

It has become a commonplace of criticism to speak of Edmund Spenser's syncretism, his skillful merger of classical and scriptural elements in *The Faerie Queene*, where he is seen as drawing "with equal freedom" on the Bible and the classical poets.[1] But that view needs to be considerably modified. The allegory on which the entire work is based is indeed scriptural in source, drawing its authority—as did the chivalric tradition at large—from the Pauline image: "Stand therefore, and your loynes girded about with veritie, and hauing on the brest plate of righteousnesse, And your feete shod with the preparation of the Gospel of peace. Aboue all, take the shielde of faith, wherewith ye may quench all the fierie dartes of the wicked, And take the helmet of saluation, and the sword of the Spirit, which is the worde of God" (Eph. 6:14–17). That biblical injunction functions throughout as the shadowy background to the battles of Spenser's knights, lending the stories a religious, allegorical significance surpassing that of Arthurian legend. It defines not only the Redcrosse Knight in the opening book but courageous defenders of the Christian virtues appearing in later books, such as Britomart, the symbol of chastity (a virtue more distinctly Christian than classical). Yet despite this obvious indebtedness to the Scriptures, a study of the literary form of his epic reveals a remarkable dearth both of images and of evocations of biblical characters, such references being dwarfed both in number and in prominence by the abundance of classical citations.

The reason for that dearth was clearly not a dislike of the Bible on Spenser's part. His personal fondness for the Scriptures is evidenced by his verse translations of biblical works which, although they have not survived, were known to the publisher of his *Complaints* who, in his "Preface to the Gentle Reader" added the comment, "I vnderstand that he besides wrote sundrie others, namelie *Ecclesiastes,* and *Canticum Canticorum* translated. . . . Besides some other pamphlets looselie scattered abroad: as . . . the *Seven Psalmes &c.*"[2]

The *Faerie Queene* suggests little of that fondness. The enemies of Una and the Redcrosse Knight are, indeed, the whore of Babylon from the Book of Revelations, envisioned there as arrayed in purple and scarlet, and her companion the seven-headed dragon, both of whom must be defeated before the coming of the New Jerusalem. But, apart from those patent allusions, the biblical references are meager. Here and there one may find a brief evocation of David calming Saul, a somewhat obscure hint of the serpent in Saint John's goblet, a reference to Debora sandwiched between a reminder of Homer's Penthelesee and Camilla's slaying of Orsilochus (4.2.2, 1.10.13, 3.4.2). Yet even such intimations, when they do occur, are in most instances only loosely connected to the scriptural source. The dwelling-place of Una's parents is, we learn, the land "which *Phison* and *Euphrates* floweth by, / And *Gehons* golden waues doe wash continually" (1.7.43); but, so far from being identical with the biblical Eden as specified by those rivers, this land is terrorized by a monstrous dragon absent from the scene of paradise. When Eden is mentioned, it is to relate a story never hinted at in Scripture: Spenser informs us that the rose was transported from there in order to adorn chaste virgins (3.5.52). The alert reader may perceive in the killing of the dragon and the release of the king and queen from its tyranny a foreshadowing of the harrowing of hell as described in 2 Thessalonians 2:8 and Revelation 12, 17, and 19, but the haziness of the allusion is in marked contrast to the overt specificity and patent delight with which Spenser adduces his classical sources, recounting, for example, in loving detail the properties of the Palmer's staff:

> Of that same wood it fram'd was cunningly,
>   Of which *Caduceus* whilome was made,
>   *Caduceus* the rod of *Mercury*,
>   With which he wonts the *Stygian* realmes inuade,
>   Through ghastly horrour, and eternall shade;
>   Th' infernall feends with it he can asswage,
>   And *Orcus* tame, whom nothing can perswade,
>   And rule the *Furyes*, when they most do rage:
> Such vertue in his staffe had eke this Palmer sage.
> (2.12.41)

For Spenser the incident provides an opportunity not to be missed for including the type of digression beloved by Homer, the introduction of an extraneous mythological allusion relished for its own sake because of its colorful classical source.

Spenser's preference for classical rather than scriptural allusion is patent throughout the epic. The list of those imprisoned in the netherworld of Duessa's dungeon includes Nimrod, but his name is swamped by the lengthy inventory of pagan figures that follows:

> Great *Romulus* the Grandsyre of them all,
>   Proud *Tarquin*, and too lordly *Lentulus*,
>   Stout *Scipio*, and stubborne *Hanniball*,
>   Ambitious *Sylla*, and sterne *Marius*,
> High *Caesar*, great *Pompey*, and fierce *Antonius*.

> Amongst these mighty men were wemen mixt,
> Proud wemen, vaine, forgetfull of their yoke:
> The bold *Semiramis*, whose sides transfixt
> With sonnes owne blade, her fowle reproches spoke;
> Faire *Sthenoboea*, that her selfe did choke
> With wilfull cord, for wanting of her will;
> High minded *Cleopatra*, that with stroke
> Of Aspes sting her selfe did stoutly kill:
> And thousands moe the like, that did that dongeon fill.
> (1.5.49–50)

The same holds true for Jonathan and David, squeezed in between a host of classical figures:

> Such were great *Hercules*, and *Hylas* deare;
> Trew *Ionathan*, and *Dauid* trustie tryde;
> Stout *Theseus*, and *Pirithous* his feare;
> *Pylades* and *Orestes* by his syde;
> Myld *Titus* and *Gesippus* without pryde;
> *Damon* and *Pythias* whom death could not seuer. (4.13)

In the same way, the ravenous, many-headed Beast in 6.12.32 that Calidore must struggle to overcome is compared not, as one might expect, to the Beast in Revelations 13:1, "hauing seuen heads, and ten hornes, and vpon his hornes were ten crownes, and vpon his heads the name of blasphemie," but to "the hell-borne *Hydra*, which they faine / That great *Alcides* whilome ouerthrew."

In any other work, the discrepancy between classical and biblical citation might be less noteworthy. But in an epic in which a hero, displaying upon his breast a "bloudie Crosse . . . / The dear remembrance of his dying Lord," whose enterprise is dedication to Una, the true Church, and who serves as a coordinating figure throughout the later books, the author's willingness to allow pagan mythology to engulf the biblical, in effect displacing it almost completely, suggests a tension between the overt religious theme and the mythology upon which the literary form relies.

To substantiate his claim that biblical imagery is pervasive throughout the epic, Angus Fletcher cites as "the most obvious example" the indebtedness of the Gardens of Adonis to the Song of Songs, although he admits at once—in a reservation that, in effect, disqualifies the claim—that the gardens are indeed, "capable of interpretation entirely within the terms of Ovidian and Neoplatonic thought."[3]

Spenser, it would seem, is so enamored of the classical world in all its rediscovered richness that the Scriptures have not been merely subordinated to it but almost forgotten, so that scriptural associations that would almost inevitably rise in the reader's mind are simply ignored. It is surely difficult for a Christian to read Spenser's lengthy account of Chrysogene's "so straunge ensample of conception," her fertilization by the warmth of Jove's sunbeams, without recalling the Immaculate Conception of the Virgin Mary, a recollection that might be thought to make that passage verge on blasphemy and therefore to demand from the author some sort of discrimination in order to avoid irreverence. Yet Spenser, absorbed in relating the story, chooses to ignore the parallel:

> Till faint through irkesome wearinesse, adowne
>   Vpon the grassie ground her selfe she layd
>   To sleepe, the whiles a gentle slombring swowne
>   Vpon her fell all naked bare displayd;
>   The sunne-beames bright vpon her body playd,
>   Being through former bathing mollifide,
>   And pierst into her wombe, where they embayd
>   With so sweet sence and secret power vnspide,
> That in her pregnant flesh they shortly fructifide.
>
> Miraculous may seeme to him, that reades
>   So straunge ensample of conception;
>   But reason teacheth that the fruitfull seades
>   Of all things liuing, through impression
>   Of the sunbeames in moyst complexion,
>   Doe life concciue and quickned are by kynd. (3.6.7–8)

Especially noteworthy is his assumption that such a form of gestation will appear strange and miraculous to the reader, requiring explanation, as though there were no precedent to which it could be related. Those who have in the past attempted to evaluate Spenser's use of the Bible have produced impressive lists of his supposed indebtedness; but they are much less impressive on close examination. It should be recalled that many biblical phrases had by now entered into the vernacular, and would therefore arouse no conscious associations. As early as 1540, Henry VIII, in granting Cromwell exclusive rights to the printing of the first Great Bible, had remarked on "the free and lyberall use of the Bible in oure oune maternall English tongue,"[4] from which time the English versions became increasingly familiar to the people, its idioms, often now translated directly from the Hebrew and Greek instead of the Vulgate, being accepted as part of common speech. Phrases such as "tender mercy" or "the powers that be" had entered everyday usage, no longer evoking their scriptural sources (Luke 1:78, Rom. 13:1). Due caution is therefore necessary in assuming that echoes of biblical phrases constituted evocations of the Bible. In the 1920s, Grace Landrum argued that Spenser was "saturated" in biblical material, and she listed some 250 scriptural allusions in *The Faerie Queene,* a number that, if valid, would indeed be considerable. A close examination, however, of the instances she cites reveals how dubious many of them are, sometimes no more than the mention of a tree referred to in the Bible.[5] Thus the passage in Isaiah 31:4, "As the lyon or lyons whelpe roareth vpon his praye, against whom if a multitude of shepheards be called, hee will not be afraide at their voyce, neither will humble him selfe at their noise," although it describes the animal's courage, she sees as the source of Spenser's description of the opposite phenomenon, its meek submission:

> The Lyon Lord of euerie beast in field,
> Quoth she, his princely puissance doth abate,
> And mightie proud to humble weake does yield,
> Forgetfull of the hungry rage, which late
> Him prickt. (*FQ* 1.3.7)

Similarly, the verse from James 4:7, "Submit your selues to God: resist the deuill, and he will flee from you," she identifies equally unconvincingly with the knight's advice to Serena: "auoide the occasion of the ill: / For when the cause, whence euill doth arize, / Remoued is, th'effect surceaseth still" (FQ 6.6.15).

Naseeb Shaheen acknowledges how far-fetched many of Landrum's claims had been, but Shaheen, providing a detailed list of such references includes under the umbrella of biblical indebtedness phrases that only a researcher determined to find such parallels could possibly conceive as invoking that source. Can one really believe, as he claims, that the lines: "The thirstie land / Drunke vp his life" (1.3.20) owe their origin to the passage from Genesis 4.10–11, "The voyce of thy brothers blood cryeth vnto me from the grounde . . . which hathe opened her mouth to receiue thy brothers blood"?[6] Or that the passage, "Is not the measure of thy sinfull hire / High heaped vp with huge iniquitie, / Against the day of wrath, to burden thee?" (1.9.46), echoes, "Fulfil ye also the measure of your fathers" (Matt. 23:32), where the only similarity is the use of the word "measure"? At times, Shaheen is aware of the tenuousness of his comparisons; after tracing "A prowd rebellious Vnicorne defies" (2.5.10) to "Wil the vnicorne serue thee? or wil he tary by thy cribbe?" (Job 39:12), he adds lamely, "The unicorn, however, was a common symbol in mythology."[7] Many of the parallels are valid but are usually little more than the use of phrases such as to "smite one's breast in repentance" or "his heart died within him," which had by then become absorbed into the language.

The merger of Christian theme and pagan imagery became a natural part of Renaissance practice, but the form the merger takes in Spenser's epic differs fundamentally from the norm, and the specific nature of his usage deserves fuller investigation than it has received. The conflation of Christian and classical in that period produced at times an eddying swirl of opposing currents and, at others, a harmonious blending of tributaries forming a new and powerful stream. Within the latter category, Christian Neoplatonism held pride of place, the influx of pagan mythology that it authorized having entered not in conflict with traditional Christianity but with the approval and, indeed, at the initiative of leading members of the church. Nicholas of Cusa, in 1449 elevated to the rank of cardinal by Pope Nicholas, had inaugurated in his *De pace fidei* the far-reaching concept that was to form the basis of the new mode, the theory that the worship of multiple deities, as in ancient Greece and Rome, was—whether the devotees realized it or not—in effect a worship of the one deity. Since theologians and philosophers of all faiths, he argued syllogistically, declare that they pursue Wisdom, and since there is and can only be one true Wisdom, then all religions, even when polytheistic, are really in pursuit of the one deity. "Just as there are no white things if whiteness does not exist, so there are no gods if the deity does not exist. Therefore, the worshiping of a plurality of gods bespeaks the deity; and he who says that there is more than one god says implicitly that there is, antecedently, one Beginning to them all . . . namely, the universe's First Cause, Beginning, or Creator."[8] That principle, however circuitous its reasoning, opened the door to the interpretation of classical myth in Christian terms, again with the inaugurators of that further stage emerging not from outside the church but from within.

There had, before the appearance of Nicholas's theory, been tentative attempts to sanction the classical Pantheon. From the time of the church fathers, the principle of a fourfold reading of Scripture, "Littera gesta docet, quid credas allegoria, / Moralis quid agas, quo tendas anagogia," had occasionally been applied to the classics too, but in a restricted sense, either christologically or in terms of general moral principles.[9] Thus, any pagan figure triumphing over an enemy could be seen as exemplifying Christ's victory over Satan, while the more general approach, as it came to be summarized in Boccaccio's *Genealogica of the Pagan Gods*, identified the classical deities as representing agencies or aspects of the one true God.[10] The revived interest in Ovid from the twelfth century onward, such as *Mythographus III* by the English scholar Albricus, even when not equating the gods with scriptural figures, had aroused the ire of the religious; but Nicholas of Cusa's theory gave a new impetus to the process, not least because it emanated from within the Church.

The person primarily responsible after Cusa for propagating the new view was also firmly within the Church. Marsilio Ficino, founder of the Florentine Neoplatonic Academy, was an ordained priest and a canon of Florence Cathedral. Not only did he sanction the Olympiad by this process but extended the principle, claiming that even Socrates and Plato were sacred figures and recommending that Plato's works should be read in all the churches. His colleague and primary assistant in propagating the system, Pico della Mirandola, was charged with heresy by a papal commission, but the rebuke was not for his Christianizing of the pagan gods. The trouble arose from a different source, from certain questionable items included in the 900 theses he prepared for presentation at a public disputation in defense of Christianity, and for that indiscretion he was eventually exonerated by the Vatican. He too was a faithful adherent of the Church and was, in fact, about to take Holy Orders shortly before his early death.

Out of Cusa's original idea and with the encouragement of these Christian scholars emerged the widely disseminated belief that the mythology of ancient Greece and Rome, so far from constituting pagan idolatry to be treated with scorn by the true believer as it had been in the Middle Ages, constituted instead adumbrations of scriptural figures and Christian concepts. These were seen through a glass darkly, by a people who had not been privileged to receive the divine revelations granted to the denizens of the Holy Land. Classical writers and thinkers were seen as groping their way toward truths that, through no fault of their own, they had been able to perceive only faintly. Among those advocating this view, some adopted a euhemeristic reading of ancient mythology, assuming that the gods of Olympus were mortal heroes later deified, others that they represented forces of nature or moral principles; but the major interpretation, that of Neoplatonism, by identifying individual mythological figures with biblical counterparts, thereby granted to the deities a vicarious sanctity or, at the very least, a means of reconciling Christian belief with their burgeoning admiration for Greek and Roman culture. As a result, Renaissance artists and writers could, with no sense of sacrilege and with the approval of the clergy, conflate the often dissolute figures of the Greek pantheon with the sacred characters of their own faith.

Some of the perceived parallels conjured up by the Christianizers demanded little ingenuity. The muscular Hercules was an obvious parallel to Samson; Apollo, the god of the Muses, was an analogue to David, the musician and author of the Psalms. Most patent of all was the identification of Jupiter, the ruler of Olympus, with the Old Testament Deity, even though the former's activities as recorded in classical legend, notably his frequent descent to earth in the guise of a swan, bull, cloud, or stream of gold in order to ravish innocent virgins, seemed to contradict the correlation. But that problem was overcome by a little manipulation. The anonymous author of the fourteenth century *Ovide Moralisé*, which had of course preceded Nicholas of Cusa's syllogism, followed the *Metamorphoses* by focusing exclusively on the process of transformation. Carefully ignoring Jupiter's lascivious intent in those stories, it highlighted the parallel involved in his adopting the human form, evocative of the Incarnation, whereby the deity wishes to come down to earth and abase himself without losing his divinity in order to ransom the race of man and to deliver us from servitude in hell. The less palatable features of those incidents were ignored. Yet it did contain a hint of later readings in commenting that Europa's clinging to one of the bull's horns symbolized firmness of faith.

Leonard Barkan, in *The Gods Made Flesh*, focuses upon the erotic or fleshly aspects of the Renaissance readings of the Pantheon. He notes especially the frequent depiction of the Europa story on Italian wedding chests, or *cassoni*, the purpose of which was to encourage the sexual prowess of the newly married couple.[11] In the instance of the wedding chests, he is undoubtedly correct. The new interpretation of pagan mythology permitted the introduction of eroticism, and there are indeed certain paintings of such scenes that bear no allegorical connotations, such as Correggio's sensual depiction of Io embraced by a cloud or Titian's voluptuous and naked *Danaë* awaiting the stream of gold. But Barkan's concern with the fleshly aspects of the divine descent leads him to ignore the numerous religious readings of such scenes, one of which Titian was himself to provide a few years after his *Danaë* in *The Rape*. For at the height of the Renaissance, the allegorizing focus turned from Jupiter's "incarnatory" descent from heaven to the rapes themselves, the god's ravishing of Leda, Europa, Io, and Danaë. The rape, however, was now perceived metaphorically as the "enrapturing" of the Christian soul by the divine spirit. Veronese's version of the Europa scene in the Pitti gallery depicts the incident in allegorical terms. There, as in the earlier version by Francesco di Giorgio, she is fully clothed and, with the happy assistance of her female friends, willingly mounting a gently submissive bull that could in no sense be conceived as a rapist. Putti hover above, holding over her the wreath of victory; and in the right-hand section of the painting, she reappears, waving joyfully as she is borne away on her savior's back. In Guido Reni's version of the same scene, Europa, affectionately embracing the docile bull on which she is seated, gazes heavenward with the ecstatic expression characteristic of Christian saints at the moment of their glorification, as she does in Titian's version of the scene. That Christian reading of divine rape had its counterpart in literature too, as in Donne's holy sonnet, "Batter my heart," where the soul, depicted as a female imprisoned in the body, longs for the divine religious ecstasy that will free her from the bonds of the flesh, the ambiguous terms "enthrall" and "ravish" shifting in meaning from their physical sense of "enslavement" and "rape" to the spiritual connotations of religious rapture:

> Divorce mee, 'untie, or breake that knot againe,
> Take mee to you, imprison mee, for I
> Except you'enthrall mee, never shall be free,
> Nor ever chast, except you ravish mee.[12]

That reading of the pagan scenes of rape would seem especially appropriate to a Christian epic employing classical sources, but it never appears in Spenser's work. Rapes, such as the forcible seizure of Amoret, take place, but there is no reference to religious enrapturement. The invocation to the god of love that opens the Amoret episode is entirely secular, complaining of his cruelty in allowing ladies to suffer the grievous trials of love:

> Great God of loue, that with thy cruell darts,
>   Doest conquer greatest conquerors on ground,
> And setst thy kingdome in the captiue harts
>   Of Kings and Keasars, to thy seruice bound,
>   What glorie, or what guerdon hast thou found
> In feeble Ladies tyranning so sore;
>   And adding anguish to the bitter wound,
> With which their liues thou lanchedst long afore,
> By heaping stormes of trouble on them daily more?
>   (*FQ* 4.7.1)

Spenser's reluctance to employ the religious interpretations of pagan myth holds true throughout the epic, not least in his frequent evocations of Jupiter. In Neoplatonism, Jupiter, as the ruler of Olympus and dispatcher of thunderbolts, clearly accorded more closely with the Old Testament deity than with Christ, and the Neoplatonic parallel was enhanced by a neat shift in nomenclature. One notes a marked preference among Renaissance writers for Jupiter's secondary name, Jove, the similarity in sound to *Jehovah* underscoring the imaginative conflation by auditory association.

A call for divine aid or an oath sworn in the name of Jove was thus legitimized even for the most pious of Christians on the assumption that the usage was simply a contraction of the divine name or, at most, an invoking of God in his classical equivalence. Spenser was certainly aware of this amalgamation. At one point, relying on the ancient worship of Jove as Lucetius, or "Bringer of Light," he praises him with patent allusion to the initial act of Creation in Genesis: "O lightsome day, the lampe of highest *Ioue*, / First made by him" (1.7.23), so that the merger of Jupiter with the Old Testament deity is accepted. But if Spenser's text were to be interpreted in that sense throughout the epic, it would become patently sacrilegious, as when he informs us that the virgins seated around *Mercillaes'* throne are "All louely daughters of high *Ioue* . . . /. . . begot in loues delight, / Vpon the righteous *Themis*" (5.9.31)[13]—a phrase scarcely consonant with the Old Testament concept of God. Even less applicable is the description of Diana as constituting an erotic temptation for Jove, as she "with her Nymphes about her, drew / To this sweet spring; where, doffing her array, / She bath'd her louely limbes, for *Ioue* a likely pray" (7.6.45).

As the process of Neoplatonic amalgamation progressed, so did its subtlety and its ramifications. Venus, on one occasion exposed by her husband, Vulcan, in the act of committing adultery with Mars, was depicted by medieval writers and artists as a despicable symbol of lasciviousness. She appears in a manuscript in the Vatican library sprawling naked in an ungainly pose clearly intended to arouse distaste.[14] When invoked in more laudatory terms during that period, it was usually, as by the Wandering Scholars, in a mood of ribaldry, of defiant, erotic carnival, as in the lines from the Goliardic song: "quicquid Venus imperat, labor est suavis, / quae numquam in cordibus habitat ignavis."[15] In the new era, however, she became transformed, sanctified not merely as a symbol of love purified to suit more effectively the revived Platonic setting, but more daringly as a homologue to the Virgin Mary herself. Both had borne male offspring due to symbolize love, that association resulting in an essentially new type of Madonna painting. No longer mournfully clasping to her breast, as in a medieval Cimabue, an infant fated to be crucified, she now appears on the canvases of Leonardo, Perugino, and Raphael as a beautiful young woman, representative of the *calocagathia,* the beautiful-and-the-good at the apex of the Platonic system, gazing benevolently at a Cupid-like child playing before her. The corollary to that equation was the emergence in so many fifteenth century Italian paintings of putti flitting above holy scenes, indicating the conflation of Cupid with the cherub of the Scriptures, the latter believed by some biblical commentators to have had the face of a child.[16] It had not always been so. In early Netherlandish art, as yet untouched by these Neoplatonic mergers, the angels hovering in blessing over sacred scenes are, as in Rogier Van der Weyden's *Seven Sacraments Altarpiece* of 1445, winged adults, like the cherub described in Scripture as guarding with flaming sword the entrance to the destroyed Garden of Eden. But that concept was swiftly superseded by that of the infant putti.

How far the equation of the two maternal figures was taken may be seen in one of the most famous paintings of the era. Botticelli's *The Birth of Venus* (1485) meant to his contemporaries, I believe, far more than it does to today's viewer, especially if we bear in mind that Botticelli was an extraordinarily pious man, reputed never to have missed attending Mass during his entire adult life. Two years before it was painted, Pope Sixtus IV had issued a ruling that validated the previously disputed doctrine of the Immaculate Conception of the Virgin, the belief that not only Jesus but she too had been conceived in purity, her birth resulting not from parental intercourse but from the infusion of a divine spirit. In terms of Neoplatonic equivalence, Botticelli's canvas was an allegorical depiction of that newly approved doctrine, as Venus is seen rising from the sea, having been immaculately generated from the *aphros* or foam of the ocean (as her Greek name, Aphrodite, implies).[17] If the nakedness of the goddess appears inappropriate for a surrogate of the Virgin, that too formed part of the new configuration; for the familiar metaphor that the body formed the "rags" or clothing of the soul meant that the soul should, legitimately, be depicted as naked. Venus, entering the terrestrial, is thus portrayed as about to assume the cloak of the flesh, held out to her by the figure on the shore, the allegory thereby merging the pagan goddess with her Christian counterpart in a manner that discarded as irrelevant the less admirable aspects of the deity's activities as recorded in classical legend.

There is, indeed, a further link with Spenser. Botticelli lived in Florence at the height of Renaissance experimentation, when artists were not only developing depth perspective but had already produced accurate renderings of space, such as Masaccio's *Holy Trinity* of 1425, which had startled contemporaries by its realistic placing of the sacred figures within a recessed, barrel-vaulted chamber. Botticelli chose to ignore such experimentation, producing instead the patently shallow perspective of this painting. Moreover, while Leonardo da Vinci was producing his meticulous study of eddying water and the complex swirling of waves, Botticelli reverted to an older tradition, the waves in this painting being mere visual tokens, chevrons symbolically indicative of waves. Spenser shared this nostalgia for outmoded systems in his use of language. Whether "E. K." was a pseudonym for Spenser may never be known, but there can be little doubt that the comments prefacing *The Shepheardes Calendar* and signed with those initials expressed what were essentially Spenser's own views, singling out his preference for the outmoded but nobler diction of a past age. That preference for the past would form part of Spenser's delight in the original forms of classical myth in the works of Homer, Virgil, and Ovid, myths as yet unaltered by humanist Christianizing.

In line with that preference, Spenser's depiction of, or allusions to, classical scenes were never intended to be construed in terms of their Christian parallels. Spenser's moral crusade against the eroticism of the pagan classics is ambiguous. Britomart and, by extension, the reader are warned of the impious and hellish nature of the House of Busyrane by means of the fire and "stinking Sulphure" that greet her at the entrance; but the description of the majesty of the arras within, the "fair tapestries" woven in gold and silk, counters the formal condemnation. Caught up in the delight of Ovidian narrative, Spenser recounts in detailed sequence the representations of Jupiter's numerous conquests of innocent maidens, with no hint of the translation of those scenes into divine ecstasies. The tapestries would not have included such religious readings of the scenes, but one could expect the insertion of a comment by the poet, condemning or dissociating himself from the heathen accounts. Instead, Spenser not only describes the scenes that the tapestries display but also does so with patent delight. Smitten by Cupid's dart, the Thunderer is compelled to descend to earth,

> to slake his scalding smart;
> Now like a Ram, faire *Helle* to peruart,
> Now like a Bull, *Europa* to withdraw:
> Ah, how the fearefull Ladies tender hart
> Did liuely seeme to tremble, when she saw
> The huge seas vnder her t'obay her seruaunts law.
> (*FQ* 3.11.30)

Jupiter has become derogated here to the level of a servant or slave to love. Cupid can therefore boast with justice that erotic love has replaced Jove as the monarch of heaven:

> Whiles thus on earth great *Ioue* these pageaunts playd,
> The winged boy did thrust into his throne,
> And scoffing, thus vnto his mother sayd,
> Lo now the heauens obey to me alone,
> And take me for their *Ioue*, whiles *Ioue* to earth is gone.
> (3.11.35)

Spenser's Venus, too, is sharply divorced there from identification with the Virgin Mary, being presented at one point as an androgynous being who "hath both kinds in one, / Both male and female, both vnder one name" (4.10.41).[18]

As Harry Berger describes it, the theme of the epic, presented allegorically, is indeed Christian in the sense of the striving for spiritual fulfillment required of the true believer. The knight must mature. Before adopting his destiny, his historical mission as a British saint, he must undergo a process of purification, being tempted by earthly glory and then overcoming the temptation, confronting his own worthlessness in the eyes of God before he can achieve spiritual stature.[19] But if the overall conception is Christian, the literary form of the epic, the events and the heroes it cites remain for the most part isolated from scriptural sources. William Empson notes how Spenser's use of archaic words keeps the reader at a safe remove from the content, allowing the author to "pour into the even dreamwork of his fairyland Christian, classical, and chivalrous materials with an air, not of ignoring their differences, but of holding all their systems of values floating as if at a distance," in a manner that prevents them from interfering with one another.[20] But if the Christian values are allowed to exist in conjunction with the classical and the chivalrous, they exist only as shadowy background allusions, rarely referred to directly, and to a large extent shunted aside while the mythology of Greece and Rome, for which Spenser displays so marked a fondness, is prominently foregrounded.

Where might one expect to find these missing scriptural allusions? In fact, opportunities arise time after time throughout the epic. There are numerous accounts of some brave warrior confronting a fearsome giant, a scene epitomized by the Redcrosse Knight's engagement with Orgoglio, a "hideous Geant horrible and hye, / That with his talnesse seemd to threat the skye" (1.7.8), yet never a hint comparing the knights to David's confrontation with Goliath. Instead, we are referred exclusively to the classics, the giant, we are informed, being the offspring of Earth and blustering Aeolus. The same holds true of Artegall's encounter with his giant opponent in book 5. When Spenser recalls a "great Champion of the antique world" to whose might he compares some dauntless knight, the champion is not Samson but Hercules—Hercules specifically distinguished from his biblical counterpart by mention of the "twelue huge labours high extold" (1.11.27). Moreover, when Samson is mentioned, it is not in praise of his championing of Israel but scornfully, for his weakness in laying his locks "before his lemans traine" (5.8.2). Similarly, the prelapsarian world, apart from the instance quoted above, is related not to Eden where Adam was the sole male, but to the golden age of Saturn as depicted in classical literature, where peace reigned:

> For during Saturnes ancient raigne it's sayd,
> That all the world with goodnesse did abound:
> All loued vertue, no man was affrayd
> Of force, ne fraud in wight was to be found:
> No warre was knowne, no dreadfull trompets sound,
> Peace vniuersall rayn'd mongst men and beasts,
> And all things freely grew out of the ground. (*FQ* 5.proem.9)

Such preferences for the classics abound. Artegall is lauded for his wisdom in judgment, for settling a seemingly insoluble conflict between Amidas and Bracidas (5.4.19), but the most famous instance of wise judgment, Solomon's skillful settling of the dispute over the baby in 1 Kings 3:16–28, receives no mention. The Britons are at one stage to fail in their task and to suffer for their misdeeds the penalty of defeat, "For th'heauens haue decreed, to displace / The *Britons*, for their sinnes dew punishment" (3.3.41). The warning seems ideal for a reference to the stiff-necked Hebrews of the Pentateuch to serve as models for divine retribution for backsliding, but there is no allusion to them. Moreover, as with Samson, on one of the few occasions when the biblical world is cited, the reference is far from laudatory. The temple at Jerusalem, "the Almighties see," is cited only to be dismissed as a structure *inferior* to the temple of Venus, classed in that lower setting with the temples of the heathen gods:

> Not that same famous Temple of *Diane*,
> Whose hight all *Ephesus* did ouersee,
> And which all *Asia* sought with vowes prophane,
> One of the worlds seuen wonders sayd to bee,
> Might match with this by many a degree:
> Nor that, which that wise King of *Iurie* framed,
> With endlesse cost, to be th'Almighties see;
> Nor all that else through all the world is named
> To all the heathen Gods, might like to this be clamed.
> (4.10.30)

Again, when the river Jordan is mentioned, its holy waters are classed somewhat derogatively with contemporary spas, as inferior to the well into which the Redcrosse Knight falls, whose properties "Both *Silo* this, and *Iordan* did excell, / And th'English *Bath*, and eke the german *Spau*" (1.11.30).

Where a parallel with the Scriptures is noted, the latter functions almost invariably as a shadowy and unspecified archetype that, it is assumed, a reader well-versed in the Bible would recall. Una's betrothal was certainly intended to be seen in terms of the marriage of the Lamb in Revelation 19, but such biblical evocations remain hazy, in no way comparable to the elaborate citations of classical mythology with which the epic abounds and where each detail is lovingly recalled and relished. Thus Florimell's girdle derives from that worn by Venus:

> Her husband *Vulcan* whylome for her sake,
> When first he loued her with heart entire,
> This pretious ornament they say did make,
> And wrought in *Lemno* with vnquenched fire:
> And afterwards did for her loues first hire,
> Giue it to her, for euer to remaine,
> Therewith to bind lasciuious desire.   (*FQ* 4.5.4)

At times, what might have been thought a scriptural allusion rather than a phrase absorbed into the language is disqualified as such by its context. In a fine study of the theological aspects of the epic, Darryl Gless (who frankly admits the "inescapable intentionalism" of his approach, that he is searching for theological implications in the text), identifies the lines describing Arthur's killing of Orgoglio— "Large streames of bloud out of the truncked stocke / Forth gushed, like fresh water streame from riuen rocke" (1.8.10)— as deriving from Moses' striking of the rock in Numbers 20:11 and thereby indicating the faith of Arthur.[21] But the scriptural story in fact conveys the opposite lesson, Moses' lack of faith, in punishment for which he was forbidden to enter the Promised Land. Were this an allusion to the scriptural account, it would have worked against the thrust of the passage. One must assume, therefore, that the water gushing from the rock was simply an image drawn from the natural world.

Spenser was under no obligation to quote scriptural counterparts to his classical citations, nor am I suggesting that a plethora of biblical allusions would have improved his epic. But the dearth of such references suggests that, in a period when classical and Christian concepts were being merged by the Neoplatonists, Spenser chose to ignore or underplay such correlations. The result is anomalous: thematic allegiance to religion and to conventional morality countered by a stylistic predilection for the pagan, the latter not in any Christianized form but in its pristine and often lascivious setting. One recalls in contrast how carefully Milton's conflation of scriptural and classical sources invariably accords primacy to the scriptural. Invoking the muse in the opening lines of *Paradise Lost*, he calls upon her not in her original form as Urania of Olympus but in her biblical equivalence situated on Mount Sinai:

> Sing Heav'nly Muse, that on the secret top
> Of Oreb, or of Sinai, didst inspire
> That Shepherd, who first taught the chosen Seed,
> In the Beginning how the Heav'ns and Earth
> Rose out of Chaos.

And later in the epic, in a second invocation, he highlights the distinction even more carefully, assuming, in line with

Nicholas of Cusa, that the muse of classical mythology, goddess of the stars, was really an adumbration of the Holy Spirit as envisioned by a people not granted biblical revelation:

> Descend from Heav'n Urania, by that name
> If rightly thou art call'd, whose Voice divine
> Following, above th' Olympian Hill I soare,
> Above the flight of Pegasean wing.
> The meaning, not the Name I call: for thou
> Nor of the Muses nine, nor on the top
> Of old Olympus dwell'st, but Heav'nlie borne,
> Before the Hills appeerd. (7.1-8)

The priorities here are reversed—the classical figure has become the shadowy allusion and the scriptural figure not merely foregrounded but displacing the classical.

In contrast, Spenser's invocation makes no attempt to grant priority to the scriptural nor even to hint at a coalescence. In his initial call upon the muse in his epic, specified there as the "chief of nine," she is merged not with the Holy Spirit but with Queen Elizabeth, the parallel relying upon their shared "virginity," while in the subsequent stanza the Muse becomes the analogue of Venus—not in any Christianized form purged of immoral associations, but arrayed in love's "jollities," as the paramour of Mars:

> And thou most dreaded impe of highest *Ioue,*
>   Faire *Venus* sonne, that with thy cruell dart
> At that good knight so cunningly didst roue,
> That glorious fire it kindled in his hart,
> Lay now thy deadly Heben bow apart,
> And with thy mother milde come to mine ayde:
> Come both, and with you bring triumphant *Mart,*
> In loues and gentle iollities arrayd,
> After his murdrous spoiles and bloudy rage allayd.
>   (Proem 3)

Spenser's preference is all the more surprising in light of a major change in attitude to the Old Testament that had been developing during the sixteenth century, transforming its characters into models for contemporary Protestant behavior. The Reformers' determination to translate the Bible into the vernacular in order to make it available to the common people and thereby to break the clergy's monopoly as interpreters of the text had produced, as an unintended corollary, a warmer and more personal relationship with the Old Testament figures. Previously, only the prefigurative function of those earlier narratives had seemed significant, Abraham, in the Brome version of *The Sacrifice of Isaac*, anachronistically calling upon the Holy Trinity since the scene's only importance for the Christian resided in the incident's adumbration of the Crucifixion. Such typological exegesis was often pursued in intricate detail, as when Augustine in his *City of God* deduced from the dimensions of Noah's ark, whose length is six times its breadth, the message that the Savior would come in the form of a man. In that typological reading, Old Testament characters were seen as insubstantial foreshadowings rather than as real people existing in a historical setting. How far that attitude prevailed is indicated by Sir Thomas More's amused recounting of the response of a certain lady (fairly typical, one would imagine) who saw the events of the New Testament as totally divorced from the world of the ancient Hebrews: "when she harde saye that our Lady was a Jew, first could not believe it, but saide, what ye mock I wis, I pray you tel trouth. And when it was so fully affermed that she at last bileued it quod she, so help me God and Halidom I shall love her the worse while I live."[22]

The advancement in the study of the Hebrew language contributed significantly to the change in attitude, its revival being one of the first tasks undertaken by Johann Reuchlin. On embarking upon it, he found to his dismay that, despite the intensive biblical exegesis prevailing in the Middle Ages, study had been confined almost exclusively to the Latin Vulgate, the philological aspects of Hebrew being so neglected that there existed no grammar book on which he could base his investigation of the language. Reuchlin was compelled, therefore, to create his own version. Once Hebrew had been mastered—Spenser, we recall, studied Hebrew under Mulcaster—the direct contact with the text that translation provided, stripping it of its prefigurative accretions, opened up a wealth of new sources, and of models that were to prove especially valuable to the Protestants. Theologically, the Reformers were still bound by the Gospel account to reject the denizens of the Hebraic world as Pharisees, as a people who had failed in their task, needing to be replaced by the adopters of the new faith. But the direct contact with the earlier narrative gradually created a new bond. Helen C. White, in her study of English devotional literature of the early seventeenth century, notes the predominance in such writings of references to the Old Testament rather than to the New. The Trinitarian viewpoint remains, she points out, but God the Father appears for the most part in the form of the Old Testament deity—although White offers no explanation for the phenomenon.[23] Yet in the context of that changed Protestant attitude to the earlier portion of the Bible, the prevalence of those references is easily explicable.

How far this new respect for the Hebrews spread is evidenced in the paintings produced in Protestant Netherlands during the early seventeenth century, contrasting markedly with those produced in Catholic Italy. Rembrandt's deep empathy with the Old Testament patriarchs is apparent throughout his work, a sympathy he expressed not only in his paintings but in his personal friendship with contemporary Jews whom he often used as models for his biblical scenes in recognition of their historical bond. Discarding the christological interpretation of Old Testament stories except where it was intrinsic to Christian belief, he saw the Hebrew patriarchs anew as real human beings, as the revered forebears of Jewish neighbors. His *Sacrifice of Abraham* (1635), by discarding the usual title of the scene—*The Sacrifice of Isaac*—deflects attention from the prefigurative reading of the event in terms of the Crucifixion to a dramatically empathic depiction of Abraham faithfully obeying an incomprehensible divine command but saved at the final moment by the intervention of an angel. Nor was Rembrandt alone in his interest in the Hebrews. Michael Zell's study of Rembrandt, again suggesting no explanation for the change of focus, notes that "it has never been adequately emphasized that Christological interpretations of the Old Testament are altogether exceptional in Rembrandt's *oeuvre*, and indeed in seventeenth-century Dutch art in general."[24]

The newly revealed reality of that ancient civilization as recorded in the Bible provided the Protestant with fascinating insights into the ancient Hebrews' everyday activities and into the problems they had confronted, insights that seemed especially relevant to the conditions prevalent in their own situation. Moses, Joshua, and subsequent leaders were now seen as forebears of the Protestants, struggling to establish the true faith in the midst of a world given over to "idolatry." In certain ways, those stories appeared even more germane to the challenges of their day than were the Gospels. Where the primary concern of the New Testament is spiritual elevation, a focus upon the inner life of the individual, the Old Testament places its emphasis upon the establishment of a viable society, a community functioning in all its daily aspects under divine authority—regulating financial transactions, protecting the poor, prohibiting sexual irregularities, and concerned even with such details as the construction of a guardrail on flat roofs to prevent mishaps. The Mosaic commandments provided for the Puritan, not only in the New World, a legal system encompassing the manifold elements of communal life, those laws no longer administered by the church or its clergy but by a civil authority appointed by the people. The sanction adduced for such a system was the injunction in Deuteronomy 16:18: "Judges and officers shalt thou make thee in all thy cities . . . & they shall iudge thy people with righteous iudgement." Such was the source cited by John Calvin to justify the appointment of civil government, his reliance on the practice of the ancient Hebrews whose leaders had held the offices of "governors, as Joseph and Daniel; others of civil magistrates among a free people, as Moses, Joshua and the Judges. Their functions were expressly approved by the Lord. Wherefore no man can doubt that civil authority is in the sight of God, not only sacred and lawful, but the most sacred and by far the most honourable, of all."[25] Similarly, the selection of Bezalel, filled "with the spirit of God, in wisdom, and in understanding, and in knowledge, and in all manner of workmanship" to devise for the sanctuary articles in gold, silver, and brass, was seized upon by the Reformers as providing scriptural justification for their own use of ceremonial art, limited though it was by their opposition to Catholic excess.[26]

Wherever the Mosaic laws had not been specifically abrogated in the New Testament, they could now be revived in time of need. Hence, Luther proposed bigamy as a solution for Henry VIII's marital dilemma on the grounds that polygamy had been practiced by the Old Testament patriarchs and never revoked in the Gospels. Moreover, the Puritan work ethic relied in large part on the biblical attitude toward the accumulation of flocks, herds, and worldly possessions as divine blessings. William Perkins was clearly not referring to the New Testament when he affirmed that the Scriptures do not condemn temporal acquisitions such as "mony, lands, wealth, sustenance, and such like," but sanction them as "the good gifts of God."[27] Where that phrase does occur in the Gospels, the message is the reverse, the need for spiritual gifts: "If ye then, being evil, know how to give good gifts unto your children: how much more shall your heavenly Father give the Holy Spirit to them that ask him?" (Luke 11:13). In England in 1603, John Dod published his *Exposition of the Ten Commandements*—so popular that it went through 18 editions in the next three decades—in which he selected not the Gospels but the Old Testament decalogue as the basis for the Puritan code of godly behavior in the manifold activities and relationships of business, household, church, and state. Some Puritans even revived the practice of circumcision, since that had been the original mark of the covenant, which Christianity claimed to have taken over from the Hebrews, a commandment never specifically annulled. There emerged individuals such as Mary Chester, a Puritan indicted in England for keeping the Jewish Sabbath and adopting the dietary separation of meat from milk, while the followers of the Puritan leader John Traske were imprisoned in 1618 for undertaking similar Old Testament observances. The observance of these practices was, in fact, neither rare nor marginal, the bishop of Exeter complaining in 1600 of the prevalence of "Jewism" in his diocese.[28]

The relevance of all this for an analysis of Spenser's work is in the absence in *The Faerie Queene* of empathy with the ancient Hebrews, but that absence has further implications in connection with the next stage in this Protestant process. For, just as the Old Testament stories were seen to be rooted in reality, the prefigurative reading began to lose its force and was replaced by personal application to the life of the individual. Instead of reading the tales of the patriarchs typologically, as a foretelling of events due to occur in the Gospels, Protestants and, even more so, Puritans, began viewing them as archetypes of behavior, seeing their own experiences as cyclical reenactments of prototypical scriptural narrative, as indeed "postfigurations." It was a process fundamentally different from *imitatio Christi*, the attempt to pattern oneself after the life of Jesus, for the new role models no longer exemplified sufferance, celibacy, and asceticism, but inspired instead principles firmly rooted in the world of actuality—militant resistance to God's enemies, the eradication of idolatrous images, and a determination to apply to the manifold aspects of daily life the examples offered by those scriptural models. The covenant with Christ, the "covenant of grace," remained the code for spiritual advancement, but there emerged a concomitant undertaking as English Puritans began to acknowledge in addition the "covenant of works." The latter, understood to be contracted initially with Adam and extended in the Mosaic laws, was perceived as adaptable, as in the Old Testament, to the conditions of contemporary society, and hence as being ideally suited to the needs of the new civil governors.[29]

That second covenant, with its emphasis upon temporal activity, provided a powerful incentive for personal achievement, an attempt to fulfill in one's own life the ideals demonstrated by the Old Testament heroes, with the added sense that such identification lent a vicarious sanctity to the aspirations of each individual. Jonathan Mitchell assured his peers, as they struggled against immense difficulties in the new land, that they stood in the tradition of Nehemiah who, like them, had boldly left the comparative comfort of his country of residence to join his compatriots in Jerusalem, where they were surrounded by ruthless enemies. Taking him as their model, the settlers should not be depressed by adversity, nor hesitate to undertake the responsibilities of leadership:

> Hence see, that difficulties and troubles do not *excuse,* nor should *discourage* Rulers from doing the work of their Places which God calls them unto, or from seeking the welfare of the people: Such things do not excuse, nor should discourage from taking and accepting the Place of Rule when called to it. As they did not *Nehemiah,* though he heard before that their condition was a condition of great affliction and reproach, *Neh.*i.3. yet he voluntarily left the Court of *Persia,* to embarque with the *Jews* at *Jerusalem,* when in so stormy a time as this was; and how is he honoured in the Book of God for it? . . . Consider a little the difficulties that lay upon the *Jews* and their Rulers at this time in *Jerusalem,* after their return from Captivity, and in the dayes of *Nehemiah.* They were a small, weak and despised people. . . . Contempt and reproach is a bitter and killing thing to ingenuous Spirits; yet this they were fain to bear and pass through. . . . They were in the midst of Enemies, and Adversaries round about them, of several sorts and Nations.[30]

Cotton Mather, like so many other Puritans, visualized the journey to America as a reenactment of the Exodus, remarking of their leader, John Winthrop, that, "when the *Noble Design* of Carrying a Colony of *Chosen People* into an *American* Wilderness, was by *some* Eminent Persons undertaken, *This* Eminent Person was, by the Consent of all, *Chosen* for the *Moses*, who must be the Leader of so great an Undertaking."

That postfigurative tendency was shared by Protestants at large, their identification with Old Testament figures having emerged as early as the sixteenth century. It manifested itself not least in the dramatic works being produced on the English scene, where contemporary events came to be seen as reenactments of archetypal stories from the Bible, often with political or religious implications. Some time before 1548, the chronicle play *Kyng John*, produced by the early Reformer John Bale, characterized the king as Moses and his successor, Henry VIII, as Joshua leading the people into the holy land of Protestantism, an association that by implication labelled any rebel against the divinely appointed monarch of his own day as a Korah defying God's will and due to perish ignominiously:

> This noble Kynge Johan, as a faythfull Moyses,
> Withstode proude Pharo for hys poore Israel,
> Myndynge to brynge yt owt of the lande of darkenesse,
> But the Egyptyanes did agaynst hym so rebell
> That hys poore people ded styll in the desart dwell,
> Tyll that duke Josue, whych was our late Kynge Henrye,
> Clerely brought us in-to the lande of mylke and honye.[31]

Nicholas Udall, the author of *Ralph Roister Doister*, wrote at approximately the same time a dramatic version of *The Historie of Jacob and Esau*, particularly interesting for its reversal of the traditional reading of the story. The medieval *Ordo de Ysaac et Rebecca* had, understandably, depicted Esau typologically as the degenerate Hebrew failing to keep the covenant, and Jacob as the Christian whose donning of his brother's clothes marked him as the rightful heir. But Udall saw the story in terms more immediately relevant, with Esau as the Catholic stubbornly claiming his firstborn inheritance, while Jacob represented the Protestant whose deeds had made him worthy to replace him.[32] Lady Elizabeth Cary, unhappily married to a harsh, unpredictable husband, chose Herod's Jewish wife as the heroine for her closet drama, *The Tragedy of Mariam*, in which she depicted a woman suffering from misfortunes similar to her own marital predicament.[33] On the continent, Theodore de Bèze, closely associated with Calvin, published in Geneva in 1550 his *Abraham Sacrifiant*, a play exemplifying this same Protestant tendency. It was extraordinarily popular, with 27 editions issued by the end of the seventeenth century, and was translated and published in England in 1577. In that play, Bèze highlighted the parallel between Abraham, exiled at God's command from his homeland in Ur of the Chaldees, and Bèze's personal situation, when he was compelled for reasons of his faith to leave his birthplace, France, for the security of Geneva. His declaration in the preface is somewhat mild: "It is now two years, since God graunted me the grace to forsake the countrie where he is persecuted, to serue him according to his holy will"; but Abraham's bitter complaint in the opening lines of the play is no doubt much closer to Bèze's own feelings than the somewhat sanctimonious phraseology of the preface:

> Alas my God, and was there euer any,
> That hath endured of combrances so many
> As I haue done by fleeting too and fro,
> Since I my natiue countrie did forgo?

His Abraham is, as one might expect, a sternly Calvinistic figure evocative of Bèze himself.

We may seem to have wandered away from Spenser, but it is surely significant that this powerful contemporary Protestant tendency to identify with the ancient Hebrews and to see either oneself or one's fictional characters as reliving the experiences of their biblical forebears is totally absent from Spenser's epic. The blind Milton was to see himself in terms of Samson eyeless in Gaza, but Spenser never sees his own exile from his country and his enforced sojourn in Ireland as a reenactment of Abraham's exile from Ur in the Chaldees or Jacob's command to leave Canaan for Egypt.

Spenser's allegiance to Protestantism would certainly have exposed him to the postfigurative tendency apparent in the writings of his Protestant contemporaries. Although he retained a certain affection for medieval hermits and monasteries,[34] his hostility to the Catholic Church as a corrupt institution is patent throughout, not least in his repeated representation of it as the Scarlet Lady. On the matter of his Puritanism, an aspect liable to expose him even further to that postfigurative tendency, there has been some debate. Early in the twentieth century, Lilian Winstanley, F. M. Padelford, and J. J. Higginson established the view that Spenser was closely allied to Puritanism; but in 1950, Virgil Whitaker challenged that concept, arguing that Spenser's sympathies lay rather with the conservative party in the Anglican church, a party striving to preserve as much as possible of the Catholic heritage.[35] While admitting that the use of allegory in *The Faerie Queene* tends to obscure the finer points of theology, Whitaker bases his reasoning on three main elements distinguishing the Puritan party, namely, its acceptance of Calvinist doctrine, its dispute over rituals and vestments, and its opposition to episcopacy, and he concludes, therefore, that the poet belonged to the middle way, arguing that Spenser hated Rome, as would "any patriotic Englishman," but showed little sympathy for the Puritans except in their demand for an honest and educated clergy. Whitaker's view held sway for a number of years, until the appearance of Anthea Hume's study in 1984 that argued in much greater detail that Spenser should be viewed in broader perspective, in terms of the contemporary crosscurrents in Elizabethan religion and politics. Viewing him in that context, she maintains that he should be restored to his previous position as a member of the Puritan group, indeed to the militant variety represented by the group of men with whom he associated. The argument that he should be disqualified from such membership because of his "mild" stance on such matters as opposition to episcopacy is, she points out, invalid, since a number of prominent Puritans of his day, including Laurence Humphrey, Thomas Sampson, John Foxe, and Anthony Gilby, took a similar line, opposing the Admonitioners' demand for the abolition of bishoprics.[36]

The view that Spenser was inclined to Puritanism certainly conforms more closely to the recorded events of his life, especially his close association with the Earl of Leicester, the leader of the Puritan faction at court, and with Sir Philip Sidney, who was at the center of a literary circle dedicated to promoting a patriotic, Protestant-oriented literature with leanings toward Puritanism. Spenser divided much of his time while composing *The Shepheardes Calendar* between the homes of Leicester and Sidney, in London and at Penshurst, relying in large part on their patronage, and it would be strange indeed if, during such periods of intense controversy, his own religious stance were at odds with theirs. Moreover, his other associations strengthen that assumption: the companion he described as his "most special freende," Gabriel Harvey, was a deeply committed Puritan, as was Lord Grey, whom Spenser, to the dismay of many historians, defended so vigorously for his harsh suppression of the Catholic rebellion in Ireland. Both in his student days, therefore, and during the time he was composing his major work, he was enveloped in an atmosphere strongly supportive of Puritan ideals.

If he was, like his mentor Sidney, in addition to his religious beliefs an admirer of Neoplatonism and a lover of Greek and Roman literature, there was no inherent contradiction in that combination, the Christianizing of classical myth having opened the way for even the most fervent Puritan to reverence its tales. Arthur Golding, whose translation of Ovid's *Metamorphoses* served as a primary source for sixteenth century writers (many of whom were happy to exploit its eroticism to the full), was in fact a staunch Puritan, a devout translator of Calvin's writings, and a man known to his peers for the strictness of his religious behavior.[37] His purpose in providing an English version of Ovid's work was to make available to the public what he saw in all sincerity as a collection of moral and Christian lessons. Apollo's pursuit of Daphne supplied in his view a model of chastity, a "myrror of virginitie," and he carefully directed attention away from the example offered by the raunchy god to that supplied by the modest maiden. But his reading is not merely a moralizing of such actions but also an outgrowth of the tradition established by Nicholas of Cusa, namely, his conceiving of the pagans as fumbling their way toward higher truths:

> I would not wish the simple sort offended for too bee,
> When in this booke the heathen names of feyned Godds they see.
> The trewe and everliving God the Paynims did not knowe:
> Which caused them the name of Godds on creatures too bestow.

In the translation, that process became even more patent, the metamorphosis being in such instances Golding's own, as when Envy is made to murmur to herself a "Divels Paternoster" or when Baucis and Philemon transform their humble cottage into a temple (in the original, presumably of the Roman kind) where the event is described in Golding's version as "The old poore Cote so base / Whereof they had beene owners erst, became a Church"[38] There was thus felt to be at that time no necessary discrepancy between religious piety and a delight in classical myth. Yet Spenser, even in the matter of postfiguration, which had become a staple of Protestant and Puritan writing, tended to see his own era not as a reliving of biblical but of classical or mythological precedent.

His epic does contain references to contemporary people seen in terms of reenactments or echoes of the ancient world. The Earl of Leicester is conflated with King Arthur, Sir Philip Sidney with Sir Calidore, Sir Francis Walsingham with Meliboeus, and Lady Sidney with Meliboeus's daughter,

Pastorella. But they are not seen in terms of biblical models. The cyclical pattern of history visible in Protestant postfiguration, which creates a bond between the present and the archetypal past, is paralleled in his attempt to establish noble ancestry for the Britons. In order to enhance the majesty of its queen, Spenser traces the origin of Britain's foundation to an august and ancient figure; but it is not to the reign of King David, even though the climactic moment in the ritual of the queen's coronation is her being anointed in the tradition of Saul and David. Instead, the foundation of Britain is attributed to Brutus of Troy, the great-grandson of Aeneas, founder of Rome. Britomart recounts with pride her feelings of empathy with those forebears: "She heard, that she was lineally extract: / For noble *Britons* sprong from *Troians* bold, / And *Troynouant* was built of old *Troyes* ashes cold" (3.9.38). From those ashes arose the Roman empire, its famed offspring destined to emerge in a city washed by the river Thames—a monarchy "That in all glory and great enterprise, / Both first and second *Troy* shall dare to equalise."

Spenser's choice of a classical lineage for his country is of special interest because the founders of the chivalric tradition on which his epic is based had taken considerable pains to provide a different context for its forebears, establishing, at times with considerable ingenuity, a connection between the British Isles and that central moment in Scripture, the Crucifixion, by means of the legendary search for the Holy Grail. Geoffrey of Monmouth's adoption of the tradition that Britain was descended from Brutus of Troy was clearly felt to be unsatisfactory once the religious pursuit of the Sangreal became of central interest. It seemed necessary to establish some genealogical linkage, however tenuous, between the British knights of the Round Table involved in the Grail legend and those involved in the earlier history of the vessel. Robert de Boron's poem, *Joseph d'Arimathie*, composed at the turn of the twelfth century, provided an initial link, connecting the as yet unnamed finder of the Holy Grail with

Joseph of Arimathea, who was believed to have collected Christ's blood in a vessel that had been used at the Last Supper. That vessel (later identified as a chalice) was in this tradition passed on to his descendants, one of whom in each generation—an individual dedicated to purity of word, thought, and deed—was assigned to protect it. In the chain of those charged with the task, a delinquent guardian, tempted by the sight of a woman's ankle, failed to preserve his chastity and the chalice was lost. Here, the anonymous author of the prose *Lancelot* (composed about 1215) provided the missing association, recounting that Lancelot, believing that he was sleeping with Guinevere, was in fact sleeping with Amite, a descendant of Joseph of Arimathea's family. From that liaison was born the British knight, Sir Galahad, destined to find the chalice. The link required further strengthening and Glastonbury provided the necessary addition. Somewhat earlier, in 1191, probably at the instigation of King Henry II, the monks at that abbey had been directed to initiate a search, during which they miraculously "discovered" in the abbey cemetery the bones of King Arthur and Queen Guinevere, which were then reinterred inside the church. Perhaps for that reason, the legend arose that Joseph of Arimathea had brought the vessel containing the blood to Glastonbury, thereby establishing an essential link between the British knights of the Round Table and the scriptural figure believed originally to have collected the blood of Jesus.[39] Such was the convoluted effort made by Spenser's predecessors to connect inventively the events of King Arthur's reign with a biblical source; yet none of this appears in *The Faerie Queene*, the sole lineage claimed to shed glory on the Elizabethan era being its supposed connection with the secular world of Troy and ancient Rome.[40]

How firmly this preference for the classics dominates the epic is evidenced in Spenser's statement to Ralegh, his declaration that he will be imitating the epic not merely in its outward form, as literary genre, but in the concept of virtue that permeated the works it produced. In choosing King

Arthur for the excellency of his person, he will, Spenser claimed, be following "all the antique Poets historicall, first Homere, who in the persons of Agamemnon and Ulysses hath ensampled a good governour and a vertuous man, the one in hisIlias, the other in his Odysseis; then Virgil, whose like intention was to doe in the person of Aeneas." Even the moral principles that his characters will demonstrate are to be those of classical definition, in "the image of a braue knight, perfected in the twelue morall vertues, as Aristotle hath deuised."

The reluctance to see his own times in biblically "postfigurative" terms reflects a further divergence from Puritan practice—his distrust of the actualities of human existence that had come to fulfill so major a role in both Protestant and Puritan writings. The focus within the latter sects had shifted to the terrestrial. Its adherents were determined, while infusing their daily affairs with spiritual devotion, to use their talents in this world, to labor industriously for the good of society and family, acknowledging, as in the Old Testament, the need to embed religious obedience in the daily actualities of earthly existence. This tendency was exemplified in their transfer of the religious term "vocation." In Catholicism it had denoted a call to the priesthood, but Protestants applied the term to all forms of daily activity on the assumption that even worldly occupations were in a sense devotional exercises, to be pursued with seriousness and responsibility. As John Cotton declared, "We live by faith in our vocations. . . . A man therefore that serves Christ in serving of men, he doth his work sincerely as in Gods presence, and as one that hath an heavenly businesse in hand, and therefore comfortably as knowing God approves of his way and work."[41]

Spenser, in contrast, attempts throughout the epic to implant in the reader a suspicion of the material and tangible, and not just through his use of allegory, a genre that by nature is at least one remove from the factual. For there was another element, introduced repeatedly throughout the epic, that ensured the distancing of its scenes from contemporary existence—a technique that might be termed the "Protean," namely, the repeated play with transpositions of bodily form, as characters disguise themselves, often adopting the appearance of others and becoming surrogates virtually indistinguishable from those they impersonate.

Behind that process lies a change in contemporary conception. *Scientia*, the search for knowledge, regarded in medieval times with grave suspicion, was allied to the curiosity that led Eve to eat of the forbidden fruit. Moreover, it was liable to encourage independent thought rather than humble acceptance of the rulings of the church fathers. Such curiosity had been especially condemned when applied to observation of the factual elements of terrestrial existence, Bernard of Clairvaux enjoining monks always to walk with head bowed and eyes fixed on the ground lest they be distracted from spiritual thoughts by their physical environment.[42] But by the fourteenth century, that disapproval began to weaken as part of the rise of empirical enquiry, the growing respect for the individual's right to examine evidence, to accumulate data, and to draw personal conclusions. There arose a new delight in observation, in scrutinizing details of the tactile world and in fostering proficiency in deducing facts from them. Chaucer provides a classic instance. Outward signs, such as eccentricities in dress, peculiarity of comportment, or oddity of gesture served as reliable indications of character—the monk's fur-lined sleeve betraying a love of luxury, the prioress's wiping of her mouth after drink revealing her aristocratic background, and the carefully curled locks and embroidered gown of the squire indicating male vanity. Such factual data were to be noted, analyzed, and interpreted. In contemporary depictions of the journey of the magi, such as the painting by Gozzoli in the Medici Palace in Florence, can be perceived the same process, each person in the procession individualized by the extravagance, the simplicity, or the professional characteristics of dress.

In Spenser the reverse holds true. The watchword for observation is wariness, suspicion of visible or tactile elements.[43] The reiterated instances of disguise and impersonation warn the observer ever to be on guard, scrutinizing outward appearance with distrust, as in all likelihood incongruent with the actuality within. In *The Faerie Queene* we meet characters—usually, but not always, the villains—transforming themselves into seemingly attractive figures in order to mislead and, for the most part, proving only too successful in the attempt. The instances are too numerous to list. Most obviously, there is Duessa, so perfect a copy of Una that even her knight fails to penetrate the disguise. Archimago, the arch-villain, frequently transforms others but adopts the same process himself, appearing on one occasion as Saint George, clad in armor, silver shield, and bloody cross identical with that of the hero's, so that "when he sate vpon his courser free, / *Saint George* himself ye would haue deemed him to be" (1.2.11). A little later, Una and the knight meet a pilgrim on their journey, the minutiae of his appearance described in full, each detail conforming perfectly to his supposed character. He is dressed

>   in simple weedes forworne,
> And soild with dust of the long dried way;
> His sandales were with toilesome trauell torne,
> And face all tand with scorching sunny ray,
> As he had traueild many a sommers day,
> Through boyling sands of *Arabie* and *Ynde;*
> And in his hand a *Iacobs* staffe, to stay
> His wearie limbes vpon: and eke behind,
> His scrip did hang, in which his needments he did bind.
>   (1.6.35)

Yet, as we are soon to learn, the seeming Pilgrim is, once again, a dissembling Archimago. On another occasion, a messenger enters, "Whom if ye please for to discouer plaine, / Ye shall him *Archimago* find, I ghesse, / The falsest man aliue" (1.12.34). Duessa is not the only counterpart designed by him, the pseudo-Florimell being so expertly devised, "That *Florimell* her selfe in all mens vew / She seem'd to passe; so forged things to fairest shew" (4.5.15). Poeana, we are warned, is outwardly beautiful but inwardly corrupt (4.8.49), and Pride "wondrously faire" in semblance (1.4.10). And so it goes on, even the noble characters participating in the masquerade. Artegall dons the armor of a pagan knight to deceive the sultan (5.8.26), and Britomart, shy at declaring her love, conceals herself in the garb of a peasant to visit Merlin—although the latter, gifted with magical powers, at once sees through the pretense (3.3.7). Ovid's *Metamorphoses*, beloved of Spenser, did, of course, recount numerous stories of mythological figures changed in form— Arachne transmuted into a spider, Daphne into a laurel bush; but the purpose of those changes differed fundamentally from Spenser's practice since the intent there was not to deceive others but to serve as punishment, rescue, or reward for the person transformed.

The message of Spenser's literary device is clear, at times phrased rhetorically to underscore the universality of the caveat:

> What man so wise, what earthly wit so ware,
>   As to descry the crafty cunning traine,
>   By which deceipt doth maske in visour faire,
>   And cast her colours dyed deepe in graine,
>   To seeme like Truth, whose shape she well can faine,
>   And fitting gestures to her purpose frame;
>   The guiltlesse man with guile to entertaine? (1.7.1)

We, who are not magicians, are instructed to exercise extreme caution, surrounded as we are by duplicity. We must learn to distrust appearances, to search beneath externals for the verities so cunningly concealed within. As Cymoent laments, "So tickle be the termes of mortall state, / And full of subtile sophismes, which do play / With double senses, and with false debate" (3.4.28).

What lay behind this new approach? In part, it marks the maturing of judgment in Spenser's generation, the emergence of a greater Renaissance sophistication as a less credulous view of the world replaces the naïveté of the past. This need for cautious discrimination becomes prominent in the writings of others of his time. Othello fails the test, insisting upon proof but being gulled by a mere handkerchief, the validity of whose evidence he does not attempt to verify; Volpone's predators prove incapable of penetrating his disguise; the Duchess of Malfi is deceived by a wax model of her supposedly dead husband—all instances intimating the authors' recognition of the need for increased circumspection. But in Spenser's work the discrimination demanded of the sophisticated has a religious dimension, the literary device he adopts constituting a strategy for coping with one of the major challenges of his time, yet in a manner very different from his co-religionists.

The names "Una" and "Duessa" chosen by Spenser to represent the single true church and its false "double"—the first instance of such substitution—indicate the main reason prompting him to formulate the technique, though it was due to reappear repeatedly throughout the work even when not related to that theme. The frequency of these substitutions suggests it was a principle of more universal significance. Religious belief had been simpler in Chaucer's day. Monks, friars, and parsons in his generation might often be neglectful of their duties, even consciously hypocritical, but there existed at that time no doubt concerning the Christian tasks that were incumbent upon them, the duties they were obligated to perform. The church had indeed seen sectarian schisms, disagreements on matters of doctrine, even the temporary emergence of antipopes, but the body of the church was unified and indivisible. In contrast, in the more complex society of Spenser's day, the need for discrimination had reached its apogee (or nadir) as two hostile churches emerged, each claiming the exclusive path to salvation. The choice was by no means easy. Rome, after all, was descended in an unbroken line from the congregations founded by Peter and Paul, its dominion was awesomely global, its threats of excommunication daunting, and the arguments for its legitimacy so persuasive that only those firmest in their belief could dare to resist, knowing that they risked thereby eternal damnation if they chose incorrectly.

Spenser's literary innovation served to ease the dilemma of those wavering in their faith. It comforted the Protestant believer not merely by suggesting the inherent fallacy of the older church's arguments but also by arguing in broader terms for the potential speciousness of all seeming truths. It urged upon its readers the compelling need for discernment, a readiness to penetrate the disguise of enemies determined to mislead them, for courage in identifying as deception the Catholic claim to exclusive authenticity. Clothing oneself in the armor of faith, as Paul had urged, and dedicating oneself to glorifying Christianity is insufficient, as the Redcrosse Knight is warned when duped by the false vision of Una: "Young knight, what euer that dost armes professe, / And through long labours huntest after fame, / Beware of fraud" (1.4.1).

In contrast to the deceptions by the human figures, the personification of abstract concepts in *The Faerie Queene* remains for the most part outwardly accordant with the qualities they represent. Loathsome Gluttony, his belly "upblown" by luxury, persistently spews up his gorge "that all did him deteast"; Avarice bears about him coffers filled with gold, yet he wears a threadbare coat and cobbled shoes; and Envy, chewing between his cankered teeth a venomous toad, gnashes his teeth at the sight of others' felicity. There can be no doubt of their characters, for the purpose of these personifications is not to deceive but, in the tradition of the morality plays, to exemplify abstract concepts in physical form. But the characters participating in the narrative line adopt instead the attribute of dissemblance for the purpose of cozening the innocent. William Empson commented that the distrust of the real world contributes to the "distancing" of the epic, but this distancing removes it as well from the validation of terrestrial concerns that had come to characterize the Puritan attitudes of Spenser's day.

Spenser's use of allegory marks a further point of difference from his peers. The Protestant attitude to the allegorizing of texts was ambivalent. The fourfold reading of Scripture dominating biblical exegesis during the Middle Ages, one of which endorsed allegory, was still valid for some of their members. That principle had, even before the Reformation, been extended to nonscriptural works as well. John of Garland's thirteenth century Latin poem, *Integumenta super Ovidium Metamorphoseos*, and the famed *Ovide Moralisé*, had both preceded Arthur Golding's version in deducing moral lessons from the pagan stories by assuming them to be allegorical. The reliance of such secular works upon the above principle of biblical exegesis is indicated in a letter written by Friar Conrad Dollenkopf some time around 1515, in which he stated proudly, "I already know by rote all the fables of Ovid in his *Metamorphoses*, and these I can expound quadruply—to wit, naturally, literally, historically, and spiritually," the latter indicating allegorical interpretation.[44]

However, for most Reformers, the fourfold technique was anathema, and not only because of its Catholic origin. Their hostility arose in addition from the Protestant insistence upon examining texts in their naked form, pared of later, especially Catholic, accretions. Certain Old Testament passages essential to Christianity and the foretelling of the Messiah, such as Isaiah's account of the suffering servant, still retained the required typological interpretation, though such verses could not have borne that meaning for the Hebrews of the day. For such passages, Calvin offered a lively comparison. The christological passages in the Old Testament were, he suggested, similar to a painter's preliminary sketch, which, in addition to its preparatory function, possesses a validity of its own:

> For painters are want to drawe that which they purpose to counterfeit or represent with a cole, before they set on the lively colours with pensill. The Apostle then puts this

difference betweene the law and the Gospell: to wit, that that which at this time is drawne and painted with fresh and lively colours, was only shadowed out under the law by a rude and grosse draught. For although it had not the perfect image of heavenly things, as if the workman had put his last endeavour to it, yet even this rough draught was greatly profitable to the Ancient Fathers.[45]

On the other hand, nonessential extrapolations into allegorical reading were generally rejected. Martin Luther condemned the technique in no uncertain terms, whether applied to sacred or to secular texts, warning that such exegetical elaboration served to detract from the primacy of the text itself: "The Holy Spirit is the very simplest writer and speaker there is in heaven and earth; therefore His words, too, cannot have more than one most simple sense, which we call the Scriptural or literal or tongue-sense." Luther regarded the application of such exegesis to the Christianizing of classical sources as a contemptible aberration:

At first allegories originated from stupid and idle monks. Finally they spread so widely that some men turned Ovid's *Metamorphoses* into allegories. They made a laurel tree Mary, and Apollo they made Christ. Although this is absurd, nevertheless, when it is set forth to youths who lack experience but are lovers and students of literature, it is so pleasing to them at the onset that they devote themselves completely to those interpretations. Consequently, I hate allegories.

William Tyndale proved no less vehement in his hostility to such allegorizing, castigating it as the invention of "sophisters with their anagogical and chopological sense, and with an antitheme of half an inch, out of which some of them draw a thread of nine days long." The Scriptures, he explained, "hath but one sense, which is the literal sense. And that literal sense is the root and ground of all, and the anchor that never faileth, whereunto if thou cleave thou canst never err, or go out of the way."[46]

If Puritan iconoclasm is generally associated with the defacing of physical images, as in the decapitation of statues in St. Paul's Cathedral under the direction of the early reformer, Bishop Ridley, in 1552,[47] their iconoclasm needs to be related also to the Puritan attacks upon verbal images, including, as part of that interdiction, allegorical extrapolations of texts. The prohibition against images, the second of the Ten Commandments, had been given added prominence when in 1561 Queen Elizabeth issued an edict that the decalogue should be displayed in all churches throughout the kingdom. Lancelot Andrewes was soon to define the second commandment as referring not only to tactile forms, such as statues, but also to mental images, the ruling applying to "any kind of conception or imagination which may arise."[48] In that context, it becomes apparent that Puritan hostility to the use of classical mythology in its Christianized form arose from a twofold impulse—opposition to the importation of pagan works on the one hand, and, on the other hand, and perhaps more importantly, from the Puritans' determination to strip away imaginative accretions to texts, as in their reading of the Bible. Stephen Gosson's *Schoole of Abuse* (1579) presents evidence of the development of that changing attitude. At first, Gosson accepted the more conventional view that allegorized classical mythology. He equates the biblical God with Jupiter, the ruler of the universe and the apex of the universal hierarchy. Just as in the body, each organ and member must fulfill its task, he proclaimed, so in the state there should be none idle: "*Iupiter* himself shall stand for example, who is euer in woork, still moouing and turning about the heauens, if he shuld pull his hand from the frame, it were impossible for the world to indure." But in his subsequent *Apologie for the Schoole of Abuse,* published in the same year, Gosson's attitude underwent radical change. He delivered a fierce assault on the contemporary habit of importing the classical pantheon to literature, exposing the profligate stories that Pico and others had conveniently allegorized and transformed into Christian lessons. With devastating effect, since none could deny his evidence, Gosson pointed to the unbridled lasciviousness of the pagan gods as recorded in the original stories and hence their blasphemous inappropriateness as counterparts of sacred scriptural figures:

> *Iupiter* which was but a mortall man and almost a parricide, that for greedinesse of the crowne, droue his owne father *Saturne*, out of his kingdome, though hee were a cruell tyrant, an vnnaturall childe, an vsurping Prince, an abhominable leacher, as wicked a wretche as euer lived, by Poets is made the king of gods. *Venus* a notorious strumpet, that lay with *Mars*, with *Mercurie*, with *Iupiter*, with *Anchises*, with *Butes*, with *Adones*, that taught the women in Cyprus to set vp a Stewes, too hyre out them selues as hackneies, for gaine, and that made her self as common as a Barbars chayre, by Poets is placed for a goddesse in heauen. Al these whome the Poetes haue called gods and goddesses, for the most part, were bastardes begotten in adulterie, or very lewde liuers, which had no soner defiled their beddes, but they were snatchte vp to the skyes and made starres, in so much that *Iuno* crieth out in *Seneca*. . . . Lets dwel in earth, for heauen is full of whores.

Those who cloaked the immorality of the pagan gods in Christian garb, incorporating them into verse and drama as models, had, he claimed, distorted the true faith:

> Whilest they make Cupide triumphe in heauen, and all the gods to marche bounde like miserable captiues, before his charriot, they belie God, and bewitch the reader with bawdie charmes. . . . Thus making gods of them that were brute beastes, in the likenes of men, diuine goddesses of common harlots; they robbe God of his honour, diminishe his authoritie, weaken his might, and turne his seate to a stewes.

In conclusion, he directed his attack on to the Neoplatonists, charging them with deliberate falsehood: "By writing of vntruthes they are open liers, but if they do faine these frantike conceates to resemble somewhat els that they imagine, by speaking of one thing and thinking another, they are dissemblers."[49]

The attack was taken up by others, no less forceful in their condemnation. William Prynne's *Histriomastix* quotes Gosson's condemnation with approval, making a similar charge that, since the pagan gods were in fact either devils, wicked men, or mere fictions, the stories spun about them by art and rhetoric in order to adapt them to Christian needs served only "to cool love for the true God."[50] That view occasionally filtered through even to some of Ovid's greatest admirers, such as George Sandys who, in the commentary he appended to his translation of the *Metamorphoses*, admitted that, in contrast to the currently accepted reading of the Io scene, Jupiter there "becomes a beast to obtain his bestiall desires." He then cites in support of that view the wry couplet from Martial: "Father of Gods, this shape of Bull then thou / Should'st have assum'd, when Iö was a Cow."[51]

In this regard too, Spenser chose his own path. He adopted neither the allegorizing of pagan mythology typified by Golding's work nor the hostility to it among mainstream Puritans, exemplified in the works of Gosson and Prynne. In rejecting those polarized responses, he was, as in his subordination of biblical imagery to classical, asserting his independence as a poet, adopting an approach that enabled him to draw upon the wealth of tales associated with the Olympic pantheon while still preserving the primacy of the Christian message motivating his work and the moral principles he intended his epic to engender. That duality emerges even in Spenser's definition of the purpose of his work. That his main purpose was religious is obvious from the characters of Una, representing the church; of the Redcrosse Knight, her defendant who functions not only in the opening book but serves as a coordinating link in the later books; of Britomart, the symbol of chastity (a virtue more relevant to Christianity than to ancient Greece or

Rome); and Orgoglio symbolizing pride, the cardinal sin in the church. Yet, in his letter to Sir Walter Ralegh, Spenser defined the aim of the work as "to fashion a gentleman in virtuous and gentle discipline," and the virtues he specified as animating the work were not those of the Puritan faith but, as has been noted, the 12 moral virtues defined by Aristotle.

The contrast between, on the one hand, the religious purpose of the epic—prominent in the opening book but reverberating throughout in its evoking of Arthurian legend and the Pauline image of knights battling to defend their faith—and on the other hand, the infusion of pagan mythology with no attempt to merge those disparate elements constitutes a perfect instance of what has come to be called intertextuality, the implanting of one text or cultural pattern within another, a process which, together with *aporia*, has been decried by deconstructionists as a seductive mode compromising meaning. As Geoffrey Hartman wrote in the collection of essays that was to serve as the school's manifesto, *Deconstruction and Criticism*, intertextuality is essentially subversive, forming a barrier that frustrates any unified or valid interpretation:

> Each text is shown to imbed other texts by a most cunning assimilation whose form is the subject both of psychoanalytic and of purely rhetorical criticism. Everything we thought of as spirit, or meaning separable from the letter of the text, remains within an "intertextual sphere." ... [Criticism] has always shown that a received text means more than it says (it is "allegorical"), or that it subverts all possible meanings by its "irony"—a rhetorical or structural limit that prevents the dissolution of art into positive or exploitative truth.[52]

In that same manifesto, Derrida confirms this negative view of intertextuality, claiming that, by moving beyond or overrunning the boundaries *(débordement)*, a writer "spoils" the previously accepted divisions so that the text "is no longer a finished corpus of writings, some content enclosed in a book or its margins, but a differential network, a fabric of traces referring endlessly to something other than itself." Later in the same essay, he declares more explicitly of such intertextuality that no meaning can be fixed or decided upon: "there is no paradigmatic text. Only relationships of cryptic haunting from mark to mark. No palimpsest (definitive unfinishedness). No piece, no metonymy, no integral corpus."[53]

Such interweaving of diverse sources functions as a major factor in Spenser's work. It was not syncretism in the sense generally applied to the epic, the assumption that it blended two cultures, drawing equally upon classical and biblical sources. Instead, the epic achieves its major effect by its separation of the two forms, deriving its theme from Christian tradition but embellishing it with imagery that is pagan in source—pagan insofar as no attempt was made to Christianize it allegorically nor to accommodate it to the theme in accordance with Neoplatonic practice. To see in that hybrid form an intertextuality disqualifying all possibility of unified reading is, I believe, to miss both the richness and the uniqueness of Spenser's poetic achievement, his refusal to remain within the restrictive borders either of the Puritan or of the secular configuration.

FOUR

Volpone, Comedy or Mordant Satire?

The laughter and applause greeting Jonson's play in its stage performances contrast markedly with its somber evaluations by literary critics. In Jonson's day, the play was received with delight and was acted frequently through the seventeenth century. Samuel Pepys, an experienced theatergoer, described it enthusiastically as "a most excellent play, the best I think I ever saw" and, in the following century, the two years 1773 and 1774 saw no fewer than 12 London productions. The play went into eclipse toward the end of the eighteenth century when the dramatic principles Jonson had espoused clashed with those of the times, but after its revival in the twentieth century it proved so popular that in the number of professional productions (35 between 1921 and 1972) it came second only to Shakespeare's most favored comedies.[1] Donald Wolfit, Ralph Richardson, and Paul Scofield provided outstanding interpretations of the leading role, with such creative directors as William Poel, Tyrone

Guthrie, Peter Hall, and Joan Littlewood offering their own notable productions.

In contrast, the views of critics have been uniformly caustic, their evaluations defining the play not as a delightful comedy but as a mordant satire on the bestiality of humankind, with Volpone himself interpreted as a reprehensible symbol of greed and corruption. He and his friends, we are told, are "villains of the stuff of which tragedy makes use, but without the dignity" of that genre.[2] His stratagems are condemned as immoral, his opening speech castigated for its blasphemy, and (contradictory as it may appear after such charges) the harshness of the punishments meted out in the final scene censured as excessive.

It was not simply the immorality of Volpone's actions that was deprecated—an unsavory character can, like Molière's miser, function with full comic effect as the object of derision. For some, the difficulty arose from the conflicting emotions the protagonist was felt to evoke, a mélange of admiration and censure implying on the author's part a failure to define his own moral criteria. This conflict resulted in a troubling sense that the vitality and vigor of his leading character in some way fascinate us even though the patent evil of his ways should repel us. Una Ellis-Fermor writes of the disgust that his "repulsive and contemptible" actions inevitably engender. Lester Beaurline refers unequivocally to Volpone and Mosca in the opening scenes as a pair of rogues. To Jonas Barish, Volpone is an "archknave" and a "monstrosity," classed by him, together with his despicable victims as representing unmitigated villainy. Jonson's editor, C. H. Herford, draws no distinction between Volpone and his victims, the legacy hunters, remarking that *all* the principal actors are criminals, gambling desperately for high stakes and representing the unlimited possibilities of evil. Never before, he concludes, had Jonson painted with such power humanity denuded of every germ of goodness. Rainer Pineas, followed by Alan Dessen, identifies Volpone as modeled on the vice of morality plays, characterized by a "love of evil for its own sake." John Enck defines Volpone as personifying "the slough of unredeemable corruption." And Gabriele B. Jackson, in a vivid metaphor, summarizes that widespread critical condemnation by describing Volpone as a character devoted to pernicious ends who, "like a spider in the center of his web of intrigue," sits waiting to destroy those around him.[3] All these responses are descriptions of Volpone not in the final scenes of the play but as he appears from the opening scene onward.

A perfect instance of the contrast between these two views of Volpone's character, those of the actor and of the critic, may be found in a review by Harold Hobson in the *Sunday Times*. He disapproved of Ralph Richardson's interpretation, suggesting that Richardson was too gentle an actor to play the part of villain effectively:

> Now the reason why Volpone is not suited to Richardson is an honourable one. It cannot be too often repeated that this actor . . . knows the simple goodness of the human heart as does no other player in the British theatre. Whatever is kindly, loving and tolerant he can portray with a moving pathos that is always saved from mawkishness by its wit and humour. . . . But there was never any goodness at all at the foundation of Volpone's avarice and lechery. The man was evil from the start. There is nothing in Volpone on which an actor like Richardson can catch hold.[4]

Exceptions to these negative responses have been very rare and limited in scope. William Empson, while acknowledging Volpone's moral turpitude, castigated critics for assuming that audiences automatically condemn him as a "loathsomely wicked individual." He argued that spectators at a Punch and Judy show, under the spell of the performance, experience a temporary suspension of moral censure, applauding Punch's beating of his wife irrespective of the revulsion such action would evoke in real life. Such deferment of ethical considerations holds true, he maintains, for comedy at large, quoting how the first audiences of *The*

Winter's Tale (audiences that were, he points out, Jonson's public too) were undisturbed by Autolycus's profession of pickpocketing, regarding him as an essentially good man, helpful to the lovers and thus forwarding the plot, even though in actuality they would have had him hanged as a thief had he been caught in the act.[5] Yet even this conciliatory view of Empson's, that we suspend ethical considerations while watching a performance, assumes that the considerations we suspend are of abhorrence, Volpone's actions being in themselves reprehensible.

Rape is certainly reprehensible, but until the actual moment when Volpone attempts to force himself upon Celia—a moment when, I propose to argue, the entire ambience of the play undergoes a profound change—the mood is one of sheer fun and good humor. During the first half of the play, the tradition of comic drama to which Jonson's audience was heir would have evoked, as it does on the modern stage, not merely a suspension of censure but a sympathy with and a delight in Volpone's actions. Later I will investigate the conflicting elements in the play, but for now I wish to note how relevant Bakhtin's perception of "dialogue" may be in this instance. For the contradictory elements motivating a work are, he points out, not always concurrent. They may function in different sections, each contributing to the complexity or subtlety of the overall effect—a factor that may explain the marked discrepancy between the audiences' response to Volpone's ruse and the negative evaluation by critics. An audience watching the first half of the play has no knowledge of the later rape scene and, unlike the critic, cannot read back into that earlier section the hostility aroused by Volpone's subsequent behavior.

There was in Jonson's day a dramatic tradition familiar to audiences that would have predisposed them to identify with Volpone. Jonson's debt to earlier theatrical sources, to Plautus, Terence, and later Italian drama including the *Commedia dell'Arte*, has long been known. But there is an aspect of that debt that has gone almost unnoticed, namely the Jacobean audience's familiarity with those sources and the ways in which that familiarity would have contributed to their appreciation of Jonson's use of them, as well as his deviation from them. One recalls the plot of Plautus's *Eunuchus* in which the young hero employs a ruse not dissimilar to Volpone's cozening of Corvino, pretending to be impotent in order to obtain the girl he loves.

In assessing how widespread that knowledge of earlier traditions was, we should recall that enlightened teachers such as Roger Ascham and Richard Mulcaster, desirous of relieving for their pupils the tedium of study, imported into England a technique that had proved highly successful on the Continent, the translation of full-length Latin comedies first into English and then back again into Latin, the process often including a stage performance by the students. The plays were either, when appropriate for schoolboys, original works by Plautus and Terence or, alternatively, comedies based upon them. These so-called "Christian-Terence" plays arose from a recognition of the moral dangers involved for the young in a study of Roman comedy with its indulgent attitude to attractive courtesans, the seduction of available young ladies, and the successful deceptions of masters by wily slaves. They realized, instead, that the Gospels could be used to authorize pseudo-Terentian scenes of carousal and misbehavior in the framework of a moral lesson, namely, the misdeeds and ultimate repentance of the prodigal son. The Scriptures merely reported that he "wasted his goods with riotous liuing," focusing upon the son's repentance, but the parable offered the opportunity of expanding the phrase to include in the play the kind of mischievous disobedience of authority that could parallel Terentian comedy. Examples include the anonymous *Nice Wanton* of 1560, Thomas Ingelend's *Disobedient Child* of 1577, and George Gascoigne's *Glass of Government* of the same year, as well as the earlier and very popular *Acolastus* by Gnaphaeus, translated and published in England in 1540.

Finally, Cornelius Schonaeus's collection, *Terentius Christianus*, was published in both Cologne and London in 1592, which became the anthology most widely used in English schools in subsequent years.[6] The preface to the English translation praised the author who, "has clothed more chaste subject-matter in the pure language of Terence, in order that along with elegance of style boys may imbibe holiness and uprightness of character." All these contained scenes of pranks and trickery occurring during the hero's earlier period of disobedience, pranks that the audience and especially the schoolboys could regard indulgently. If the schoolboys were restricted to these Christianized versions, one may assume they were not unacquainted with the less chaste originals, either read on the sly or after they had left school. On the professional stage, elements drawn both from Plautus and Terence and from the later Italian comedies were routinely incorporated into English drama, including Shakespeare's, such as the plots of Plautus's *Menaechmi* and *Amphitryon* borrowed for *The Comedy of Errors* and, from other plays, the exchange of lovers in *A Midsummer Night's Dream*, the bedroom substitution in *Measure for Measure*, and the characterization of the braggart soldier in Falstaff.[7] There can be little doubt, therefore, of Jacobean audiences' familiarity with the plot elements and comic contrivances imported from these Roman plays.

Jonson took a firm stand on the author's right to borrow from his predecessors, stating in an oft-quoted passage in his *Discoveries* that such ability formed a cornerstone of successful composition:

> The third requisite in our *Poet*, or Maker, is *Imitation*, to bee able to convert the substance, or Riches of an other *Poet*, to his owne use. To make choise of one excellent man above the rest, and so to follow him, till he grow very *Hee:* or so like him, as the Copie may be mistaken for the Principall. Not, as the Creature, that swallowes, what it takes in, crude, raw, or indigested; but that feedes with an Appetite, and hath a Stomacke to concoct, divide, and turne all into nourishment.[8]

It was a tendency that his detractors were quick to seize upon, Henry Parratt satirizing him caustically:

> Thou think'st thy skill hath done a wondrous feat,
> For which the world should give thee many thancks:
> Alas, it seemes thy feathers are but loose,
> Pluckt from a Swanne, and set upon a Goose.[9]

Yet Jonson continued to imitate his models, borrowing not only from Latin drama but also from plays of a later period too.

An admirer of Italian comedy in general, he held in special esteem one of the most influential of its playwrights, Niccolò Machiavelli, whose work is especially germane to our present concerns. The latter's *La Mandragola*, highly popular from its first performance in 1514, engendered a host of followers. It is to the tradition they established and its infiltration into England that the response of Jonson's audience to his own play needs to be related,[10] as audiences recognized and relished his variations on the models he was employing.

The basic plot element of *La Mandragola*, which was to serve many writers of comedy in subsequent generations, was the outwitting, by an ardent young lover, of a mean-spirited *senex*, a husband who keeps his wife under close guard and thereby blocks the fulfillment of the young man's desires. In Northrop Frye's terms, that theme of the triumph of youth over age archetypally represents the victory of springtime fertility over the barrenness of harsh winter, the male hero in such scenes being generally assisted by an *eiron* or resourceful adviser (in Machiavelli's play a friend, but more often in plays by Plautus and his followers an astute slave) by whose help the *senex* is eventually outmaneuvered and the lovers happily united.[11] In such plays, there can be no question where the audience's sympathies are intended to lie as they witness the success of the ruse, the hoodwinking of the older generation that enables the young man to consummate his love. Indeed, if comedy is a form of fertility rite, symbolizing hope for a rich harvest, the eventual union of the lovers must evoke a positive reaction, a sense of fulfillment and gratification.

A brief reminder of Machiavelli's plot may serve to highlight the parallels. When Callimaco falls passionately in love with the attractive wife of the elderly Nicia, his friend Ligurio concocts a wily stratagem. He offers Nicia a potion that is "guaranteed," when administered to his wife, to produce a male heir, but with the grave drawback that whoever first sleeps with Lucrezia after she has partaken of the potion will die. The gullible Nicia, eager for an heir, is happy to learn that there is, newly come to town, a young man whom no one would miss, and the play concludes, to the delight of the audience, with an account of the elderly husband ushering the young man not only into the bedroom but actually into the bed of the wife he has been so carefully shielding from just such an intrusion. Outside the theater, the audience may or may not approve of adultery; but within the ambience of the comedy, the success of Ligurio's trick and Lucrezia's eventual acceptance of her lover evoke full audience approval. Callimacho's account of his victory contains no hint of remorse, no sense of adultery as an immoral act, as he records how he revealed his love to Lucrezia, assuring her that, because of the simple-mindedness of her husband, they would now be able to enjoy continued happiness without danger of being discovered, to which he adds the promise that he will make her his wife as soon as the elderly Nicia passes on. As he himself puts it, when

> she had tasted the difference between my embrace and that of Messer Nicia and between the kisses of a young lover and those of an old husband—after sighing a little, she said: "Since your cunning, my husband's stupidity, my mother's foolishness, and the wickedness of my confessor have led me to do what I would never have done of myself, I'm ready to believe it was heaven's will that it should all happen in this way, and I don't have it in me to reject what heaven wants me to accept. Therefore, I receive you as lord, master, guide; I want you to be my father, my protector, my every good;

and what my husband has wanted for one night I want him to have always. . . . You'll come and go as you please, and we'll be able to meet at any time, without arousing the least suspicion."[12]

Callimacho concludes by declaring himself to be "the happiest and most contented man that ever was in the world." Machiavelli had, in fact, already indicated in the prologue where his own sympathies lay, as well as the empathy he expected from the audience:

> A lady of propriety
> Was passionately loved by this young swain,
> And tricked by him, as you shall see.
> I wish that you might someday be
> Tricked just as was she.

That situation recurs, with variations, throughout subsequent Italian drama, as in Cecchi's *The Owl (L'assiuolo)* first performed in 1550. A young man, Giulio, becomes enamoured of Oretta, the charming young wife of the lawyer Ambrogio who, as usual, keeps his wife under lock and key. Ambrogio, it transpires, is himself in pursuit of another woman who, unknown to him, is his wife's friend. Oretta, in league with this friend, arranges an assignation in which she will take her friend's place (the familiar bedroom substitution). But Giulio's astute servant, uncovering the plan, alters it to assist his master who, disguised as a chambermaid, locks up Ambrogio and himself joyfully keeps the assignation with Oretta. She, like her predecessor, Lucrezia, readily adapts to the situation and accepts Giulio as her lover. Similarly, Luigi Groto's *The Treasure (Il Thesuro)* of 1583 presents a young wife, Licinia, married to an elderly, long-winded lawyer. She requires no astute servant to assist her, as she herself devises a method of cuckolding her husband, sending him off on a treasure hunt to enable her to enjoy her romance.

How entrenched that situation was in the public imagination in Jonson's day may be seen in its infiltration into so unlikely a work as *The Faerie Queene*, where an old and miserly Malbecco, married to the beautiful young Hellenore, keeps her under close watch, denying all knights entry to his castle in the vain conviction that he will thereby avoid being cuckolded:

> Thereat Sir *Satyrane* gan smile, and say;
> Extremely mad the man I surely deeme,
> That weenes with watch and hard restraint to stay
> A womans will, which is disposd to go astray.
> In vaine he feares that, which he cannot shonne:
> For who wotes not, that womans subtiltyes
> Can guilen *Argus*, when she list misdonne?
> It is not yron bandes, nor hundred eyes,
> Nor brasen walls, nor many wakefull spyes,
> That can withhold her wilfull wandring feet.   (3.9.6–7)

The comic theme of the cuckolded *senex* persisted throughout later years, in comic opera as well as drama, as in Donizetti's *Don Pasquale* and Rossini's *Barber of Seville*, that continuation ensuring that it would be familiar to audiences of Jonson's play in later periods too, including those of our own era.

In the light of that established tradition, the events leading up to the rape scene in *Volpone* need to be read very differently from the accounts of critics. The overall pattern is indeed identical with that of the above plays—a lover, Volpone, smitten by the charms of a lady burdened with a barren, elderly husband, Corvino, needs to devise a stratagem to obtain access to her. The plan, provided here by Mosca, is as ingenious as Ligurio's, exploiting Corvino's hope of being inscribed as heir to convince him to use his wife, like the biblical Avishag, to warm the bed of a supposedly impotent Volpone (here with echoes of *Eunuchus*). As Mosca assures Corvino, "A long forgetfulness hath seized that part" (2.6.66). The audience, having watched the plans devised by Volpone and Mosca to outwit the legacy hunters, is now looking forward eagerly to the culmination of this new plot, when, it is hoped, the repulsive Corvino will willingly lead his attractive wife into Volpone's bedroom, just as Nicia did in Machiavelli's play. Jonson, lest the audience forget the Italian tradition upon which that plot element is based, has Corvino, after Celia's appearance at the window, berate her for having made him appear (he uses the Italian term) "the PANTALONE *di besogniosi*," namely, the figure of the senile, cuckolded husband of a young wife in the version popularized by the *Commedia dell'Arte*.

Seen from that viewpoint, the situation is broadly comic, and by echoing a traditional theme in drama, it corresponds to what Mikhail Bakhtin terms the "centripetal" impulse, until the "centrifugal" moment when Celia unexpectedly reverses the play's mood—a reversal to which we shall soon return.[13] Before that moment, everything seems to be moving in the established direction. Volpone, performing brilliantly in the guise of a mountebank and obviously directing his request primarily at Celia, begs the spectators for a handkerchief as "a pledge of your loves." Celia, situated at the window despite her husband's stern injunction never to show herself there and watching with interest the mountebank's performance, obligingly drops him her handkerchief, being, indeed, the only spectator to do so. At that point in the play, her action can only be interpreted as encouragement of his suit. For Jonson has been careful to phrase the invitation not as a request for customers but as a pledge of love. Subsequently, we may understand that she had not paid attention to the exact phrase and was merely interested in the medicinal oil; but for the audience, at the time when the phrase is uttered, the implications are obvious. Volpone is, accordingly, rapturous, responding with all the passion, vigor, and lavish imagery of a Renaissance lover:

> angry Cupid, boulting from her eyes,
> Hath shot himselfe into me, like a flame;
> Where, now, he flings about his burning heat,
> As in a fornace.   (2.4.5–8)[14]

It is here that we are repeatedly informed by critics of the lasciviousness of Volpone's passion, Daniel Kay defining it as "lust" and Helena Baum as part of his "glittering evil."[15] One wonders, however, if they would apply the same terms to Callimicho's love for Lucrezia.

In the context of that Italian tradition, the alleged inconsistency between the charm of Volpone's serenade to Celia immediately before the rape and the revulsion we are supposed to feel toward the singer emerges as baseless.

> Come, my Celia, let us prove,
> While we can, the sports of love,
> Time will not be ours for ever,
> He, at length, our good will sever;
> Spend not then his gifts in vain;
> Suns, that set, may rise again;
> But if once we lose this light,
> 'Tis with us perpetual night. (3.7.165–72)

F. S. Boas complains that this song was too exquisite to suit the "lecherous" Volpone, and Lester Beaurline found difficulty in reconciling the gorgeous language of the rape scene with the audience's "moral disgust."[16] But until the moment of the reversal, there should be no disgust at all, except that directed at the despicable Corvino, viciously berating his wife as a whore for exposing herself at the window, and threatening in the foulest language to affix a chastity belt on her, all this quite apart from his readiness, even on the misguided assumption that Volpone is impotent, to force her against her will into another man's bed.

It should be noted that Celia's resistance to Corvino's demand in no way contradicts traditional expectations. The wives in the Italian versions had also resisted initially. Lucrezia rejects Nicia's proposal that she sleep with the young man, only yielding to Callimacho's entreaties after she has learned from him the nature of the plot. But Celia's reluctance in this scene is even more understandable, as the proposed *amorato* is, to the best of her knowledge at that time, a repulsively emaciated creature. What is more, she believes that her husband's project is an unsavory and totally unwarranted test of her marital fidelity:

CELIA. Sir, let me beseech you,
Affect not these strange trials; if you doubt
My chastitie, why locke me vp, for euer:
Make me the heyre of darkenesse. (3.7.23–27)

Audiences familiar with the patterns of Italian comedy could thus expect that in this play Celia will soon, like her predecessors, happily submit to "destiny" when Volpone reveals his identity and would join him in the joyful consummation consequent upon it. As Volpone leaps from the bed thrusting aside his repellent disguise and revealing himself as a virile, eager lover, not only does he woo her with one of the loveliest of serenades, echoing Catullus's tribute to his beloved Lesbia, but proceeds to offer her a wealth of superlative delights in language such as had won for Marlowe's Tamburlaine the love of the beautiful Zenocrates. Where Tamburlaine promises:

A hundred Tartars shall attend on thee,
Mounted on steeds swifter than Pegasus;
Thy garments shall be made of Median silk,
Enchased with precious jewels of mine own,
More rich and valurous than Zenocrate's.
With milk-white harts upon an ivory sled,
Thou shalt be drawn amidst the frozen pools,
And scale the icy mountains' lofty tops,[17]

so Volpone conjures up rich visions of love:

heare me, Celia.
Thy bathes shall be the iuyce of iuly-flowres,
Spirit of roses, and of violets,
The milke of vnicornes, and panthers breath
Gather'd in bagges, and mixt with *cretan* wines.
Our drinke shall be prepared gold, and amber. (3.7.211–16)

All, therefore, points toward the auspicious fulfillment of his love, his song assuming her readiness to respond. When she demurs, he understandably attributes her response to shyness, gently assuring her, just as Callimacho had assured Lucrezia,

VOLPONE: Why droops my Celia?
Thou hast, in place of a base husband, found
A worthy lover: use thy fortune well,
With secrecy and pleasure.

It is only when her resistance turns to outrage and horror, a demand for poison or disfiguring leprosy rather than dishonor, that the romantic ambience suddenly evaporates.

The time-honored comic theme of the cuckolded husband not only supplies the main theme but also is entertainingly reflected in the subplot, although this has never been noted. In a manner anticipating Fielding's parody of Richardson, when, amusingly reversing roles, he replaces Mr. B's pursuit of a chaste young housemaid with a harridan's attempted seduction of a virtuous Joseph, we have here Lady Politique-Would-Bee grotesquely trying to flirt with Volpone. His faithful Mosca rescues him from her unwelcome advances with the resourceful fabrication that her husband has been seen on a gondola in the company of a courtesan. In a comment intended only for Volpone's ears, Mosca adds that he knew the ruse would succeed as those who use themselves with most license are always the most jealous—a remark recalling such jealous husbands as Ambrogio, keeping his wife under lock and key while himself pursuing other women. Paralleling Corvino's suspicion of his wife's infidelity, Lady Would-Bee rushes off, so convinced of her husband's betrayal as absurdly to assume that his male companion, Peregrine, is a courtesan in disguise. The traditional scene of unwarranted outrage, such as Corvino's castigation of Celia for innocently appearing at the window, is thus reproduced with reversed gender-roles, Lady Would-Bee scolding her perplexed husband for his "concupiscence" in patronizing a lewd harlot, a base fricatrice, a female devil in a male outside, and swearing that she will persecute and discipline that wretched whore. Brilliantly, the two themes of main plot and subplot are made to converge, as the supposed "lewd harlot" she wishes to persecute turns out to be Celia herself, soon to be accused in court of whoredom both by her jealous husband Corvino and by the jealous wife, Lady Would-Bee.

If we may postpone once more discussion of the dramatic tergiversation at the time of the attempted rape, I should like to move back, to view the initial scenes of the play, once again as they would have impressed Jonson's audience, since those scenes have formed the basis for most critical attacks on the ethical depravity of its leading character. Volpone's opening speech, while generally admitted to be poetically splendid, has been repeatedly censured for its disclosure of his inordinate greed, and for its blasphemous application of religious imagery to the materialistic acquisition of gold.

> Good morning to the day; and, next, my gold:
> Open the shrine, that I may see my *saint*.
> Hail the world's soul, and mine! more glad than is
> The teeming earth to see the long'd-for sun
> Peep through the horns of the celestial Ram,
> Am I, to view thy splendour darkening his;
> That lying here, amongst my other hoards,
> Shew'st like a flame by night, or like the day
> Struck out of chaos, when all darkness fled
> Unto the centre. O thou son of Sol,
> But brighter than thy father, let me kiss,
> With adoration, thee, and euery relique
> Of sacred treasure in this blessed roome. (1–13)

Douglas Duncan, while admitting that the speech is theatrically compelling, condemns it as "morally outrageous"; S. L. Goldberg, like so many others, sees it as evidencing Volpone's corruption, a speech unmistakably "blasphemous"; and Robert E. Knoll views it as revealing Volpone's "corrupted soul."[18] Yet a great deal depends on the way the actor performs it. It can surely be read as a charmingly boisterous self-parody, an amusing paean of joy at the success of his schemes and the wealth with which they supply him. Moreover, does it really indicate greed? As Jonson takes care to inform us a moment later, it is not the wealth itself that gives him pleasure so much as the sport involved in obtaining it, the ingenuity required for tricking his evil victims: "Yet I glory / More in the cunning purchase of my wealth, / Than in the glad possession." Critics, of course, pounce upon the word "cunning," forgetting that its meaning then was no more than "ingenious" or "skillful," as in Viola's reference in *Twelfth Night* to "beauty truly blent, whose red and white / Nature's own sweet and cunning hand laid on."[19] He glories therefore less in his gains than in the adroitness of his stratagems, the kind of tricks that make Plautus's plays so successful.

There is the inevitable charge that Volpone's idolization of wealth was in itself immoral, a condemnable greed—a charge somewhat perverse when in our own day the hope of attaining unearned wealth through stocks and shares forms a universal focus of attention. Jonson is here condemning Volpone for cupidity. Yet within society at this time there had arisen a new and powerful validation of acquisitiveness that had emerged not as a vice but as a commendable and very natural desire. Bassanio in *The Merchant of Venice*, as was noted in chapter 1, proudly compares himself in his quest for riches to Jason heroically pursuing the golden fleece, and Antonio happily invests there in wealthy argosies. Richard Ehrenberg informs us that the general atmosphere of the time was permeated with such a desire for wealth that the ambition to share in the successful financial dealings centered on Antwerp and Lyons had, from the late sixteenth century onward, affected an ever-widening circle. Even the most violent increase of demand failed to exhaust the supply, whole classes of the European people being eager to obtain possession of those magic parchments known on the world's exchanges as king's bonds, court bonds, or bonds of the receivers general.[20] In England, Sir Thomas Gresham's founding of the Royal Exchange in 1568 gave new impetus to this desire for monetary gain. In Volpone's speech, the pursuit of wealth is, of course, exaggerated, presented as an intoxication with the joy of riches; but even in that form it is redeemed by a Renaissance sense of the opportunities opening up before the people as it emerged from the more ascetic milieu of the Middle Ages, a longing for power and wealth such as had motivated Faustus, a craving valid in its own right on the condition, as in Volpone's case, that it did not involve the selling of one's soul. Thus we have the speech promising Celia, in terms echoing Tamburlaine's, the luxuries with which he generously proposes to endow his love.

Moreover, Jonson takes special care to place in his protagonist's mouth a justification of the methods he adopts for obtaining wealth. Those methods involve, he assures us, no harm to the innocent. He employs no mills to grind men to powder, he spurns usury, and risks no men's lives at sea in order to fill his own coffers. To that exoneration Mosca adds that his master lays no snares to catch prodigal heirs, and abominates evoking the tears and cries to heaven of widow or orphan, the latter encomium bestowing a hint of scriptural approval for his actions. Of course, Mosca is interested in being in his master's good graces, but the initial statements concerning the legitimacy of Volpone's actions are his own, and he fully approves of Mosca's addenda. For his purpose is to entrap only the crafty, to fleece the evil schemers of society, the debauched and the corrupt, a pursuit (as Herford has pointed out) authorized by classical precedent, the duping of *captatores*, those legacy hunters forming a central theme in Lucian's witty *Dialogues of the Dead* and Petronius's *Supper of Trimalchio*. Unlike Robin Hood, who in the process of aiding the poor did commit the crime of robbing the wealthy, Volpone robs no one; rather, by a little deception, he inveigles his victims into voluntarily showering him with gifts. In *The Alchemist*, Jonson was to satirize exploiters of the innocent and gullible by portraying a Face and Subtle who defraud a naïve, innocent grocer of his money; but here the objects of Volpone's scheming are, as their names imply, characters fully deserving of such treatment. They are the carrion crows and vultures of society, despicable not only in their legacy-hunting but, as Jonson makes clear, potential murderers, ready to hasten Volpone's death by poison or suffocation. Alvin Kernan, quite unjustifiably, remarks that in the opening scene, "Master and servant are confederated to cheat the world, and one another if possible." But they are certainly not cheating the world, only those warranting such treatment; and so far from cheating each other, there is in those early scenes a camaraderie and mutual loyalty between Volpone and Mosca that is only breached in the latter half of the play.[21]

L. C. Knights first identified the contemporary response to the rise of capitalism as a central theme in English Renaissance drama. Jonson's response to the social volatility produced by the transition from feudalism to capitalism lies at the core of his work, as he documents, often satirically, the frenzied pursuit of wealth among his peers, from the ingenious cony-catchers of the underworld to the avaricious merchants of the emerging middle class.[22] Yet in *Volpone* Jonson's attitude is different. He takes pains to justify Volpone's accumulation of wealth not only in the passages cited above but also in the excellent use he makes of his money. He is, as Mosca points out, no miser filling his vaults with expensive wines while he himself drinks vinegar, but a generous patron of the arts. That claim Volpone at once confirms by calling forth the entertainers whom he maintains as part of his permanent household.

The interlude the entertainers provide has, like so many other aspects of the play, drawn strong adverse criticism; it has been generally regarded as a distasteful exploitation of the physically handicapped. Herford, for example, condemned in no uncertain terms the "contortions of a dwarf, a eunuch, a hermaphrodite, whose splayed or stunted ditties are made with horrible ingenuity to reflect their several deformities." That response certainly holds true for a modern audience, sensitized as we have become to the misfortunes of the disabled; but it is a reading, as Herford should have known, inappropriate for Jonson's day. Velasquez's 1656 portrait of *The Royal Maids of Honour* (*Las Meninas*), with a richly appareled female dwarf as a member of the princess's personal entourage, as well as the admired status of *castrati* in Italian music circles indicates that such persons were frequently introduced into public events or entertainments without being regarded as "horrible" monstrosities. Their employment, in contrast to our own day, provided them with a respectable livelihood. But whatever the general attitude of Jonson's contemporaries, both for them and for a modern audience, the play's text counters possible discomfort by clearly indicating both Volpone's and Jonson's personal respect for them. For the interlude culminates in a song expressing their pride at being professional performers, claiming that they are members of society deserving, like the amusing court jester, to be called blessed. They will celebrate that learned opinion "with all our wit, and art / To dignifie that, whereof our selues are so great, and speciall a part" (1.2.62–63). As Nano reminds us in a later scene, a dwarf is "little, and wittie, / And euery thing as is little, is prittie" (3.3.9–10).

Like Hamlet's generous welcome of the itinerant players, Volpone's delight in the interlude and his patronage of the arts would have endeared him to a theater-loving audience. Moreover, he is himself a consummate actor, not only in his impersonation of a dying man. His performance as mountebank is a theatrical tour de force, a hilarious parodying of the contemporary fashion of euphuistic word coinage and the richly inventive vocabularies of the pamphleteers, combined with a burlesque of the flamboyant charlatanry of the mountebanks themselves: "These turdy-facy-nasty-paty-lousy-farticall rogues, with one poore groats-worth of un-prepar'd antimony, finely wrapt up in seuerall scartoccios, are able, very well, to kill their twentie a weeke, and play; yet these meagre staru'd spirits, who have halfe stopt the organs of their mindes with earthy oppilations, want not their fauourers among your shriuel'd, sallad-eating artizans" (2.2.59–65).

There arises, however, a further question concerning Volpone's opening speech. Would the references to saints have appeared as blasphemous to a Jacobean audience as it has to modern critics? Volpone is comparing his adoration of gold not to genuine Christian worship but to the superstitious veneration of saints' relics that was, in the England of Jonson's day, so often regarded as a perversion of Christianity, a practice treated with disdain and even ridicule by his contemporaries. John Bale, in his *Kyng John,* had depicted a personified *Sedition* as ludicrously offering for sale a series of relics, including a louse of Saint Francis, a scab of Saint Job, a maggot of Moses, and, he adds, a fart of Saint Fandigo. Similarly, Donne mused scornfully on the fate likely to befall a lover's bones, with their bracelet of bright hair about the wrist, if the grave were opened at a time when "misdevotion" does command:

> Then, he that digges us up, will bring
> Us, to the Bishop, and the King,
>   To make us Reliques; then
> Thou shalt be'a Mary Magdalen, and I
>   A something else thereby.[23]

Volpone's imaging of gold as a saint's relic and of the chest containing it as its shrine would have seemed to his audiences not profanity but an amusing burlesque of an outmoded and distasteful practice.

Jonas Barish establishes the view that all the chief characters, including Volpone, have, from the beginning of the play, descended to the level of beasts, their actions brutishly travestying humanity.[24] As their names suggest, they belong, he maintains, to the genus "monster"—half-man, half-animal—that order of fabulous creatures whose common denominator is their unnaturalness, their lack of humanity. Barish, however, fails to note, as D. A. Scheve had already demonstrated when Barish wrote his article, that Volpone would, to his audience, have been set apart from his victims in that regard.[25] Voltore, Corvino, and Corbaccio are indeed predatory vultures, crows, and ravens; but in the legend to which these names directly refer, a legend widely known at the time and recounted in Conrad Gesner's *Historia Animalium* of 1557 of which Jonson owned a copy, the fox was in fact the hero of the story (heroine in the original), the clever animal who "out-foxes" the potential predators:

> When she sees the flocks of birds flying about, she lies prone on the ground and at the same time shuts her eyes, and places her snout on the ground, and holds her breath, and at once assumes the appearance and likeness of one sleeping or dead. But when the birds see her thus stretched out upon the ground, thinking her dead, they glide down in flocks, and sitting on her, they mock her. . . . When ravens, crows, and other birds that are particularly ravenous see her lying thus, rejoicing as it were over a dead enemy, they fly near and are seized.

It was a legend that appeared repeatedly in bestiaries and other collections, as well as in medieval illuminations, stained glass, and misericords, becoming especially popular in England after Caxton's translation of *The History of Reynard the Fox* in 1481. Here, too, Jonson is careful to remind the audience of the reference. When Volpone is informed that Voltore has brought him a plate engraved with his supposed benefactor's name and coat of arms, he asks jokingly, "not a foxe / Mocking a gaping crow?" Indeed, if there is little room for sympathy toward Volpone's odious predators, by reverse reasoning there can be little cause to condemn him for fleecing them.

And what of Mosca who, like Volpone, is scheduled later to betray his master? Again, we should be wary of confusing his subsequent portrayal with his earlier one. In those opening scenes he is as resourceful, wily, and amusing a servant as any Plautine slave, beloved by his master who thoroughly enjoys the clever ruses conjured up for his delectation and profit, and who is duly grateful to his servant when the latter rescues him from the flirtatious assaults of Lady Would-Bee. Mosca may be flattering his master at times, but that forms part of his wiliness, paralleling the repeated instances in Shakespeare's plays of court jesters wittily extorting handouts. Repeatedly, he performs acts that would win the audience's amused approval, such as in the entertaining scene when, having convinced Corvino of Volpone's total deafness, he encourages the visitor to shout into his master's ears the most crude and gross insults, thereby tricking Corvino into revealing his true feelings toward a supposedly beloved benefactor. Mosca manages similarly, and with remarkable skill, slyly to insult the profession and hence the character of one of the most obnoxious of the predators, the lawyer Voltore, without exposing himself to reproof:

> I, oft, haue heard him say, how he admir'd
> Men of your large profession, that could speake
> To euery cause, and things mere contraries,
> Till they were hoarse againe, yet all be law;
> That, with most quick agilitie, could turne,
> And re-turne; make knots, and vndoe them;
> Giue forked counsell; take prouoking gold
> On either hand.   (1.3.52–59)

Could the audience hear this with anything but amusement? In the play's list of characters he is termed a parasite, but Jonson is careful to have Volpone dismiss the pejorative aspects of the appellation in the opening scene, claiming "they are envious that term thee parasite," while later Mosca himself distinguishes between the fawning type of parasite he abhors and the fine, elegant rascal, a Jonsonian form of Puck, who can

> rise,
> And stoope (almost together) like an arrow;
> Shoot through the aire, as nimbly as a starre;
> Turne short, as doth a swallow; and be here,
> And there, and here, and yonder, all at once;
> Present to any humour, all occasion;
> And change a visor, swifter, then a thought.   (3.1.23–29)

Indeed, it is Mosca's ingenuity that motivates much of the plot, as when he turns to his own advantage Bonario's potentially catastrophic exposure of his scheme. The only act he commits that can be termed villainous in the context of Plautine comedy is his unexpected betrayal of his master, an idea that occurs to him only in act 5, when Volpone has ceased to be the attractive figure he was at the opening, when his master, now caught up in deceit and denial, fully deserves to be betrayed in his turn.

I have referred a number of times to the moment of the attempted rape as marking the division between the two sections. Stephen Greenblatt claims that the turning point in the play occurs not at that moment but much later, at the end of act 4, when Celia and Bonario are being led off for sentencing and Volpone seems to have achieved complete success. That scene constitutes, he suggests, a "false ending" at which point spectators are constrained to ask themselves what kind of world would eventuate if such characters were left unpunished.[26] But the break had occurred much earlier, at the time I have suggested, in so marked a fashion that their subsequent behavior becomes devoid of any justification. Volpone, on his exposure by the concealed Bonario, is immediately transformed from confident, witty, and amusing manipulator to terrified victim, the erstwhile *magnifico* reduced to cringing impotence before the threat of the branding iron:

> Fall on me, roofe, and bury me in ruine,
> Become my graue, that wert my shelter. O!
> I am vn-masqu'd, vn-spirited, vn-done,
> Betray'd to beggery, to infamy.   (3.6.276–79)

Mosca experiences a similar reversal, the erstwhile entertaining and ever-resourceful servant crying in terror, "Where shall I run, most wretched shame of men, / To beat out my unlucky brains?" They may continue to invent new stratagems and attempt to escape their punishment, but they are now in a vastly different setting, no longer justified by the hypocrisy and greed of their odious victims. Nothing can possibly extenuate Volpone's readiness to condemn as a lewd adulteress the Celia he had just serenaded so passionately, nor the plan to dispatch her and Bonario to their deaths. If Volpone resorts once again to playing the dying man, the purpose of the disguise has changed radically. No longer a means of tricking his evil predators, it is now adopted in full concord with the villains. He has, in effect, changed sides, the pretense no longer a source of delight but distasteful even to himself:

> I ne're was in dislike with my disguise
> Till this fled moment; here, 'twas good, in private,
> But, in your publike, *Caue,* whil'st I breathe.
> 'Fore God, my left legge 'gan to haue the cramp,
> And I apprehended, straight, some power had strooke me
> With a dead palsy.   (5.1.2–7)

From that point, therefore, and not from the point Greenblatt suggests, he is stripped of the role of self-assured outwitter. The play's climacteric had occurred at the moment of his unmasking by Bonario, and is so complete that no restoration to his previous status remains possible, his journey thenceforth being ineluctably downhill.

All these aspects, then, suggest that the play would, until the moment of the rape scene, have been greeted in its day not with the "moral disgust" permeating twentieth century criticism but with humor and delight. From the dedication included in the 1607 quarto we know how warmly the play was received at both Oxford and Cambridge. And that warm response to the stage performances seems to have carried through to our own time, the play's popularity during the twentieth century evidencing that modern actors, producers, and audiences have in their evaluation been closer to their Jacobean counterparts than to twentieth century critics. The depiction of Volpone in the most famous of these productions was by no means that of a vicious or corrupt individual. Donald Wolfit's version of 1935, frequently revived by him in later years, portrayed Volpone as a young man of tremendous gusto and joie de vivre. In Tyrone Guthrie's 1964 Minneapolis production, Douglas Campbell was so amusing in the scene of seduction that the audience actually applauded the attempted rape. As J. C. Trewin records, Campbell "dances, struts like a turkey-cock, throws open his treasure chests to woo the lady, seeks to crown her, twiddles a bare foot in delighted anticipation, serenades Celia with operatic gestures, coos, roars, and when all persuasion fails, seizes her and dumps her unceremoniously on the bed."[27] At the Great Lakes Shakespeare Festival in 1970, John Milligan, to the delight of the audience, played Volpone's attempted rape in the style of Groucho Marx. And Peter Hall's 1977 rendering at the National Theatre, with Paul Scofield in the lead, was far from a depiction of corruption and evil. The characters were clothed in gorgeous Renaissance costumes, with Volpone depicted as a distinguished aristocrat with a gift for poetry. In the seduction scene, Scofield, certainly no despicable villain, was described by a reviewer as "shifting with virtuoso skill from one extreme to another of his enormous vocal range and singing *Come, my Celia* unaccompanied, in a strong, sweet baritone—something no previous Volpone seems to have been capable of doing."[28]

How, then, are we to explain the discrepancy between this essentially attractive Volpone and the reprobate he suddenly becomes at the moment when Bonario, hearing Celia's plea for help, leaps from his hiding place with the melodramatic cry, "Forbeare, foule rauisher, libidinous swine"? The answer lies, I suspect, in a paradoxical element in Jonson himself, though not the paradox that his biographer David Riggs suggests. Riggs sees in Volpone a projection of the dramatist himself. He points out that Jonson also used his wit to inflict pain on others as Volpone does to the legacy hunters, even when the cost of doing so was unacceptably high, and he too was an insatiable womanizer. Riggs argues that Jonson was therefore able to identify with his villain-hero because his own instinctual drives had taken him down the very path that leads Volpone to ruin; his fictional character offers "a vicarious experience of vice that teaches his audience the power of discrimination," instructing them, in effect, in how not to live.[29] But that view, reiterated throughout Riggs's biography, assumes that

Volpone's infliction of pain on the predators was intended to be seen by the audience as a vice, the interpretation I have here attempted to discount. Moreover, if Riggs believes that Jonson was offering in the play a condemnation of womanizing, that interpretation means that Volpone's pursuit of Celia is from the first, like Jonson's pursuit of other men's wives, to be regarded as a moral failing, a reading that entirely ignores the tradition of Italian comedy and the light-hearted outwitting of senile husbands.

The reason for the sudden change in direction derives, I would propose, from a different conflict, between two elements prominent in Jonson's character, producing respectively the main text and subtext of the play. In the first half, Jonson's instinctive sense of comedy, emanating from his love of the classics and of Italian drama, allows him to present with delight Volpone's amusing resourcefulness patterned on the plays he so admired. But there was a contrary impulse at work. Although Jonson did not devote his major writings to religious themes, he was, as George Parfitt has shown, genuinely devoted to Christianity.[30] His conversion to Catholicism had taken place at a time when that act endangered him personally, at the time of the Gunpowder Plot; and his return to the Anglican church occurred after protracted theological meditation, as he recorded in "An Execration upon Vulcan": "twice twelve years stored up humanity / With humble gleanings in divinity; / After the Fathers, and those wiser guides."[31] That religious penchant led him to write often and in considerable detail on his conception of the ethical principles that should direct literature at large and comedy in particular. In his *Timber, or Discoveries* he condemns slapstick and vulgar humor as appealing only to the "beast, the multitude," suggesting that instead the writer should aim to instruct and inform. And he declared there of the Poet: "wee doe not require in him meere *Elocution;* or an excellent faculty in verse; but the exact knowledge of all vertues, and their contraries; with ability to render the one lov'd, the other hated."[32]

However, in the preface to this very comedy, Jonson gives fullest expression to his insistence on a moral purpose, demanding both from himself and from his peers not only that literature should, in the words of Horace, profit as well as delight *(aut prodesse volunt aut delectare poetae)*, but that its teachings should be ethically impeccable. With echoes of Sidney's attempt in the *Defence* to counter Plato's exclusion of poetry from the ideal republic by claiming that it was possessed of a high and noble purpose, Jonson here goes a step further, declaring that not only the work produced but also the author must be morally worthy. No one, he argues, can be a good poet without first being a good man; and the literary work itself must have the loftiest of aims, "to informe yong-men to all good disciplines, inflame growne-men to all great vertues, keepe old-men in their best and supreme state, or as they decline to childhood, recouer them to their first strength." In brief, the dramatist is, as he puts it, to be "a teacher of things diuine." His peers or, as he contemptuously terms them, the "poetasters," had debased their profession, offering "nothing but ribaldry, profanation, blasphemy, all licence of offence to god, and man," while he in contrast, as he assures the reader, had striven in *Volpone* to fulfill the principal end of poesy, namely, "to inform men how to live best."

Jonson's declared aim to be a corrector of morals could in no way accord with the condoning of adultery, with the seduction of other men's wives that had formed so central an ingredient of the theme initiated by the Roman dramatists and revived by Machiavelli. The method he adopted to ensure the morality of the play's message was to temper the secular comedy by providing a heavily didactic ending. The first half of this play, therefore, offers, in the tradition of the Italian theater, a lively, rambunctious comedy skating close to the periphery of misdemeanor, while the "profanation" and "blasphemy" (as he termed it above) of granting success to reprobates he avoided by a sober conclusion, recognizing the need to provide there an especially harsh series of punishment in order to counterbalance the sympathy aroused by his leading character in the earlier part of the play when in amorous pursuit of Celia.

Of special note in this regard is a further comment in the preface, where Jonson explains that, although the "catastrophe" of his play, the stern sentences passed on the characters at the end, may, "in the strict rigour of comick law, meet with censure," critics should be charitable enough to recognize that the frustration of normal expectations was deliberate, "my speciall ayme being to put the snaffle in their mouths, that crie out, we neuer punish vice in our enterludes." He frankly admits, therefore, the existence of a discrepancy between the humorous intent in the first half of the play—which accords, in his words, with the principles of "comick law"—and the more solemn conclusion demanded by commitment to the moral doctrine of virtue triumphant. His acknowledgment that the first half follows the principles of comic law clearly militates against the critics' labeling of Volpone as a villain from the opening scene. And Jonson's admission of the existence of a dichotomy between the first and second halves of the play confirms that this play has both a centripetal impulse in line with traditional comedy as well as a centrifugal impulse, the imposing of Christian morality upon that tradition.

The terminology employed in the rape scene highlights the transition from a secular to a religious setting. Feminist criticism has justly pointed to the Elizabethan and Jacobean view of rape as being essentially male-oriented, an offense less against the woman than against the husband who "owns" her, Deborah Burks noting that the rape statutes were designed "to redress a wrong committed against a woman's male relatives."[33] But the focus here is upon Celia herself, the deeply offended victim. The moment she resists and Volpone utters his savage cry: "Yeeld, or Ile force thee," the love scene is metamorphosed into one of lechery, a representation of male physical power about to triumph over the physical weakness of the victimized female, an act utterly reprehensible, instantaneously robbing the play from that point onward of its comic force.[34] The changeover to a Christian setting is marked as Celia now sees herself in the tradition of the female martyrs who had preferred death to sexual submission, as described in the thirteenth century homily, *Hali Maidenhead:* "Think of St. Katherine, St. Margaret, St. Agnes, St. Juliana, St. Lucy, St. Cecilia, and of the other holy maidens in heaven; how they not only refused kings sons and earls with all worldly wealth and earthly joys, but endured strong pain rather than accept them."[35] From this moment she becomes the prototype for countless heroines of nineteenth century melodrama, symbols of purity and piety calling upon heaven (as her name indicates) to help her defend her innocence and her chastity. She conjures up images of the torture and suffering she is prepared to undergo rather than submit:

> If you have touch of holy saints—or heaven—
> Do me the grace to let me 'scape—if not,
> Be bountiful and kill me . . . flay my face,
> Or poison it with ointments, for seducing
> Your blood to this rebellion.   (3.7.242–53)

Her reply suddenly thrusts into the previously lighthearted atmosphere of the play a reminder of the morally directed world that the lively Plautine and Machiavellian comedy had, until now, so casually excluded. As the impulse of Christian morality drives out the evocations of traditional Italian comedy, both Celia and Bonario repeatedly assure us of their trust in celestial mercy, calling upon "God, and his good angels" to support them, and devoutly expressing their confidence, in the face of all contrary indications, that "heaven never fails the innocent."

But Jonson had a further reason for the abrupt tergiversation, an impulse arising from a more personal cause. If he had long made it clear to his readers that he wished to be recognized as the restorer of morality to the contemporary stage at this juncture of his life, he felt prompted to take upon himself the role of moral castigator with augmented seriousness—the added factor being the enthralling possibility of obtaining formal academic recognition. The lengthy epistle prefacing *Volpone* confirms not only that such was his purpose but also that the contrast between the main part of the play and its graver conclusion derived in large part from this aspiration, that he was altering the play to fit the requirements of that role. As all Jonson's biographers note, he carried with him throughout his life a deep sense of frustration at having been denied a university education. His family had lacked the financial resources to send him to a grammar school and, for some strange reason, brilliant as he was, he failed to win a scholarship to Westminster school. He had, indeed, the good fortune to be supported there financially by a family friend, but the school restricted candidacy for further grants to its scholarship holders, enabling only them to continue their studies at Oxford or Cambridge. That restriction prevented Jonson from advancing to the next stage, and the avenue to a university education was thus closed to him. With no further source of assistance forthcoming, his dream of a formal academic training vanished. Embittered by the deprivation, he was determined by a process of self-education to outclass his university-trained peers in scholarly studies, eventually becoming acknowledged in his day as one of the most learned men of his time. He yearned nonetheless for some official acknowledgment of his scholarship, experiencing a deep-seated desire for academic recognition which, apart from the honor it would bring, in those days carried with it a significant rise in social status, providing the possessor of a university degree with the rank of gentleman.

It was precisely at this time that there arose in his mind the possibility of his being awarded an honorary university degree—an admirable compensation for that sense of loss. *Volpone* had been performed with great success at both Oxford and Cambridge, probably in July 1606 when the King's Men were forced out of London by an outbreak of the plague. As F. S. Boas notes, it was rare for either university to host a performance by a professional company, and the warmth with which the play was received would have strengthened his hope of success.[36] Hence Jonson prefixed a fulsome dedication to the 1607 quarto of this play at a time when dedications of quarto texts were extremely rare.[37] Jonson's dedication is very serious and stresses the equal fame of the universities in a manner that leaves open the possibility for either, or for both, to respond as he had hoped:

> TO THE MOST NOBLE AND MOST EQUAL SISTERS,
> The Two Famous Universities,
> FOR THEIR LOVE AND ACCEPTANCE SHEWN TO HIS POEM IN THE
> PRESENTATION,
> Ben Jonson
> THE GRATEFUL ACKNOWLEDGER,
> Dedicates Both it and Himself

Jonson had written the play very quickly—within five weeks, as the prologue informs us—obviously enjoying to the full the vitality, energy, and wit of both Volpone and Mosca in the context of the Italian tradition he so admired. But he would have recognized that neither university would bestow an honorary degree on a writer condoning or promoting immorality. Those universities were, until the late nineteenth century, acknowledgedly religious establishments, and during Jonson's time were centers of religious controversy, the problem of the legitimacy of the theater being a matter of central concern. In Oxford during the 1590s, there had erupted a conflict that was to arouse interest throughout the country. The learned theologian John Rainoldes had attacked William Gager of Christ's College for arranging the performance of a Latin play, Rainoldes's main complaint being that the wearing of women's clothing by male students offended the prohibition in Deuteronomy, chapter 22. Gager replied that the biblical ruling was intended to prevent cross-dressing for purposes of gender deception only, and hence that the temporary donning of female garments for a stage performance was permissible. The dispute produced sufficient eddies in the public domain to prompt Rainoldes in 1599 to publish an account of the controversy, understandably from his own viewpoint, in *Th' Overthrow of Stage-Playes, By the way of controversie betwixt D. Gager and D. Rainoldes.* The problem continued to be debated, with Nashe defending the practice on the grounds that such cross-dressing was preferable to allowing women to play the parts, as was the practice on the Continent: "Our players are not as the players beyond the sea, a sort of squirting baudie Comedians, that have whores and common Curtizans to play womens parts and forbeare no immodest speech or unchast action." And, we may note, it was Jonson himself who persuaded Selden to join the fray in defense of the theater.[38]

The universities were thus very much involved in the religious aspects of theatrical performances, a controversy that was closely connected with the Puritan attacks on the stage. In general, Cambridge, while not capitulating to the control of the Puritan preachers in its midst, had, especially since the arrival of William Perkins at Emmanuel College, become a focal point for the dissemination of Puritan doctrine—that aspect perhaps explaining why Jonson's hope of academic recognition from that university was never to be fulfilled. But Oxford, despite the Rainoldes dispute, was less exposed to such influences. For example, in 1603 Robert Cecil set up a commission to investigate and limit Puritan activities at Cambridge, while he established no parallel commission at Oxford, probably because of his reliance on its chancellor, Lord Buckhurst, who had the reputation of being a staunch conformist, opposed to sectarian dissent.[39] With both universities involved in the religious disputes of the time, there would be no doubt in Jonson's mind that the extent to which his play conformed to the precepts of Christian morality would be a prerequisite for university approval. His strategy of placating the dons by a morally instructive conclusion and thereby forestalling potential censure by its conformity to ethical principles was, of course, crowned with success when in 1619 Oxford University awarded him that long-coveted degree, an honorary master of arts.

The conclusion of the play, when Volpone's fortunes are reversed, has evoked numerous condemnations for the severity of the punishments meted out, a harshness out of all proportion to the crimes. The punishment is indeed harsh, Mosca being condemned to a whipping and to spending the rest of his life as a galley-slave, while Volpone, after the confiscation of his property and its transfer to the hospital for Incurables—"since the most was gotten by imposture, / By feigning lame, gout, palsy, and such diseases"— must lie in prison, cramp'd with irons until he too becomes sick and lame. Edward Partridge remarks with considerable justice that the tone of this ending "seems closer to tragedy than comedy," while Northrop Frye deduces from the closure that the play is hybrid in genre, "a kind of comic imitation of a tragedy."[40] It is, however, in full accord with Jonson's remark in the preface that he expected such censure from the critics but was determined to proceed, "my speciall ayme being to put the snaffle in their mouths, that crie out, we neuer punish vice in our enterludes."

Disappointment has also been expressed that the conclusion of the play offers no romantic union of Celia with Bonario, such as one might have expected in the usual fertility closure of comedy. But the reason emerges once its indebtedness to the Machiavelli tradition is recognized. In order to evoke the secular pattern derived from Italian comedy, it was essential for Celia to be married to an unsavory *senex* keeping her under lock and key. But the ending characteristic of those plays—the wife's happy acceptance of her lover—had been nullified the moment Jonson decided to impose a moral conclusion. As the wife of Corvino, the pious Celia could not be permitted to reveal any hint of fondness for another man, and the only possibility, divorce from her husband, was, prior to Milton's famed defense of it, forbidden even to Protestants.[41] Jonson chooses for her, therefore, an ending tailored to fit those limits, that she return to her father with her dowry trebled, presumably to remarry when her elderly husband eventually passes on.

But the play does not end on a harsh note. In the epigram Jonson inserted on the title page of the 1607 edition, he defined as his twofold aim, *simul et iucunda et idonea dicere vitae,* to present both the pleasurable principles of secular comedy *(iucunda)* with what is right or proper, the *idonea* of Christian morality. Lest we (or, more importantly, the university dons) miss the religious aspects of the *idonea,* he inserts Celia's frequent invocation of heaven, of the good angels, of a just God for aid and, when the situation seems temporarily to improve, to cry in gratitude, "O heau'n, how iust thou art!" Even in the most threatening situations, both she and Bonario proclaim their confidence in the ultimate manifestation of divine justice. As a true Christian, Celia, at the end, asks the judges to be merciful to her persecutors, and Bonario points out to the audience with some satisfaction that their acquittal marks the fulfillment of the trust they had expressed throughout, that "Heau'n could not, long, let such grosse crimes be hid." But the duality that underlies the play finds its consummation in the epilogue. After the audience has been assured that all crimes and vices have been duly punished, and after Volpone has been condemned to his grim fate, Jonson suddenly reverses the mood. The last word he grants to Volpone himself, assigning to him the traditional plea for applause in order to recall to mind in those final moments the witty, congenial, and amusing Volpone whose joviality had captivated us in the earlier scenes and whose early attractiveness we might otherwise have forgotten:[42]

> VOLPONE: The seasoning of a play is the applause,
> Now, though the FOX be punish'd by the lawes,
> He, yet, doth hope there is no suffring due,
> For any fact, which he hath done 'gainst you;
> If there be, censure him: here he, doubtfull, stands.
> If not, fare iovially, and clap your hands.

Volpone does not sound in this concluding speech like the "monstrosity," the "unmitigated villain," or the "archknave" of critical commentary, sitting, we are told, "like a spider in the center of his web of intrigue." Instead, we leave the theater in a more cordial mood, remembering Volpone as he was prior to his fall from grace, and recollecting the *iucunda*, the comic tradition of the theater that had amused us before the advent of the counterimpulse, the more solemn lessons of the *idonea*. Again, therefore, we find a leading literary work based upon an unresolved conflict, both on Jonson's part and, by extension, on the part of the audience. The attempt of critics to unify the whole by interpreting it as a grim satire on the bestiality of mankind not only ignores the laughter that stage performances consistently evoke but leaves little room for recognition of the play as a dramatic masterpiece.

To return to the coordinating theme of this study, the play would seem on two counts to conform to the palimpsestic multiformity of reader-response that has become the target for deconstructionists. First, by its importation of Italian patterns of comedy together with the legend of Reynard the Fox into a supposedly contemporary setting, the play offers a perfect instance of intertextuality condemned by them as a seductive mode compromising meaning. Second, the inconsistency between the amusing licentiousness of the opening section and the somber moral conclusion creates a hybrid form in which the conflict of text and subtext would seem to produce *aporia*. In this instance, however, there is a factor that differentiates it from the earlier instances and places it outside that category; for the polarization here is not concurrent, evoking a simultaneous polarized response, but sequential, evoking amusement in the first half and a somber sense of the meting out of justice in the second. As such, it conforms closely to Bakhtin's approval of *heteroglossia*, which may occur in different sections of a work, as it so frequently does in the novel. Moreover, if there is indeed a *débordement* in Jonson's play, a transgressing or rejection of the normal division between comedy and tragedy, it is the fault of the critic if Jonson's carefully worded preface to this play is ignored, his warning that the harshness of the ending was integral to his purpose, intended to counter the relaxation of strict moral principles in the opening section. With that warning in mind, the play needs to be seen as a fully unified work, combining in sequential form a delight in comedy with the moral lessons he believed should be intrinsic to all literary productions.

FIVE

Donne and the Meditative Tradition

The heady excitement engendered by the Grierson-Eliot revival of interest in metaphysical poetry during the twenties had begun to wane midcentury, when Louis Martz's *The Poetry of Meditation* restimulated interest, offering an essentially new tool for evaluating and analyzing the verse. The intense imaginative sensibility characterizing English devotional poetry of the early seventeenth century was, he argued, indebted in large part to the contemporary revival within religious circles of a medieval practice. Ignatius Loyola's *Spiritual Exercises,* intended for members of the Jesuit order and approved by the pope in 1548, not only lent new impetus to an ancient mode of religious contemplation among its followers but also soon generated a multitude of similar manuals for Protestant as well as Catholic sects. With many of these manuals published in England, they encouraged Christian votaries to adopt a regular practice of devotional regeneration, of temporary withdrawal from the world into the sphere of religious self-reassessment. Those manuals were seen as fostering elements close to the distinguishing characteristics of metaphysical verse. At fixed times and in fixed sequence, the devotee was to conjure up imaginatively an event from the Gospels, a scene of martyrdom, or an instance of saintly beatitude with such vividness as to transform the agony or bliss into a personal experience. The ultimate purpose of that exercise was to lead the visionary to a sharpened awareness of his or her own spiritual deficiencies and a determination to undertake a process of penitence and self-purification.

In applying that insight to the poetry of Donne, Vaughan, Herbert, and Marvell, Martz argued that the three "powers" of the soul the manuals encouraged the votary to actuate in sequence—*memory* (the imaginative recalling of a sacred event), *understanding* (pondering the significance of that event), and *will* (the evoking of a personal, emotional response)—formed the underlying pattern of much seventeenth century religious verse, and that the encouragement of self-examination or interiority was responsible in large part for the contemplative elements in such poetry.[1] It was an enormously stimulating work, providing a fertile area for further critical investigation, and sensitizing readers to a relationship largely ignored until then. Although it was not one of the poems he discussed, George Herbert's *Aaron* fit this pattern remarkably well. The speaker, a country parson visualizing the biblical high priest and his successors auspiciously performing their holy office, is led, as in the meditational manuals, to an awareness of the gap between those archetypal models and his own deeply felt inadequacy:

> Holinesse on the head,
> Light and perfections on the breast,
> Harmonious bells below, raising the dead
> To leade them unto life and rest.
> Thus are true Aarons drest.
>
> Profanenesse in my head,
> Defects and darknesse in my breast,

A noise of passions ringing me for dead
Unto a place where is no rest.
Poore priest thus am I drest.[2]

In the course of his study, Martz, in drawing attention to the flood of translations or adaptations of Jesuit, Salesian, and other Catholic manuals that poured into England in the early seventeenth century, commented that Protestants failed to produce effective treatises of their own and were generally content to employ the Catholic manuals despite the taint of their source. The collections of prayers and precepts in the English versions were, he maintained, poor and ineffectual compared with the richly imaginative works coming from the Continent, so that the tracts produced by the continental Counter-Reformation were readily adopted in England as the primary texts for exercises in inward devotion.[3]

That comment was to evoke an equally influential study, Lewalski's *Protestant Poetics and the Seventeenth-Century Religious Lyric*, which, while acknowledging the validity of Martz's theory in general, challenges him on that point. She adduces impressive evidence that the Protestants not only had produced numerous meditative manuals of their own and had, even when adopting Catholic manuals, introduced significant changes in adapting them to their own needs, but argued also—and this was crucial—that the main indebtedness of the English metaphysical poets was not to the Jesuit or other Catholic manuals but to the Protestant versions. Calvinist theology, Lewalski points out, dominated English thought in the seventeenth century and, if there existed certain sectarian discrepancies within the various Protestant sects, the concept of predestination deduced from the Pauline epistles—namely that no one was righteous by law and only some elected by grace—became the primary distinguishing factor of Protestant thinking in all its varied forms. Lewalski found that concept characteristic of the English religious verse of the time and accordingly argued in contrast to Martz that the fixed stages in the process of achieving grace—election, calling, justification, sanctification, and glorification—formed the true pattern structuring metaphysical poetry, a pattern deriving essentially from the Protestant manuals.

The problem I wish to confront concerns Lewalski's treatment of Donne's meditations, which she places unequivocally within that latter group. Although admitting that his theological interpretations were at times individualistic, she notes that his religious views remained within the parameters of formal Protestant doctrine and she deduces that, since they permeate his writings, he is to be identified both in his poetry and his prose with those versions indebted to the Protestant and not the Catholic forms of meditation. Although her work became accepted as the authoritative reading, it was recently challenged on that score by R. V. Young who, in a well-based study, argues that the doctrine of "prevenient grace" identified by Lewalski as a distinguishing factor in determining the Protestant affinity of seventeenth century poetics is considerably less definitive than she suggests, since the Catholics held an essentially similar view. The Council of Trent, following Aquinas, had stated explicitly that grace can only be achieved after God's prior granting of it; or, as the mystic Saint John of the Cross put it, "Without His grace one is unable to merit His grace."[4] There are, Young agrees, passages that reveal Donne's allegiance to the more severe interpretation of grace in accordance with Calvinist doctrine, such as the plea concluding *Holy Sonnet III:* "Impute me righteous, thus purg'd of evill, / For thus I leave the world, the flesh, and devill,"[5] where the word "impute" suggests that the individual can only obtain grace by reliance upon divine sanction. Yet, Young points out, even the most zealous searcher after Calvinist elements in the poems, John Stachniewski, hedges his argument with reservations, acknowledging the presence of many Catholic elements.[6] Young then transfers his doubts concerning the specifically Protestant form of seventeenth century poetry to the seventeenth century meditation, questioning Frank Huntley's claim that they are philosophically Platonic rather than Aristotelian, psychologically Augustinian, not Thomistic, theologically Calvinistic and public rather than private. All of these assumptions, Young points out in considerable detail, are ultimately oversimplifications.[7]

Without entering into lengthy discussion, one may perceive the force of those arguments leveled against Lewalski's view, opposition suggesting that theological labeling is in the final analysis ineffective. Characteristic is Young's argument concerning Donne's attitude to the Eucharist—that in the Fourth Prebend Sermon, Donne states in clearly Thomistic terms, "how fearfull, how terrible, how reverentiall a thing is the blood of this immaculate Lambe," yet elsewhere rejects as heresy the view "that the body of Christ must necessarily be in all places at once, by communication of the divine Nature," that is, by means of transubstantiation,[8] a contradiction Young ascribes to Donne's "unsettled religious conscience."[9] On the other hand, insistence upon his Catholic leanings has recently been countered by a collection of essays highlighting his debt to the Protestant tradition. Daniel W. Doerksen argues there that Donne reveals in his writings a Calvinist piety such as prevailed in the leadership of the Jacobean Church of England. Jeanne Shami focuses upon his appointment as proculator to the convocation as indicating his doctrinal fidelity to his adopted church, and Mary Papazian traces his theology to Augustinian teaching, with its emphasis upon original sin, election, and grace as espoused by many of the English Reformers of his day.[10]

What emerges from this debate, above all, is the inadequacy of the theological criterion as such, since, within the Catholic and Protestant churches, treatment of doctrinal elements varies so greatly in wording and in application, especially in this period, that evidence can too easily be adduced for either side. The fact that Donne's patron, James I, had, as mentioned earlier, expressly instructed preachers to avoid controversial elements of church doctrine makes it even more unlikely that Donne would have included in his sermons statements identifying him with problematic issues.[11] Where his personal beliefs differed from those of his adopted church, he was, as Jeanne Shami has shown, careful to situate himself at the borderline of the new creed without actually crossing it.[12] Thus Mariology, debarred by Protestantism, is carefully avoided in Donne's sermons, although there remain in his poetry clear indications of an emotional attachment to her worship, as in the sonnet series *La Corona*.[13]

The use of theology in determining Donne's sectarian allegiance is further weakened by the fact that he deplored the tendency to elevate minor points of theology into dogma, a practice he saw as fostering divisiveness within the church. He urged his congregants to distinguish between fundamental tenets of the faith, on which there should be unanimous accord, and those elements open to individual preference, adding that, in the latter category, one should choose in a manner that would avoid acrimonious dispute:

> nothing becomes a Christian better than sobriety; to make a true difference betweene problematicall, and dogmaticall points, betweene upper buildings, and foundations, betweene collaterall doctrines, and Doctrines in the right line: for fundamentall things, *Sine hesitatione credantur,* They must be beleeved without disputing; there is no more to be done for them, but beleeving; for things that are not so . . . we must hold them so, as our brother be not justly offended, nor scandalized by them; wee must weigh them with faith, for our own strength, and we must weigh them with charity, for others weaknesse. Certainly nothing endangers a Church more, then to draw indifferent things to be necessary; I meane of a primary necessity, of a necessity to be beleeved *De fide,* not a secondary necessity, a necessity to be performed and practised. (*Sermons* 2:20)[14]

To hunt, therefore, for phrases in his writings that may suggest Calvinist or Catholic leanings and to deduce from them that he belongs to one group or another is to deny him the discrimination he insists upon, the contrast between fundamental matters of doctrine that must be believed *de fide*, and those of lesser significance needing to be weighed carefully in order to avoid splitting the church into hostile groups.

The attempt to determine Donne's literary or religious models on the basis of the structural patterning of his work has proved equally inconclusive, producing two opposed critical camps. Helen Gardner endorses Martz's view that Donne, both in his meditations and in his holy sonnets, adopted the classic tripartite pattern of the Ignatian version, converting the traditional material to his own use, "with the freedom of a poet whose imagination is not tied to an initial plan," while N. J. C. Andreasen, well before Lewalski's book appeared, argued that the meditations were closer in structural form to the Protestant versions, as exemplified in the writings of Donne's friend, Bishop Hall. In contrast, Thomas F. Van Laan claimed to have identified close parallels with the Jesuit pattern in his analysis of certain of the *Devotions* (although his thesis required considerable rearrangement of the structural order to produce that conformity), while, more recently, Kate Frost has taken a more neutral stand, suggesting that their generic affinity is to a tradition earlier than the Ignatian, the tradition of spiritual autobiography and self-scrutiny leading from Paul, through Augustine's *Confessions*, and reaching its closest approximation to Donne's version in the self-revelatory *Life* by the fourteenth century Dominican mystic Henry Suso—a theory which, if correct, would place Donne's work in a larger Catholic grouping than the Ignatian.[15]

Since both the theological and the structural tripartite bases for such research have proved inconclusive, it may be helpful to look elsewhere. For if Donne carefully avoided—not least because of the king's specific directive—any theological tenets that could be regarded as controversial, certain processes of thought of which he had imbibed in the Catholic environment of his younger days, especially from the Jesuit meditations, remained with him, affecting the quality and direction of his writing. Whatever controversy there may be over his sectarian affiliation, his reputation rests not on his status as a theologian but on his achievement as poet, preacher, and meditator. The literary aspects of that achievement should be our primary focus.

I shall be suggesting that there exists in Donne's avowedly Protestant writings a profound Catholic indebtedness, a rich mingling of two seemingly contradictory elements—that although he was consciously advocating the Protestant cause and preaching to members of the new church, the quality of his writing was deeply indebted to his Jesuit upbringing and, especially, to the Catholic manuals of meditation on which he was reared. If that view is held by many critics, I propose to adduce here essentially new evidence based upon close reading of the manuals themselves. However, in examining that dual commitment, I would like to dissociate myself from the widely accepted view of Donne's so-called "unsettled conscience," the theory, as John Carey terms it in what has become a standard work in the field, that Donne was a "muddled" thinker whose conversion, arising primarily from personal ambition, was a betrayal of his inherited faith for the purpose of career advancement, a betrayal that left him with a feeling of guilt. It produced, we are informed, a dual allegiance, responsible for the "almost comic contradictions" in his sermons, a confused attempt on his part to conform to the demands of his adopted church while being incapable of deserting that of his birth.[16] While Carey's view has remained dominant, it has been challenged by both Annabel Patterson and Dennis Flynn, who maintain that his account of Donne's "time-serving" is insufficiently grounded historically.[17] To me, the argument that Donne converted for reasons of expediency seems to be gainsaid by a moving passage from the *Pseudo-Martyr* in which Donne calls upon his God to witness (and when Donne does so, one may take him seriously) how intensely and for how long he had struggled in his youth with the problem of religious allegiance, refraining from any violent and sudden determination, till I had, to the measure of my poore wit and judgement, survayed and digested the whole body of Divinity, controverted betweene ours and the Roman Church. In which search and disquisition, that God which awakened me then, and hath never forsaken me in that industry, as he is the Author of that purpose, so is he a witnes of this protestation; that I proceeded therein with humility and diffidence in my selfe and by that, which by his grace, I tooke to be that ordinary meanes, which is frequent prayer and equall and indifferent affections.[18]

According to Izaak Walton, he was closeted early each morning from the hours of four to ten immersed in investigating the sources as he tried to determine his final allegiance. One significant gain during that lengthy period of spiritual search was his extraordinary erudition in matters of theology. Once his decision was reached, his familiarity with the doctrinal distinctions between the two churches meant that he was at all times fully aware of them, and hence was capable of ensuring his conformity to the articles of faith belonging to Anglicanism. Charles and Katherine George have rightly concluded that "his revolt from the Church of Aquinas is in some ways the most absolute of that of any English divine."[19]

Moreover, it would be hard to think of any less confused thinker as one reads the magnificent sermons and meditations, with their penetrating awareness of the subtle paradoxes and problems in matters of faith. Once he took the fateful step of conversion, the Catholicism of Donne's youth became hateful to him, henceforth regarded by him as a form of profanity. He not only discarded his earlier allegiance but did so with satirical vigor, defining the Catholics in his vitriolic attack, *Ignatius His Conclave,* as being at a moral level below that of the infidel, and visualizing their daily entry into a hell of *"Turkes,* as well as *Papists,"* the latter having a special room reserved for them there, as being even more impious than the pagans.[20]

This public and contemptuous rejection of his previous faith would seem to counter my sense of his debt to Catholicism. But I would argue that, if he had discarded faith in the doctrines of Rome, in the infallibility of the pope and the efficacy of priestly absolution, there are elements of his childhood upbringing among a persecuted Jesuit minority that remained with him, elements related to patterns of thought that lie outside the narrower areas of theological dogma and tripartite form. The result is a devotional literature combining predominantly Anglican theology with a process of thought distinctly Catholic in source, providing once again a tension between traditional and innovative elements that, so far from detracting from the poetry and prose, enormously enhances them—a factor that has a distinct bearing on the nature of his debt within his meditational writings.

One aspect has long been recognized. Stylistically, Donne's predilection for casuistic argument remained characteristic of his writings long after he had converted, proclivities that place him closer to the "equivocation" of Father Garnet than to the simpler, unadorned prose or "plain style" developing in Protestant England. Luther, echoing Paul's statement that "my speech and my preaching was not with enticing words of man's wisdom, but in demonstration of the Spirit" (1 Cor. 2:4), had set the tone for his followers by declaring categorically, "The Holy Spirit is the plainest writer and speaker in heaven and earth, and therefore His words cannot have more than one, and that the very simplest, sense which we call the literal, ordinary, natural sense."[21]

Donne, however, like his Catholic mentors, was responsive to the multilayered meanings of scriptural text and the subtleties to be deduced from them, which he saw as validating his own textual intricacies. In contrast to Luther, he maintained that God, in addition to being a literal God, is "a figurative, a metaphorical God too; a God in whose words there is such a height of figures, such voyages, such peregrinations to fetch remote and precious metaphors, such extensions, such spreadings, such curtains of allegories."[22] And that penchant for remote and precious metaphors, often ingeniously pursued into their complex ramifications, characterized his own writings, as in the last and greatest of his sermons written long after he had left the Catholic Church:

> when these bodies that have beene the children of royall parents, and the parents of royall children, must say with Job, *Corruption thou art my father,* and *to the Worme thou art my mother and my sister.* Miserable riddle, when the same worme must bee my mother, and my sister, and my selfe. Miserable incest, when I must be maried to my mother and my sister, and be both father and mother to my owne mother and sister.[23]

Donne's contemporary, Richard Sibbes, who commanded a devoted following at Gray's Inn where his audience consisted "besides the learned lawyers of the house many noble personages and many of the gentry and its citizens,"[24] preferred the plain style despite the intellectual level of his audience, stirring his listeners by the simplicity and directness of his language:

> A frantic man, when he is bound in chains, he laughs, when they that are about him weep at his misery. So you have men frolicking in sin. They will swear at liberty, and besot themselves at liberty, and corrupt their consciences, even for base trifles. They think they are in no bondage, and they do all wondrous cheerfully and well; whenas indeed the more cheerfully and readily any man performs the base service of sin, the more he is in bondage.[25]

That preference for casuistic argument holds true of Donne's *Meditations* too, where the progression is deliberately convoluted, the images startlingly incongruous, producing a prose extraordinarily challenging to the mind. Thus, in *Meditation XII* he contemplates the strange self-originating fever or "vapour" of sin that so frequently corrupts man:

if this vapour were met withal in an ambush, and we surprised with it, out of a long shut well, or out of a new opened mine, who would lament, who would accuse, when we had nothing to accuse, none to lament against but fortune, who is less than a vapour? But when ourselves are the well that breathes out this exhalation, the oven that spits out this fiery smoke, the mine that spews out this suffocating and strangling damp, who can ever, after this, aggravate his sorrow by this circumstance, that it was his neighbour, his familiar friend, his brother, that destroyed him, and destroyed him with a whispering and a calumniating breath, when we ourselves do it to ourselves by the same means, kill ourselves with our own vapours?

However, if this casuistic tendency is well known, there are other aspects of his prose writing, highly relevant for investigations of his affiliation, that have not been noted. As has been documented by A. C. Southern,[26] numerous English translations of Catholic books, including manuals of meditation, were smuggled into England from the Continent and were secretly printed on English presses. The most influential of the manuals was the *Spiritual Exercises* of Loyola, so it would seem likely that that manual, the major source of the Catholic revival of such exercises, written specifically for the Jesuit order, would have been a primary influence upon Donne during his Jesuit upbringing. One should note, for example, how closely the situation presented in "Batter my heart" approximates to Loyola's image in the Thirteenth and Fourteenth Rules. In Donne's sonnet, the soul is depicted as a chaste maiden betrothed to God but held prisoner in a fortified town conquered by Satan:

> I, like an usurpt towne, to'another due,
> Labour to'admit you, but Oh, to no end,
> Reason your viceroy in mee, mee should defend,
> But is captiv'd, and proves weake or untrue,
> Yet dearely'I love you', and would be lov'd faine,
> But am betroth'd unto your enemie. (5–10)

In Loyola's manual, the devil, endeavoring to seduce the soul, is portrayed as a licentious lover paying court with evil intent to the daughter of some good father or the wife of a good husband without her father's or husband's knowledge, acting like

> a military leader who wishes to conquer and plunder the object of his desires. Just as the commander of an army pitches his camp, studies the strength and defenses of a fortress, and then attacks it on its weakest side, in like manner, the enemy of our human nature studies from all sides our theological, cardinal, and moral virtues. Wherever he finds us weakest and most in need regarding our eternal salvation, he attacks and tries to take us by storm.[27]

But whatever the specific version may have been, I propose to argue that Donne's meditations have the greatest literary affinity to the Catholic manuals despite his religious conversion, and they left a deep impression upon him, affecting both the themes and the style of his poetry and prose, including the meditations themselves.

In an often quoted passage, Donne wrote of the difficulty he had experienced in struggling to discard ideas inculcated in him during his Jesuit training. But it is important to note to which elements he refers:

> I had a longer work to doe then many other men; for I was first to blot out, certaine impressions of the Romane religion, and to wrastle both against the examples and against the reasons, by which some hold was taken; and some anticipations early layde vpon my conscience, both by Persons who by nature had a power and superiority ouer my will, and others who by their learning and good life, seem'd to me iustly to claime an interest for the guiding, and rectifying of mine vnderstanding in these matters.[28]

The elements he was attempting to eradicate, he tells us specifically, were the doctrinal arguments in favor of Catholic belief, namely the "examples and reasons" of his earlier indoctrination, while our concern here is not with dogma but with modes and patterns of thinking that remained implanted in his being, the continued presence of which constituted no theological contradiction to the creed he had espoused. There emerges from his poetry and prose a fascinating duality, as Donne dedicates his writing to his Protestant beliefs while employing the thought processes he had developed in his Catholic youth. This duality produced not "muddled" theological conceptions but a poetry and prose extraordinarily impressive in their fervor, intensity, and literary distinction.

Perhaps the most striking difference between the Catholic and Protestant manuals is one entirely ignored in the debates briefly summarized above, yet reflecting one of the major shifts in concept introduced by the Reformation. The rise of Protestantism, in many respects paralleling within the church changes in sensibility characterizing the Renaissance at large, was of course, marked by its increased focus upon the tactile world and its consequent rejection of the medieval *contemptus mundi*. William Perkins advised his readers to regard as blessings such temporal possessions as money, lands, and wealth, adding that "these earthly things are the good gifts of God, which no man can simply condemne, without injurie to Gods disposing hand and providence, who hath ordained them for naturall life."[29] Donne's obsession with death as casting its shadow over the whole of life left him much closer to the older tradition of *media vita in morte sumus*, without involving any deviation from the doctrines of the Reformed church:

> But then this *exitus a morte*, is but *introitus in mortem*, this *issue*, this deliverance from that *death*, the death of the *wombe*, is an *entrance*, a delivering over to *another death*, the manifold deaths of this *world*. We have a winding sheete in our Mothers wombe, which growes with us from our conception, and wee come into the world, wound up in that *winding sheet*, for wee come to *seeke a grave*. (*Sermons* 10:233)

Donne and the Meditative Tradition 185

This leads us into a fundamental point. Since the Jesuit movement, founded to stem the spread of the Reformation, was committed to reaffirming the medieval view, it is, I believe, of major significance that the Catholic manuals were intended not merely as exercises in spiritual discipline but as exercises in *withdrawal* or sequestration from the realities of mortal existence. In fact, in Catholic circles, the meditational programs came in time to be known as "retreats," opportunities for laypersons to isolate themselves, if only temporarily, from the pressures of daily life and to experience a strengthening of spiritual commitment in such segregation from the tactile world.

Included in the Catholic manuals was a recommendation of primary concern to us here, which concerned the location in which the exercise was to be performed. Loyola's treatise, like so many of its successors, recommended the following setting for the meditation: "I will deprive myself of all light, closing the shutters and doors when I am in my room." Meditators were enjoined to ignore their physical surroundings, focusing instead upon the inner experience. Loyola encouraged meditators to conjure up in the mind, employing all five senses, a scene from Holy Writ or from a saint's life with such vividness as eventually "to smell and taste in my imagination the infinite fragrance and sweetness of the Divinity." He advised them to refrain from gazing at any object in the room as they concentrate on the imagined scene. How influential that advice was to prove, echoed as it was throughout subsequent Catholic manuals, is evidenced in the religious art it produced, where, on the canvases of El Greco and Tintoretto, scenes of the Last Supper or the Resurrection were depicted not as they might have occurred, but as mystically envisioned in the mind of a meditator, in a dream-world isolated from physicality. Hence the unearthly, luminescent colors, the bodies strangely elongated beyond the proportions of human anatomy as they stretch upward in ecstatic longing for the celestial, the entire scene vibrating with the passionate intensity of the meditator. Hence, also, the depiction in El Greco's *Resurrection* of the witnesses of that scene twisting in agonized excitement when, in fact, according to the Gospels, there were no witnesses at all, the body's disappearance being discovered only after the event. For the Catholic meditator, however, it was essential to experience the scene with immediacy, as if he or she were actually present; and it is the intensity of that imagined presence that is depicted in El Greco's painting. In some Mannerist paintings, such as Tintoretto's *Removal of the Body of St. Mark*, the meditator himself is depicted in the foreground ecstatically pulling aside a curtain to reveal the iridescent vision of ghostly figures fleeing from the miraculous event. The indebtedness of such depictions to the Catholic meditational practice of withdrawal from reality is evidenced by a friend's account of a visit to El Greco. Surprised to find the painter on a bright, sunny afternoon seated in a darkened room with the shutters drawn, he urged him to join him in a walk through the town, only to be met by El Greco's firm refusal on the grounds that "the daylight blinded the light within him."[30]

The process of intense identification with an imaginatively conceived saint, to be followed by a recognition of one's own moral failings, clearly motivates certain of Donne's religious poems. *Holy Sonnet VII* opens with what seems to be a vivid depiction of Jesus on the way to Calvary: "Spit in my face yee Jewes, and pierce my side, / Buffet, and scoffe, scourge, and crucifie mee." But in the following line the reader stumbles over the speaker's strange admission of sin, an admission inappropriate to the figure of Christ:

> For I have sinn'd, and sinn'd, and onely hee,
> Who could do no iniquitie, hath dyed:
> But by my death can not be satisfied
> My sinnes, which passe the Jewes impiety:
> They kill'd once an inglorious man, but I
> Crucifie him daily, being now glorified.

The speaker in the opening of the poem, one realizes retrospectively, was not, after all, Jesus himself, but a meditator momentarily projecting himself into the experience of the Christ figure and then withdrawing to focus upon the chasm between his Savior's perfection and his own deplorable sins.

That process of intense visual reenactment within a darkened room has no place in Protestant meditation. In the many manuals produced by the Protestants that I have examined, the instruction to close the shutters and withdraw mentally from this world is not only missing but replaced by a contrary recommendation, to move outside into the heart of nature in order to enjoy its beauty. As an anonymous Protestant treatise noted in 1568, *A short and pretie Treatise touching the perpetuall Reioyce of the godly, euen in this lyfe:* "The right and true Christians doe take incredible delectation especially among other men, at this wonderfull ornature and beautie of the worlde, at the varietie, grace and order of heauenlye bodies, at the most pleasant sight of ye sunne, at the starres shining by night, and the amiablenesse of the earth, and the most faire, & as it were, springing countenaunce of naturall things."[31] In accordance with that advice, Richard Rogers, in his *Seaven Treatises* of 1604, established a new tradition that was to be echoed repeatedly in later works. He recommended Protestants remove themselves from the company of others and from "troublesome occasions" that might distract, citing as scriptural authority the patriarch Isaac, of whom it is written, "that he went out into the field towards the euening to meditate."[32]

It should be stressed here that the contrast I am suggesting is not with Catholicism at large but with its meditational manuals, the rules suggested for Loyola's revival of the spiritual exercises. Within Catholicism, despite its *contemptus mundi,* there is at times a positive response to the physical world. Saint John of the Cross was a lover of nature, frequently taking his fellow friars for walks in the mountains to be refreshed by the views and, during his period at

Segovia, often repairing to a grotto hollowed out from a rock to enjoy from there a vista including a great stretch of sky, river, and landscape. Such then was Saint John's practice; but his meditations follow the Loyolan pattern in deliberately excluding the tactile and visible, and in advising his followers to do the same. He had attended the Jesuit College from 1559 to 1563, shortly after Pope Paul III had approved Loyola's manual in 1548, and had left the college to assist Teresa of Avila, another of Loyola's disciples, in founding the Order of the Discalced, there developing his system of meditative, mystical experience. The meditator, he insisted in accordance with Loyola's advice, was to purge away all spiritual longings in order to be open to a closer contact with the divine; but as a prerequisite for such ascent, he was urged to experience a total "withdrawal from the life of the senses," the ascent itself being termed, as he entitled the chapter devoted to it, and as he described it metaphorically in his verse, a journey of the "dark night," a movement away from the house into darkness and secrecy:

> One dark night,
> Fired with love's urgent longings,
> —Ah, the sheer grace!
> I went out unseen,
> My house being now all still
> In darkness, and secure,
> By the secret ladder, disguised,
> —Ah the sheer grace!
> —In darkness and concealment.[33]

Teresa of Avila, describing in her *Vida* both her own meditative practice and the rules she proposed others should follow, explained the necessity of shutting out the real world: "Beginners must accustom themselves to pay no heed to what they see or hear, and they must practise doing this during the hour of prayer; they must be alone."[34] Fray Luis de Granada's *Book of Prayer and Meditation* (1554), one of the most popular of such Catholic manuals, attempts throughout to instill a similar disdain for actuality, reminding his readers that this house of earth, which is our grave, teaches above all things the vanity of mortal existence. In that, he was reflecting the earlier advice both of the *Imitatio Christi* and the *Ars Moriendi*, that one should have the hour of death constantly before one's eyes in order to achieve perfect contempt of this world. Similarly, Luis de la Puente's *Meditations on the Mysteries of our Holie Faith* recommended as a prelude to meditation the ability "to despise all things created."[35]

In Protestantism, in contrast, what Puente had termed "all things created," namely the world of Nature, so far from being despised, was to become a text second in importance only to the Holy Writ. The instruction to move out into the fields reflected the Protestants' reverence for the Book of Nature, the metaphor indicating the belief that the Deity had inscribed upon the birds, trees, and flowers moral lessons placed there for the Christian to decipher. The devout were urged to study nature closely in order to discern the messages it contained. Sir Thomas Browne declared that there are "two bookes from whence I collect my Divinity; besides that written one of God, another of his servant Nature, that universall and publik Manuscript, that lies expans'd unto the eyes of all." He reproved those Christians "who cast a careless eye on those common Hieroglyphicks and disdain to suck Divinity from the flowers of nature."[36] And this tendency displaced the contrary injunction of Loyola and of the Catholic manuals that served so often as sources for the Protestant versions. Behind the recommendation to meditate not in a darkened room but out in the field was, therefore, as Joseph Hall put it in his own manual of meditation, the belief that "Every herb, flower, spire of grass, every twig and leaf, every worm and fly, every scale and feather, every billow and meteor speaks the power and wisdom of their divine Creator. We shall spend our time ill in this great school of the world if, in such store of lessons, we be non-proficient in devotion." Accordingly, Hall included in his *Occasional Meditations* such topics as "Upon the Sight of a Raine in the Sun-shine," "Upon the Singing of Birds in a Spring-morning," "Upon the Crowing of a Cocke." Richard Baxter declared that every creature contains a divine message "which a considerate believer may as truly discern, as he can read upon a post or hand in a cross way the name of the Town or City which it points to."[37]

George Herbert provided, of course, the classic example of that Protestant principle, employing such "hieroglyphics" throughout his verse. The sudden emergence of spring flowers forcing their way through the cold snow is for him a divine message, an assurance that the most wintry despair of man can be followed by a heartwarming renewal of faith. To view the visual elements in this world as mere objects, he insisted, is fallacious. The Christian must spell out or decode the divine and moral lessons they contain: "We say amiss, / This or that is, / Thy word is all, if we could spell."[38] Hence, his Protestant peer, Marvell, perceives in a translucent drop of dew, resting lightly on a petal and awaiting the evaporating warmth of the sun, the lesson of the soul's need to prepare for its final ascent: "How loose and easie hence to go: / How girt and ready to ascend. / Moving but on a point below, / It all about does upwards bend."[39]

Such delight in nature is absent from Donne's prayers and meditations. He finds no inspiration in meadow or forest, rich as they may be to others in moral instruction. Nature and the physical world are, in that mood, only a deplorable distraction as the mind struggles to free itself from actuality and focus on the celestial:

> I throw my selfe downe in my Chamber, and I call in, and invite God, and his Angels thither, and when they are there, I neglect God and his Angels, for the noise of a Flie, for the ratling of a Coach, for the whining of a doore; I talke on, in the same posture of praying; Eyes lifted up; knees bowed downe; as though I prayed to God; and, if God, or his Angels should aske me, when I thought last of God in that prayer, I cannot tell: Sometimes I finde that I had forgot what I was

about, but when I began to forget it, I cannot tell. A memory of yesterdays pleasures, a feare of to morrows dangers, a straw under my knee, a noise in mine eare, a light in mine eye, an any thing, a nothing, a fancy, a Chimera in my braine, troubles me in my prayer.[40]

In the same way as the Catholic meditator was urged to disregard his or her physical surroundings and grant exclusive priority to the induced vision, so throughout Donne's *Meditations* cogitation spurns reality, searching for eternal verities beyond:

> our creatures are our thoughts, creatures that are born giants; that reach from east to west, from earth to heaven; that do not only bestride all the sea and land, but span the sun and firmament at once; my thoughts reach all, comprehend all. Inexplicable mystery; I their creator am in a close prison, in a sick bed, any where, and any one of my creatures, my thoughts, is with the sun, and beyond the sun, overtakes the sun, and overgoes the sun in one pace, one step, everywhere.[41]

This world is, for him, a close prison from which he yearns to escape into the world of meditation.

Logic itself, the rational pattern underlying earthly affairs, is equally distracting and fallacious—"Reason your viceroy in mee, mee should defend, / But is captiv'd, and proves weake or untrue."[42] Donne is not antirational—he delights in playing with logic, as in his amusing poem, *The Flea*, whose appeal is not in the theme (it was a commonplace idea at the time he wrote it, a contemporary anthology containing 50 flea poems) but in the subtle elisions leading to patently absurd conclusions. However, in matters of religious belief, he regards logic or reason as no more than a threshold to ultimate truth: "Faith is not on this side Knowledge, but beyond it; we must necessarily come to *Knowledge* first, though we must not stay at it, when we are come thither. For, a regenerate Christian, being now *a new Creature*, hath also *a new facultie of Reason:* and so believeth the Mysteries of Religion, out of another Reason"

(*Sermons* 3:359). Truth, he argues elsewhere, cannot be reached by direct means, only circuitously:

> On a huge hill,
> Cragged, and steep, Truth stands, and hee that will
> Reach her, about must, and about must goe;
> And what th' hills suddennes resists, winne so.[43]

When Donne does turn to the physical world of sense perception, it is in search of the contradictions inherent in the terrestrial, that justify his turning away from the tactile in yearning for the irrational, the paradoxical, the truths of spiritual experience that transcend the physical limitations of this world. Shadows, he argues perversely, are aspects of light. They are "not utter darknesse, but a thicker light; shadowes are thus much nearer to the nature of light then darknesse is; shadowes presume light, which darknesse doth not; shadowes could not be, except there were light" (*Sermons* 7:360). From that inversion of conventional concepts he deduces that God's condemnation of sinners, despite its dark foreboding, contains within it the bright hope of redemption.

How different such passages are from the eminently rational arguments of the Protestant manuals. M. A. Symson declares in the *Heptameron,*

> Now the Light is most excellent in five respects: First, because it is necessary for the direction of our actions: for he that walketh in darknesse knoweth not whither hee goeth. Secondlie, the Light is moste pleasant, for it addeth beautie unto all inferiour creatures; who if they had no light shining vpon them, they would bee vnder disgrace. But there are other foure thinges, wherein our Sauviour exceedeth this materiall Light: First, the Light is created; and he is an vncreated Light. Next, the Light cannot pierce thorow all things: for there are secret places in the Earth, to the which it can neuer attaine.[44]

Donne's focus upon the incongruities of the natural world becomes a principle in his writing, employed as a means of undermining confidence in empirical reasoning and thereby justifying faith in spiritual experience which so frequently defies logic. Thus, in an image of the hill of truth slightly different from that quoted earlier, he suggests that at a certain point reason must be deserted as no longer of value: "though our natural reason, and human arts serve to carry us to the hill, to the entrance of the mysteries of religion, yet to possess us of the hill itself, and to come to such a knowledge of the mysteries of religion as must save us, we must leave our natural reason and human arts at the bottom of the hill, and climb up only by the light, the strength of faith."[45] Hence, he seeks within the natural scene only the phenomena that contradict rational expectations: "I can better know a man upon the top of a steeple, than if he were halfe that depth in a well; but yet for higher objects, I can better see the stars of heaven, in the bottom of a well, than if I stood upon the highest steeple upon earth."[46] The natural world as it impinges directly upon the senses is thus regarded by him as unreliable or enigmatic, and his meditations, therefore, in accordance with the Catholic conception of them, are essentially a withdrawal from reality.

Important as that disparity between the manuals may be, it as yet arises only from specifying the locality, the provenance in which the meditation should take place. But there was a profound distinction too in the purpose animating the two types of manual, a distinction affecting the quality of the respective exercises. Although the aim of both versions was the encouragement of self-discipline and self-improvement—a shared element that made the Catholic manuals, despite their origin, acceptable as a basis for the Protestant versions—they differed in one essential aspect of that aim, the difference this time arising from a doctrinal divergence, although Donne's allegiance here is not, as we shall see, to the doctrine but to the stylistic implications. The concept of Calvinist predestination might well be thought to have produced a miasma of despair among Protestant believers, as indeed it did for many. The principle that only very few were destined to be saved, and that the performance of good works could not alter one's fate, left little room for optimism. But, as historians have noted, that tenet produced an inverse result, a process of circular reasoning. If the performance of good works and the attainment of faith were of no avail in a world where the prospect of salvation is preordained, those virtues were seen as, at the very least, placing one within the category of those persons from whom the elect had been chosen, the *Thirty-Nine Articles* noting that those who are called must indeed be drawn from those who "walk religiously in good works." As James Ussher assured his readers, "they that doe no good workes, doe declare that they neither are justified nor sanctified and cannot be saved."[47] The reverse did not mean that the virtuous were saved but indicated that they were, at least, eligible. Moral behavior was thus not regarded as entirely ineffective in the shadow of predestination, being regarded as a prerequisite, if not a guarantee, of salvation.

The principle, however, went much further and is especially relevant to the present discussion; for the Protestant, confronted by the knowledge of the very small proportion of humankind due to be saved, needed urgently to know whether he or she was indeed included among those who would stand at the right hand of God on the last day. In Catholicism, conviction of personal salvation had been regarded as a very rare occurrence, usually dependent upon some miraculous revelation, whereas for the Protestant it formed part of a defined process, available to all. Martin Luther had set the pattern. Profoundly depressed by a sense of his miserable inadequacy before the majesty of the divine and haunted by a terrifying vision of his stern rejection by Christ on the Day of Judgment, he chanced upon the phrase in Romans: "The just shall live by faith." In a flash, the phrase provided him with new joy and confidence, a sense, as he recorded, that he had been born again and had entered the gates of Paradise.[48] Based on that experience, he conceived of justification not as a prolonged process of cleansing by divine grace but as an almost instantaneous act whereby the true believer would, in a surge of faith, sense his redemption and thereby appropriate to himself the righteousness earned by his Savior.

The consecutive stages in the process termed "Calling" were: a recognition of personal sinfulness, genuine repentance of one's sins, and, after that, a conviction like Luther's of being spiritually reborn. Without such conviction, the Protestant, it was now believed, was doomed. The result was a peculiarly Protestant search, a compelling craving for confirmation of one's personal salvation. Arthur Dent's 1601 treatise made its point unambiguously in its title, *The Plaine Man's Pathway to Heaven: wherein every man may clearley see, whether he shall be saved or damned.* The pamphlet stressed, moreover, the urgency of obtaining such knowledge, warning the reader that "he who knoweth not in this life that he shall be saved, shall never be saved after this life."[49] William Perkins too gave prominence to that anxious concern, entitling his treatise of 1605, *A Case of Conscience, the Greatest that ever was: How a man may know whether he be the child of God or no.* Thomas Morton's *A Treatise of the Threefolde State of Man* (1596) declared that the mark of true faith was "the assurance of salvation, which is the undoubted persuasion and certaine knowledge of a faithfull man, that he is one of those who shall be made partakers of eternall glorie. . . . Every faithfull man may be and ought to be assured of his owne salvation and that by the wonderfull worke of regeneration wrought in him by the holy spirite."[50] Accordingly, the primary purpose of the Protestant manuals as opposed to the Catholic versions was to help the meditator to achieve that consoling assurance—a factor that provides us with a valuable criterion for distinguishing between the two types and, by extension, for distinguishing to which type a writer such as Donne was most indebted.

With this consolation as the acknowledged aim of the Protestant manuals, they are, again in contrast to the Catholic versions, essentially optimistic and reassuring. Calvin had set the tone by viewing the meditation as a means of mentally emerging from the sorrows of this world to a vision of the reward awaiting the true believer: "the only prop for our faith and patience is to disregard the state of our present life and direct our minds and senses to the last day, and pass through the world's hindrances until the fruit of our faith at last appears."[51] In the *Meditations and Praiers* of Sir John Conway, first published about 1570 and republished in 1611, a passage entitled *Wherewith Christe dooth comforte the soule of the Sinner* assures the reader of the reward that awaits the penitent, discouraging doubts and scruples in favor of an optimistic trust in the salvation duly granted by divine mercy:

> Thou shalte vndoubtedly feele a farre more bewtiful fruite, if thou diligentely care howe to loue, please, and folowe me, then by brosinge thy Selfe with scruples of thy confessions, for deeminge to search out, and abolishe doubtes, thou dooste rather engender to thee doubtfuller thinges; thou canst not thinke mee too pitieful, or mercifull, so that thou doe not presume vpon my mercies, neither canst thou geue mee ouer much credite. Wherfore accustome thy selfe to thinke wel of mee, and beleue that I wil not condemne thee: For truly, who so euer is willing to correcte his Life, and dispaireth not, him wil I saue. I am well pleased, O Daughter, that thou arte sorry thou haste offended, and that thou wilt not sinne hereafter. Now thou arte in state of Saluation, why fearest thou? I am ritche in infinite mercies.[52]

In line with the encouraging tone of such manuals, Richard Rogers comforts his depressed readers before they embark on the proposed spiritual exercise with the exhortation that "God doth, as it were, hide himselfe sometime for a season, that they may with more earnest desire mourne for God's wonted grace; and that when they have obtained it again, they may with more joyfulnesse of heart praise Him."[53] Joseph Hall, after apprising the reader of the latter's seemingly hapless condition, at once moves across to the radiant salvation that due faith will guarantee:

The soule that sinnes shall die: Hell claimes his due; Justice must bee satisfied; where art thou now, O my soule? What canst thou now make account of but to despaire and die? surely, in thy selfe, thou art lost; there is no way with thee but utter perdition. But looke up, O soule, look up above the Hills whence commeth thy salvation; see the heavens opening upon thee; see what reviving, and comfortable raies of grace and mercy shine forth unto thee from that excellent glory.[54]

His *Art of Meditation* concludes with a chapter entitled, *A cheerful Confidence of obtaining what we have requested and enforced.*

Indeed, what had prompted Richard Baxter to compose his popular *Saints Everlasting Rest* was compassion for those dreading damnation because of the principle of predestination, his perception that there were "so many forlorn, uncomfortable, and despairing Christians" about him whom he wished to encourage, through meditation, to envision the promised happiness of heaven so that thereby they would be provided "both with Assurance, and with Joys."[55] That purpose of the manual, to enable the meditator to obtain such assurance, could not be more clearly stated than it was in the wording of the title page:

The
Saints Everlasting Rest:
OR, A
TREATISE
Of the Blessed state of the SAINTS
in their enjoyment of GOD in Glory.
Wherein is shewed its Excellency and Certainty
the Misery of those that lose it, the way to Attain it,
and Assurance of it; and how to live in the continual
delightful Foretasts of it, by the help of Meditation.

In contrast, the Catholic manuals are considerably less heartening. They employ scenes of eternal damnation to alarm the meditator into repentance, offering no comfort or assurance of redemption. The scenes of suffering are accordingly depicted not as applicable to others, to those who have failed to achieve salvation, but as intensely personal, applicable to the meditator. Loyola warns the meditator to avoid thinking of "pleasant and joyful things such as heaven, the Resurrection, etc., for such consideration of joy and delight will hinder the feeling of pain, sorrow, and tears that I should have for my sins. It would be better for me to keep in mind that I want to feel sorrow and pain, remembering death and judgment."[56] Similarly, François de Sales, considered one of the mildest of Catholic mentors, provides in the *Meditations VI* and *VII* not a promise of reward but a grim warning of the need to continue the spiritual struggle unremittingly if the abhorrent end is to be avoided:

> Consider the final sentence of the wicked. *Go far from me, you that are accursed, into that eternal fire which has been prepared for the devil and his angels.* Try to realize how terrible these words are. *Go far from me.* A sentence of everlasting banishment from his presence; then, to be called *accursed* by God is the most terrible and final of all maledictions, and an eternal one for he adds *into eternal fire;* an eternity of suffering; nothing could be more terrible.... Remember these things, my soul, and tremble. Who can save me, my God, on the day when the very *pillars of heaven* tremble with fear? ... Stir your soul to terror. Could I endure *the devouring flame ... of fires that burn unceasingly?* Am I really prepared to cut myself off for ever from God?[57]

Donne has not a trace of the optimism evinced by the Protestant manuals. In diverging from that point, he was not offending against any doctrinal requirement since the matter of divine grace that formed the basis of the optimistic Protestant tracts had been deliberately left open. King James, apart from his general request that doctrinal elements be avoided by preachers, made the injunction more specific when he informed the Bishop of London at the time of the Hampton conference that "he wished that the doctrine of predestination might be very tenderly handled, and with great discretion, lest on the one side, God's omnipotency might be called in question, by impeaching the doctrine of his eternal predestination, or on the other, a desperate presumption might be arreared, by inferring the necessary certainty of standing and persisting in grace."[58] For Donne, salvation was no process achieved by a sudden sense of being reborn, but a hard and agonizing struggle continuing to the last moment of life, and then by no means assured. Hence his somber misgivings:

> And will God say to me, My son be of good cheer, thy sins are forgiven thee? Does he mean all my sins? He knows what original sin is, and I do not, and will he forgive me sin in that root, and sin in the branches, original sin, and actual sin too? . . . Will his mercy dive into my heart, and forgive my sinful thoughts there? Will he contract himself into himself and meet me there, and forgive my sins against himself, and scatter himself upon the world, and forgive my sins against my neighbor, and imprison himself in me, and forgive my sins against my self? (*Sermons* 2:67)

If his lugubrious view remained within the parameters of Protestant belief, it marked nonetheless a clear deviation from the mood of contemporary manuals, such as Arthur Dent's exhortation to the meditator that, with the help of the Holy Spirit, he should attempt to soar aloft, "whereby we may be carried above this world, into the mountains of Myrrhe, and the mountains of Spices. For how happie a thing it is, to have our conversation in heaven, that is, to have an inward conversation with God, by much prayer, reading, meditation, and heavenly affections."[59]

A corollary of the distinction between Protestant and Catholic manuals in the matter of salvation is to be found in their depictions of hell—not in the depictions themselves, which are equally daunting in the tracts of both churches, but in the function they perform within the manuals. In the Protestant versions, the aim of the description of hell is less to intimidate the meditator than to comfort and encourage him by contrasting the dire fate of the unrepentant sinners condemned to eternal agony with the bliss that awaits the faithful. Richard Sibbes's *Soules Conflict* (1635) asks, "If *fire* be so terrible, what is *hell* fire? If a darke *dungeon* bee so lothsome, what is that *eternal* dungeon of darknes? If a feast be so pleasing, what is the *continuall feast of a good conscience?* If the meeting of *friends* be so comfortable, what will our meeting together in heaven be?"[60] One notes that concluding phrase "*our* meeting together in heaven." The meditator is invariably, together with the writer of the manual, placed securely in the company of the godly, hell's fires being assigned to others, to the reprobates who have failed to join their church and achieve salvation within it. M. A. Symson's *Meditation of Death* (1621) declares, "Indeed Death is terrible to the Worldling; and no maruell, for it separateth him from all his comforts, and entereth him to all his paines: but it possesseth the godlie in all their joyes, and maketh an end of all their troubles."[61] One is left in little doubt who are to be included among "the godlie."

Behind that growing confidence lay a further distinction between the two churches; and here we shall need to return to that "postfigurative" tendency discussed in an earlier chapter whereby, once the Protestant had been granted access to the text itself, the stories of the patriarchs and their descendants became less typological and more real, and with that more vivid experience there came an increased empathy with them as living beings. In reading those biblical tales of the patriarchs, prophets, and kings and of their struggle for moral probity in the midst of worldly temptation, the Protestant looked for their true meaning in his or her own spiritual and even political exertions. As an embattled minority, they experienced a profound empathy with the chosen people of the biblical text, directed to fulfill a mission on earth under divine guidance, with the promise of a heavenly Jerusalem beyond. Implicit in this postfigurative awareness was the encouraging conviction that the victorious destiny of the biblical hero was, by virtue of the other parallels, the destiny of the postfigurer too— a conviction that underlay the Protestant sense of justification by faith and rebirth into salvation as depicted in the manuals.

Such cheerfulness forms no part of Donne's outlook. In only one devotional poem, written in a rare mood of trust, his *Hymne to God my God, in my Sicknesse,* does he contemplate his own death with calm assurance, preparing his soul at the door of everlasting life for the new role in which "I shall be made thy Musique"; yet even that poem concludes with a plea that God in his mercy will wrap him in the purple of Christ's blood, the prerequisite for such salvation since his own repentance will never suffice.

> As the first *Adams* sweat surrounds my face,
> May the last *Adams* blood my soule embrace.
>
> So, in his purple wrapp'd receive mee Lord,
> By these his thornes, give me his other Crowne.[62]

In general, however, the picture Donne provides is far less sanguine, hellfire depicted not only as terrifying in itself but as the fate that awaits his own sinful soul unless he can, by some agonizing effort of will, persuade the Deity to offer him the forgiveness he knows he can never deserve. In one of the most vivid passages in his sermons, he recounts his dread lest God should

> leave me, and cast me away, as though I had cost him nothing, that this God at last, should let this soule goe away, as a smoake, as a vapour, as a bubble, and that then this soule cannot be a smoake, a vapour, nor a bubble, but must lie in darknesse, as long as the Lord of light is light it selfe, and never sparke of that light reach to my soule; What Tophet is not Paradise, what Brimstone is not Amber, what gnashing is not a comfort, what gnawing of the worme is not a tickling, what torment is not a marriage bed to this damnation, to be secluded eternally, eternally, eternally from the sight of God? (*Sermons* 5:267)

How differently this reads from Henry Bull's advice to the Protestant in a meditation on awakening from sleep, where the awakening is compared to the joys awaiting one in heaven after the tribulations of this world: "Here call to mind the great mirth and blessedness of the everlasting resurrection. Also remember to muse upon that most clear light and bright morning, and new clearness of our bodies, after the long darkness they have been in: all then shall be full of joy." And Bull's advice for meditating at bedtime, when one should compare the charms of sleep after a tiresome day to the pleasures awaiting one after death: "even so after the tumults, troubles, temptations, and tempests of this life, they that believe in Christ have prepared for them an haven and rest most pleasant and joyful. As you are not afraid to enter into your bed, and to dispose yourself to sleep, so be not afraid to die, but rather cheerily prepare yourself thereunto."[63]

Is it to this more congenial tradition of the Protestant manuals that Donne is indebted or to the harrowing versions he would have studied in his Catholic youth? Loyola urges the meditator to meditate on hell, to visualize the great flames, the souls enveloped in fire; to hear the wailing, the screaming, and the cries, in order to experience to the full an abhorrence of sin and the urgent need to repent before it is too late:

> To see in imagination those enormous fires, and the souls, as it were, with bodies of fire. To hear in imagination the shrieks and groans and the blasphemous shouts against Christ our Lord and all the saints. To smell in imagination the fumes of sulphur and the stench of filth and corruption. To taste in imagination all the bitterness of tears and melancholy and a gnawing conscience. To feel in imagination the heat of the flames that play on and burn the souls.[64]

And such is Donne's meditation, in which hell is not for others but envisioned as intended for himself unless God be merciful:

> When I look upon God, as I am bid to doe in this Text, in those terrible Judgements, which he hath executed upon some

men, and see that there is nothing between mee and the same Judgement, (for I have sinned the same sinnes, and God is the same God) . . . I cannot breake off this terriblenesse, and say, Hee hath beene terrible to that man, and there is an end of his terror; it reaches not to me. Why not to me? In me there is no merit, nor shadow of merit; In God there is no change, nor shadow of change. I am the same sinner, he is the same God; still the same desperate sinner, still the same terrible God. (*Sermons* 8:123-24)

Moreover, where the Catholic versions encourage the meditator to envision the Crucifixion, Terence Cave notes how that scene of suffering is replaced in the Protestant manuals (as, indeed, it is in the passages by Henry Bull quoted above) by evocations of the Resurrection, although Cave offers no reason for the change. In the present context, the reason seems clear, namely that the Protestant preference is for the more comforting scene of Resurrection presaging the meditator's own hoped-for salvation, rather than the suffering of Jesus.[65] One recalls, in Donne's poetry, the contrary predilection, his frequent envisioning of the Crucifixion, as when the speaker in *Goodfriday 1613, Riding Westward* senses with awe the vivid spectacle in the east behind him, the scene of Christ hanging on the cross. Donne's careful inclusion of the year in the title is to remind us that the scene is not that of the Crucifixion itself, but a recall of the scene envisioned by a meditator on that holy day in 1613, conjuring up a sight so intimidating in its picturing of the agony that the speaker dare not turn to gaze upon it, and leading to the intensely personal conclusion, the recognition of his own unworthiness and his plea for mercy:

> O thinke mee worth thine anger, punish mee,
> Burne off my rusts, and my deformity,
> Restore thine Image, so much, by thy grace,
> That thou may'st know mee, and I'll turne my face.[66]
> (39-42)

In addition to his thematic indebtedness, Donne's style too is patently traceable to Catholic sources. Brent Nelson has recently argued that his "passionate preaching" parallels such Protestant models as inspired Joseph Hall's meditations, but it is surely the contrast between them that is most striking.[67] Hall's *Upon the Tolling of a Passing-bell* has often been compared to Donne's more famous devotion on the same theme.[68] They are indeed similar in their message, counseling that, on hearing the knell tolled for another's death, one must prepare for one's own demise; but the difference in presentation places them worlds apart. Hall's meditation is impressively solemn, logically sequential, and conveying with simplicity and directness the lesson to be learned:

> How doleful and heavy is this summons of death! This sound is not for our ears but for our hearts. It calls us not only to our prayers but to our preparation; to our prayers for the departing soul, to our preparation for our own departing. We have never so much need of prayers as in our last combat. Then is our great competitor most eager, then are we the weakest, then nature is so overlabored that it gives us not leisure to make use of gracious motions.[69]

Although Hall termed the collection from which this passage comes *Occasional Meditations*, the form is not that of a soliloquy, of a soul conversing in solitude with God. His meditations, as Frank Huntley points out, are, like most of the Protestant versions they inspired, public rather than private, the speaker functioning as a spiritual mentor advising his auditors on their responsibilities.[70] Hall proceeds with clarity from point to point, providing neither innovations nor intellectually challenging notions but confirmations of established truths. And the same holds true for Lancelot Andrewes, whose sermons, authoritative in their restatement of Christian doctrine, contain little that is personal in exposition: "When we behold the state of the world, and see that good men are trodden under feet, and the vessels of wrath and sin are exalted and prosper, then we may know that that is not the true Kingdom, and therefore we pray that God will set up His Kingdom in our hearts, and govern us by His Spirit."[71]

Donne's sermons and meditations differ in two major respects. They exemplify in their introspective and intensely personal presentation the final stage in Loyola's *Spiritual Exercises*, the meditator's turning inward to enquire how far he or she falls short of the example set by the envisioned martyr and what effort is required to move closer to that spiritual standard. As he reminded his auditors, his intention was not to moralize but to share with them his own agonizing sense of spiritual deficiency. "I preach but the sense of Gods indignation upon mine own soul, in a conscience of mine own sins, I impute nothing to another, that I confesse not of my selfe" (*Sermons* 2:53). Elsewhere, Donne declared that his sermons grew out of his own devotional exercises, so that the distinction between the two genres was minimal: "as a hearty entertainer offers to others, the meat which he loves best himself, so doe I ofnest present to Gods people, in these Congregations, the meditations which I feed upon at home" (*Sermons* 2:49). In accordance with that declaration, the sermons emerge as fervent personal dialogues with God, creating the impression for reader and auditor that one is eavesdropping upon a private meditation in progress, a meditation unfolding dynamically as its author shifts anxiously from thought to thought:

> when I shall need peace, because there is none but thou, O Lord, that should stand for me, and then shall finde, that all the wounds that I have, come from thy hand, all the arrowes that stick in me, from thy quiver; when I shall see, that because I have given my selfe to my corrupt nature, thou hast changed thine; and because I am all evill towards thee, therefore thou hast given over being good towards me. (*Sermons* 7:57)

His presentation, however, differs in a second major regard. The progression of thought is not linear; rather, it consists of a series of twists and turns, reliant upon a validation of paradox rather than confirmable truths, a technique reflecting the casuistry that became typical of Jesuit thought— casuistry not in its technical, theological sense but as a process of argument dependent upon a subtle undermining of seemingly self-evident truths in order to assert some overarching spiritual verity. At the time of the Gunpowder Plot, this element in Father Garnet's reasoning aroused the scorn of his Protestant accusers—the "equivocation" that allowed him to declare to his captors that he was not a priest by mentally adding the reservation "of Apollo." However absurd that might have appeared to those attending his trial, his statement arose from a genuine belief intrinsic to Jesuit thinking, namely that final validity lay not with the factual (in this instance the words articulated), but with the spiritual undertaking (the addendum audible only to God). That form of reasoning may appear strange to us, but as Mario Praz has pointed out, it formed the Catholic version of the *concetto* or dazzling wit, producing the emblems, devices, anagrams, and riddles that came to be seen in the late sixteenth and early seventeenth centuries as supreme achievements of art, although in its Jesuit form it was serious in intent.[72] In Donne's prose, that convoluted, paradoxical form of reasoning is paramount, as when, in the above passage, he reminds himself that it is not only mercy that comes from God, but that from him derive also the wounds and arrows that have compelled the speaker to beg for mercy.

Hence his most famous meditation, on the passing-bell, consists, unlike Hall's, of a challenging of normal assumptions, an inversion of logic that repeatedly compels the meditator to discard conventional responses and to acknowledge more urgent, disturbingly revelatory ideas. It marks a use, in fact, of the labyrinthine reasoning of the Jesuits, challenging the conventional and searching for verities transcending, and often contradicting, appearances. Each sentence, indeed each phrase, forces us as readers to confront an apparent absurdity, that confrontation compelling us to discard normative response in favor of a new and hitherto unperceived concept, as in the opening sentence of his *Meditation XVII:* "Perchance hee for whom this *Bell* tolls, may be so ill, as that he knowes not it *tolls* for him."[73] The word "ill" applied to the deceased, the person "for whom the bell tolls," conjures up the preposterous image of the dead person as a "sick corpse" listening out anxiously to the bell that proclaims its death. That impossibility compels us to rethink the obvious, and eventually to realize in the course of the meditation the ambivalence of a seemingly insignificant word we had previously taken for granted—that although the knell is being rung *for* (in honour of) a dead man, its true purpose is *for* (intended for) the listener who is alone capable of hearing it.

It is a process of intellectual challenge repeated with often startling variations throughout the meditation, as in the later passage which, though it may seem at first a mere echo, in fact presses the argument a stage further: "As therefore the *Bell* that rings to a *Sermon,* calls not upon the *Preacher* onely but upon the *Congregation* to come; so this *Bell* calls us all; but how much more *mee,* who am brought so neere the *doore* by this *sicknesse.*"

The incongruous image of a preacher needing to be reminded to deliver his sermon forces us to reevaluate the situation, confirming our rejection of the normal assumption that the bell is intended "for" the dead; but it also compels us suddenly to perceive that the "preacher" here is, in a very real sense, the corpse itself, delivering to us the most compelling sermon of all, the tolling of the bell calling us to hearken to his sermon. And Donne, as always, concludes that section by turning inward—"but how much more mee," the intensely personal application to self so characteristic of the culmination of the Loyolan exercise, the enquiry, "What have I done for Christ? What I am now doing for Christ? What ought I to do for Christ?"

If the Protestant meditational manual came to resemble the sermon, becoming increasingly didactic as the author instructs the meditator to join those who are saved, Donne's sermons and meditations, also merging stylistically, were animated not by didacticism but by an impassioned interiorization, remaining close to the concept of the Catholic meditation as a retreat from actuality into a process of self-analysis. They are, moreover, characterized not by the confident exposition of an ecclesiastical counselor assuring his readers of their resurrection but by the dissatisfaction and agony of one deeply aware of his personal failings, seeing himself, as Loyola had advised, as "a great sinner, bound in chains and worthy of death," confronted by the impossibility of ever earning divine forgiveness and hence utterly reliant on God's granting of gratuitous mercy. The satisfaction of knowing one is saved, the main purpose of the Protestant meditations, is not for him:

> Even in spirituall things, there may be a fulnesse, and no satisfaction, And there may be a satisfaction, and no fulnesse; I may have as much knowledge, as is presently necessary for my salvation, and yet have a restlesse and unsatisfied desire, to search into unprofitable curiosities, unrevealed mysteries, and inextricable perplexities: And, on the other side, a man may be satisfied, and thinke he knowes all, when, God knowes, he knowes nothing at all; for, I know nothing, if I know not Christ crucified, And I know not that, if I know not how to apply him to my selfe, Nor doe I know that, if I embrace him not in those meanes, which he hath afforded me in his Church, in his Word, and Sacraments. (*Sermons* 5:276)

The poetry and prose Donne dedicated to the new church and its sacraments employed, therefore, literary and thematic forms drawn from a church he had not only forsaken but had come to regard with contempt. Acknowledgment of that indebtedness is by no means new, but the evidence here adduced from a close study of the meditational manuals not only provides considerable support for the view but also suggests that the differences between the Catholic and Protestant manuals are more fundamental than has been thought. Martz claims that the latter are variations of the Catholic versions with only minor sectarian emendations, but they should be seen as disparate in both purpose and form. If, as I have argued, Donne's meditations conformed more closely to those he was acquainted with in his youth, we need no longer rely upon somewhat vague theological distinctions to substantiate his stylistic indebtedness; for the major characteristics of the meditational manuals designed by the Protestants are indeed absent from Donne's writings. For him, the physical world of nature was not, as for Herbert and his peers, a divine book providing religious inspiration but an irksome distraction from religious contemplation. And Donne's process of meditative practice was not to achieve a conviction of personal salvation but the opposite, to intensify his awareness of potential damnation, with hell not assigned for others but ominously awaiting himself unless he could in near desperation persuade his God to show him mercy. Doctrinally he conformed, after his conversion, to the tenets of the Anglican church, eschewing controversial elements; but stylistically and in the intensity of his personal vision, Donne remained indebted to the spiritual exercises in their original Catholic form.

In that contrast between doctrine and style may be perceived once again the confluence of centripetal and centrifugal impulses. In a paradox not unlike those that Donne favored in his writings, it was his affinity to the manuals of a church he had come to regard as profane that was ultimately responsible for endowing his Anglican sermons and meditations with their extraordinary effectiveness, a tension contributing profoundly to the brilliance of his writing.

One final comment. In one of his most convoluted essays, Jacques Derrida applied to the concept of death the deconstructionist principles he had adopted for literary texts, arguing, with frequent reference to Heidegger, that the idea of death was in itself an impossibility. Just as a text disintegrates as it is dispersed into its contradictory readings, so "my death," since it cannot be generalized, is meaningless: "'My death' is an absolute singularity (no one can die in my place), so that the term is always a matter of *hapax legomenon*, of what is only said *one time each time*, *indefinitely* only one time." As a result, Derrida declares,

Fundamentally, one knows perhaps neither the meaning nor the referent of this word. It is well known that if there is one word that remains absolutely unassignable or unassigning with respect to its concept and to its thingness, it is the word "death." Less than for any other noun, save "God"— and for good reason, since their association here is probably not fortuitous—is it possible to attribute to the noun "death," and above all to the expression "my death," a concept or a reality that would constitute the object of an indisputably determining experience.

Accordingly, Derrida maintains in this late formulation of his philosophy that such disintegration of meaning even goes beyond *aporia*, the latter being a situation that requires some idea over which there is a conflict of interpretation. And he concludes that in "place of aporia, *there is no longer any problem* . . . because one could no longer even find a problem that would constitute itself and that one could keep in front of oneself, as a presentable object."[74]

For Donne, not only is death an actuality, vividly conceived both in the gruesome putrefaction of the body and in the soul's subsequent ascent to a Day of Judgment, but it is always his own death that serves as the exemplar and lesson for his audience, the awareness of the sinfulness of his own life and his own agonized longing for mercy before death comes upon him. Where Derrida sees no possibility of generalizing from the particularity of "my death," Donne focuses intently upon that individualistic experience in order, by implication, to extrapolate it into an archetype for the predicament of his auditors and humankind at large. As "any man's death diminishes me because I am involved in mankind," so, in reverse order, his own death, like the tolling of the bell for another, should, as he proposes in "Death's Duell," provide warning to all of what awaits them.

What applies to the concept applies also to the literary form. The combination of Catholic meditative tradition with Protestant belief creates in Donne's writings a merger of past tradition with present doctrine. Such co-presence of earlier and later "texts" within a literary work is again interpreted by deconstructionists as producing a critical stalemate. The joint presence, we are told, of

> previous and later texts is a version of the relation of parasite to host. It exemplifies the undecidable oscillation of that relation. It is impossible to decide which element is parasite, which host, which commands or encloses the other. It is impossible to decide whether the series should be thought of as a sequence of elements each external to the next or according to some model of enclosure like that of the Chinese boxes. When the latter model is applied it is impossible to decide which element of any pair is outside which is inside.[75]

Donne's meditations have no relation to a Chinese puzzle with an inside and an outside, but mark an impressive integration of two traditions. Where the Protestant manuals recommended meditation within the natural beauties of the countryside and encouraged in the meditator a conviction of personal salvation and joy, Donne's sermons and *Devotions Upon Emergent Occasions* owed to Loyola's *Spiritual Exercises* and its progeny two opposite qualities—withdrawal from the tangible world and vivid contemplation of his own threatened damnation. The importation into his sermons and devotions of qualities so alien to Protestant meditative practice, his extraterrestrial thought processes and his everpresent dread of the Day of Judgment, accounted in large part for their remarkable literary power.

Epilogue

If the main focus in this study has been upon *aporia*, the doctrine concerning the final insolubility of the text, that theory was symptomatic of a broader devaluation of interpretive processes. I should like, in conclusion, to examine briefly one further aspect, the model that has been cited repeatedly by the exponents of deconstruction as a means of authorizing their approach. Both J. Hillis Miller and Geoffrey Hartman have turned to biblical commentary and, more specifically, to Hebraic Midrash to demonstrate the diversity of readings that emerge from the study of a text, pointing to the multiplicity of such textual interpretations as evidence for the invalidity of choosing any single reading in preference to others. Under Hartman's aegis and with his personal participation, a forum was established devoted to that theme, from which emerged under his joint editorship the volume of essays, *Midrash and Literature*.[1]

The aspect that attracted the participants in that forum, as well as others developing its themes, was the freedom with which midrashic commentators could approach the biblical text, extrapolating its narratives, reinterpreting the wording, and often changing its import in the process, those variegated readings gathered in such respected anthologies as the *Midrash Rabbah*. To offer one example of the way in which the import of the original passage is changed and multiple incompatible readings emerge: when Isaac is about to bestow his blessing on the disguised Jacob and requests confirmation of his identity, Jacob replies, "I am Esau thy firstborn." One commentator admits the reply was a falsehood but provides an accompanying explanation to allay the harshness of the misdemeanor, while another interpreter takes a contrary view, ingeniously rereading the phrase to acquit him of falsehood. A punctuational pause (they are never marked in the Hebrew text) is inserted, for the reply to be read exoneratingly as: "I am [Jacob]. Esau is thy firstborn." And the two interpretations are presented side by side.

Gaps in narrative are filled imaginatively, wordplay and anagram exploited to produce amplifications or explications of the scriptural account, this authoritatively approved process being adduced by the deconstructionists as evidence of the ultimate indeterminacy of all texts, even the most sacred. The rabbis, Susan Handelman claims, "sought to penetrate the inner meaning of the law; the interpretation was an exegesis, a reading 'in' what was already there. Thus any new halakha [legal ruling] was tied to the Written Law in an internal way, considered to be embedded in the letter and disclosed in the Midrash. The Rabbis were not, to their minds, adding anything new but only bringing forth what was already there."[2] To offer an example of "gap-filling," on the passage describing Rebecca's pregnancy, "And the children struggled within her" (where the text offers no explanation of the nature of the struggle), the Midrash comments that whenever she passed a place of idolatrous worship Esau struggled to emerge, and whenever she passed a center of Hebrew learning Jacob strove to emerge. Accompanying that explanation is an entirely different view, that they were fighting each other in the womb. Quoted approvingly in the Hartman collection is the remark by Max Kadushin that essentially the Midrash implies that other interpretations are possible, thereby confirming the principle of indeterminacy.[3]

The *Midrash Rabbah* does indeed provide richly imaginative interpretations and extrapolations of the text, often offering a collection of diverse, mutually contradictory readings; but to argue that they undermine the determinacy of the original is to ignore two factors. The first is an axiom well known to its readers, that such extrapolations and interpretations, charming and educational as they may be, are not to be taken literally (*ein meshivin al hadrash*). More significant, however, are the recurrent statements by leading commentators warning against such misinterpretation. Maimonides ridiculed "those ignorant persons" who take the midrashic interpretations literally, explaining that the Sages were simply extrapolating from the biblical text in order to teach ethical lessons.[4] And the most celebrated of biblical commentators, Rashi, while frequently quoting such legendary accretions with approval, adds the reservation, "There are many such midrashim, *but the literal meaning of the text is. . . .*" (e.g., Gen. 3:24). The midrashic commentaries may be instructive, conveying moral teachings loosely connected to the narrative, but they are acknowledged as fanciful elaborations, in no way invalidating or replacing the import of the text. Even within *halakhah,* the deriving of a law from the precise wording of the text was by no means arbitrary; it did not encourage multiplicity or freedom of interpretation, being strictly controlled by 13 principles of exegesis to which every such derivation needed to conform. And even then the new ruling did not replace that of the text but expanded it, as in the prohibition against seething a kid in its mother's milk (Exod. 23:19), where its threefold appearance in the Pentateuch was interpreted as prohibiting not only the act itself but also the consumption of meat and milk together and the deriving of any benefit from such seething. The text itself, one notes, remains legally binding and has in no sense been supplanted by the Midrash.

The danger involved in this claim for the indeterminacy of texts and the freedom to elaborate or interpret without limit is evidenced in its impact outside the sphere of literature.

One of my own interests in recent years has been the relationship between literature and contemporary changes in the visual arts of painting, architecture, and sculpture, all such media responding to developments in the cultural configuration of the time; and it is apparent that deconstructionism has affected the plastic arts no less than literature. In an article in the *New York Times Book Review*, Barry Geween notes how even those art critics who had, until the last decades of the century, proved most supportive of innovative trends in art, encouraging the public to appreciate experimentation—among them Clement Greenberg, Michael Fried, and Harold Rosenberg—have despaired of postmodernist trends, especially the abandonment of all previous evaluative criteria concerning the nature and function of art. In a manner deriving in large part from Derrida (as Geween specifically notes), the principle has been adopted on the basis of this "indeterminacy," that any interpretation of the meaning of "art" is valid:

> In 1974, Chris Burden had himself crucified on the roof of a Volkswagen. He was creating a work of art. A decade later, Herman Nitsch staged a three-day performance in which participants disemboweled bulls and sheep and stomped about in vats, mixing the blood and entrails with grapes. In another work of art, Rafael Ortiz cut off a chicken's head and beat the carcass against a guitar. Ana Mendieta, who had a retrospective at the Whitney last year, also decapitated a chicken and let its blood spurt over her naked body. . . . [Artists] have sliced themselves with razor blades, inserted needles in their scalps, rolled naked over glass splinters, had themselves suspended by meathooks and undergone "surgical performance operations."[5]

After that lurid, but factually justified opening, Geween proceeds to a very sober and sobering examination of recent scholarship, of academic studies by specialists in the field that indicate how grave is the present condition of the arts, with art criticism itself having become irrelevant—reduced to mere descriptions of works or performances that claim to be art, since the criteria for any form of evaluation have been negated.

Hillis Miller offers a defense of the deconstructionist approach on the grounds that it reveals what he terms hitherto unidentified meanings within each work. But he claims also, as if that were its major achievement,

> Analysis becomes paralysis, according to the strange necessity which makes these words, or the "experience," or the "procedure," they describe, turn into one another. Each crosses over into its apparent negation or opposite. If the word "deconstruction" names the procedure of criticism, and "oscillation" the impasse reached through that procedure, "undecidability" names the experience of a ceaseless dissatisfied movement in the relation of the critic to the text.[6]

Various challenges to the deconstructionist approach have appeared during the last few years, but they have been essentially theoretical, discussing the implications of polysemy, as in the recent collection of essays, *Arguing with Derrida*.[7] Instead, I have attempted here to examine one of its central doctrines by focusing upon specific works, suggesting that literature, even when—or perhaps especially when—there exists within it a clash between text and subtext, when subversive elements militate against the overt theme, the conflict produces at its best not the deadlock that has been claimed but, as in *Hamlet* or in Donne's meditations, a reflection of and response to the complexities and paradoxes of life itself. I have restricted the works examined in this book to the period of the Renaissance, but the above principle applies, I believe, to the finest writing of all eras.

Notes

NOTES TO INTRODUCTION

1. J. Hillis Miller, "The Critic as Host," *Deconstruction and Criticism* (New York: Continuum, 1986). For the origins of the theory, see also Jacques Derrida, *Writing and Difference,* trans. Alan Bass (Chicago: University of Chicago Press, 1978), and Paul De Man, "The Rhetoric of Temporality," *Blindness and Insight* (Minneapolis: University of Minnesota Press, 1983).

2. Roland Barthes, *Image—Music—Text,* ed. and trans. Stephen Heath (New York: Hill & Wang, 1977), 147, and *S/Z,* trans. Richard Miller (New York: Hill & Wang, 1975), 120, 98.

3. M. M. Bakhtin, *The Dialogic Imagination,* ed. Michael Holquist (Austin: University of Texas Press, 1981), 272, 276, 285. Although most of Bakhtin's work was written in the early to mid-twentieth century (and for a long time suppressed by the Soviet authorities), its remarkable applicability to postmodernist theory has been widely acknowledged. See, for example, Terry Eagleton, *Literary Theory* (Minneapolis: University of Minnesota Press, 1989), 119ff.

4. *King Lear* 1.2.119ff. Shakespeare quotations throughout this book are from the *Riverside Shakespeare,* ed. Hardin Craig and David Bevington (Glenview: Scott Foresman, 1973).

5. Dwight Eddins, ed., introduction to *The Emperor Redressed: Critiquing Critical Theory* (Tuscaloosa: University of Alabama Press, 1995).

NOTES TO CHAPTER 1, "SACRED AND SECULAR IN
THE MERCHANT OF VENICE"

1. Noted in John S. Colley, "Launcelot, Jacob, and Esau: Old and New Law in *The Merchant of Venice,*" *Yearbook of English Studies* 10 (1980): 181.
2. Barbara K. Lewalski, "Biblical Allusion and Allegory in *The Merchant of Venice,*" *Shakespeare Quarterly* 13 (1962): 327. Nevill Coghill, "The Governing Idea," *Shakespeare Quarterly* 1 (1948): 9, had noted that the play constituted an allegory of Justice and Mercy, of the Old Law versus the New, but in very general terms, suggesting that Shakespeare's source was the medieval *Processus Belial.* See also Douglas Anderson, "The Old Testament Presence in *The Merchant of Venice,*" *Journal of English Literary History* 52 (1989): 119.
3. Biblical quotations throughout this book are from the Geneva Bible, the text most probably used by writers of this period. I have here made a slight change, substituting for the antiquated and misleading "againe" the more modern phrase, "in return."
4. The *Oxford English Dictionary* cites this line from Shakespeare under the heading "infected with disease"; but, as the dictionary itself records, "taint" was used from as early as 1471 with the simple meaning, "to colour or dye."
5. L. L. Schücking, *Character Problems in Shakespeare's Plays* (London: G. G. Harrap, 1922), 171, and John R. Brown's note on these lines in his Arden edition of *The Merchant of Venice* (New York: Arden, 1964), 4. Joan O. Holmer, *The Merchant of Venice: Choice, Hazard, and Consequence* (Basingstoke: Macmillan Press, 1995), 131, adopts E. K. Chambers's suggestion in his *Shakespeare: A Survey* (London: Oxford University Press, 1925), that Antonio's melancholy arises from the imminent departure of his friend Bassanio; but Holmer admits that his mood remains a "mystifying melancholy."
6. Paul Gaudet, "Lorenzo's Infidel," in *The Merchant of Venice: Critical Essays,* ed. Thomas Wheeler (New York: Garland Press, 1991), 352, is puzzled by Antonio's celibacy.
7. Leslie A. Fiedler, "These Be the Christian Husbands," in *The Merchant of Venice: Modern Critical Interpretations,* ed. Harold Bloom (New York: Chelsea House, 1986), 66, and D. M. Cohen, "The Jew and Shylock," *Shakespeare Quarterly* 31 (1980): 53. Although James Shapiro's *Shakespeare and the Jews* (New York: Columbia University Press, 1996), has been widely admired and frequently quoted for its reading of the play in New Historical terms, it adopts the practice of that school in finding some obscure

historical reference which is then read into the literary work. I can find not the slightest indication in the text of this play that would associate Shylock with castration.

8. Harold Fisch, *The Dual Image* (London: World Jewish Library, 1971), 31.

9. Hijman Michelson, *The Jew in Early English Literature* (Amsterdam: H. J. Paris, 1926).

10. See Ruth Mellinkoff, *Outcasts: Signs of Otherness in Northern European Art of the Late Middle Ages* (Berkeley and Los Angeles: University of California Press, 1993), 1:151, and the illustrations in the accompanying volume.

11. Hermann Sinsheimer, *Shylock: The History of a Character* (New York: Citadel Press, 1964), 137.

12. Commentators differ on the precise meaning of Antonio's stipulation that half be reserved for Jessica's eventual use, but to an audience it comes across clearly as an act of charity.

13. See E. C. Pettet, "*The Merchant of Venice* and the Problem of Usury," *Essays and Studies* 31 (1945): 19. Norman Jones, *God and the Moneylenders* (Oxford: Oxford University Press, 1989), offers a detailed account of the situation in sixteenth century England, and Lawrence Stone, *The Crisis of the Aristocracy, 1558–1641* (Oxford: Oxford University Press, 1967), 532–35, records both the insolvency of the upper classes and the consequent proliferation of moneylending. There is a useful summary in Lawrence Danson, *The Harmonies of "The Merchant of Venice"* (New Haven: Yale University Press, 1978), 144–45.

14. Thomas Wilson, *A Discourse upon Usury* (London, 1572).

15. S. Schoenbaum, *Shakespeare's Lives* (Oxford: Oxford University Press, 1970), 32.

16. R. H. Tawney, *Religion and the Rise of Capitalism* (1922; reprint, Harmondsworth: Penguin Books, 1948), 58. The quotation from Gratian appears on 47.

17. Jerome, *Commentary on Ezekiel.*

18. See G. G. Coulton, *The Medieval Panorama* (Cambridge: Cambridge University Press, 1962), 335–45.

19. Benjamin Nelson, *The Idea of Usury* (Princeton: Princeton University Press, 1949), esp. 29–35.

20. Ibid., 93–94.

21. Wilson, *A Discourse upon Usury.* See also Miles Mosse, *The Arraignment and Conviction of Usury* (London, 1595).

22. Daniel Price, *The Merchant: A Sermon Preached at Paul's Cross on Sunday the 24th of August . . . 1607* (Oxford, 1608).

23. Immanuel Bourne, *The Godly Mans Guide* (London, 1620), 26–27.

24. Laura Stevenson, *Praise and Paradox: Merchants and Craftsmen in Elizabethan Popular Literature* (Cambridge: Cambridge University Press, 1984), 97.

25. Philip Stubbes, *The Anatomie of Abuses*, ed. M. J. Kidnie (Tempe: Renaissance English Text Society, 2002), 180.

26. William Perkins, *A Treatise of the Vocations* in *Workes* (London, 1612), 1.

27. Quoted in R. H. Tawney's introduction to his edition of Wilson's *Discourse* (London: G. Bell & Sons, 1925), 75.

28. Richard Sibbes, *The Saints Cordials* (London, 1637), 188.

29. John Dod and R. Cleaver, *A Plain and Familiar Exposition of the Ninth and Tenth Chapters of Proverbs* (London, 1612), 139–40.

30. Tawney's *Religion and the Rise of Capitalism* followed Max Weber's "The Protestant Ethic and the Spirit of Capitalism," first published in 1912. Tawney's approach has been challenged, but for a summary of the dispute confirming the emergence of a capitalist tendency in Puritanism by 1640, see Charles H. George and Katherine George, *The Protestant Mind of the English Reformation, 1570–1640* (Princeton: Princeton University Press, 1961), 144–73.

31. William Harrison, *Chronology* (c. 1570). See G. J. Parry, *A Protestant Vision: William Harrison and the Reformation of Elizabethan England* (Cambridge: Cambridge University Press, 1987), 282–83.

32. George and George, *Protestant Mind*, 178.

33. Karoline Szatek, "*The Merchant of Venice* and the Politics of Commerce," in *The Merchant of Venice: New Critical Essays*, ed. J. W. and E. M. Mahon (New York: Routledge, 2002), 325.

34. Schoenbaum, *Shakespeare's Lives*, 33–34.

35. Mosse, *Arraignement*, sigs. F4–F4v. For a valuable examination of the subject, see Helen C. White, *Social Criticism in Popular Religious Literature of the Sixteenth Century* (New York: Octagon Press, 1973).

36. Joan O. Holmer, "When Jacob Graz'd his Uncle Laban's Sheep: A New Source for *The Merchant of Venice*," *Shakespeare Quarterly* 36 (1985): 64–65.

37. In 1598, the play was entered in the Stationers' Register as *The Marchaunt of Venyce or otherwise called the Jewe of Venyce*, although all surviving quartos use the former title alone. The entry in the Register suggests that the public linked it to Marlowe's play and that the official at the Stationers' Register wished the connection to be acknowledged; but that it was not the title Shakespeare himself chose.

Notes to Pages 36–45 223

38. Paul De Man, *Allegories of Reading* (New Haven: Yale University Press, 1979), 11–12.
39. Jacques Derrida, "Before the Law," trans. A. Runnell and C. Roulston, in *Acts of Literature*, ed. Derek Attridge (New York: Routledge, 1992), 187.

NOTES TO CHAPTER 2, "HAMLET AND THE STOIC"

1. T. S. Eliot, "Hamlet," in *Selected Essays* (London: Faber, 1934), 141–44.
2. Harley Granville-Barker, "From Henry V to Hamlet," reprinted in *Studies in Shakespeare*, ed. Peter Alexander (Oxford: Oxford University Press, 1964), 85.
3. James L. Calderwood, *To Be or Not to Be: Negation and Metadrama in "Hamlet"* (New York: Columbia University Press, 1983), xv.
4. J. Dover Wilson, *What Happens in "Hamlet"* (Cambridge: Cambridge University Press, 1960), 30–34; Francis Fergusson, *The Idea of a Theater* (Princeton, N.J.: Princeton University Press, 1949); Ernest Jones, *Hamlet and Oedipus* (New York: Methuen, 1949); Jacques Lacan, "Desire and Interpretation of Desire," in *Literature and Psychoanalysis*, ed. Shoshana Feldman (Baltimore: Johns Hopkins University Press, 1982); and Janet Adelman, *Suffocating Mothers: Fantasies of Maternal Origin in Shakespeare's Plays* (New York: Routledge, 1992). See also K. R. Eissler, *Discourse on Hamlet and "Hamlet"* (New York: International Universities Press, 1971), and Avi Ehrlich, *Hamlet's Absent Father* (Princeton, N.J.: Princeton University Press, 1977).
5. A. C. Bradley, *Shakespearean Tragedy* (New York: Meridian Books, 1955), 101–02; G. Wilson Knight, *The Wheel of Fire: Interpretations of Shakespearean Tragedy* (New York: Meridian Books, 1957), 28.
6. J. Dover Wilson, *What Happens in Hamlet* (Cambridge: Cambridge University Press, 1936), xlviii.
7. Jan Kott, *Shakespeare, Our Contemporary*, trans. B. Taborski (London: Methuen, 1964), 49–53.
8. T. S. Eliot's "Shakespeare and the Stoicism of Seneca," in *Selected Essays*, is a very general discussion of the possible influences of Machiavelli, Montaigne, and Seneca on the dramatist and makes none of the points suggested in this essay.
9. Epictetus, *Golden Sayings*, vol. 44 in Harvard Classics (New York: Collier, 1909–14), 2:2.
10. Seneca, *On Providence*, 6.4–7, in *Seneca*, trans. John W. Basore, Loeb Classical Library (London: Heinemann, 1928).

11. See, for example, J. H. F. Sandbach, *The Stoics* (Bristol: Bristol Press, 1989), 82–83.

12. J. M. Rist, *Stoic Philosophy* (Cambridge: Cambridge University Press, 1969), 256–58, discusses the "mistiness" on this point in the writings of such early Stoics.

13. Seneca, *Epistle* 54, in the Loeb edition, 363.

14. Cicero, *De finibus bonorum et malorum*, trans. H. Rackam (London: W. Heinemann, 1951), 3.18.60.

15. Seneca, *Letter 70*, trans. Moses Hadas, in his *The Stoic Philosophy of Seneca* (Garden City, N.J.: Doubleday, 1958).

16. Seneca, *De Ira*, 3.15.3–4.

17. The quotation is from the translation by A. J. Church and W. J. Brodribb (London, 1864), 16:64. On the impact of Savile's translation, see James Shapiro, *1599: A Year in the Life of William Shakespeare* (London: Faber, 2005), 140, and the relevant bibliographical note.

18. Gordon Braden, *Renaissance Tragedy and the Senecan Tradition* (New Haven: Yale University Press, 1985), 63–114. He mentions suicide briefly on 23–24 and 228, but never as an influence on Renaissance concepts. That does not hold true for Gilles D. Monsarrat, *Light from the Porch: Stoicism and English Renaissance Literature* (Paris: Didier-Erudition, 1984), but his discussion of *Hamlet* (136–39) focuses upon the latter's conception of destiny, the only mention of suicide there being in connection with Horatio's frustrated attempt at the conclusion of the play. See also J. A. Cunliffe, *The Influence of Seneca on Elizabethan Tragedy* (New York: G. E. Stechert, 1925), 80, and *Notes & Queries* 226 (1981): 129.

19. Hiram Haydn, *The Counter-Renaissance* (New York: Grove Press, 1960), 628.

20. Seneca, *Epistle 70*. See also E. A. J. Honigmann and D. A. West, "With a Bare Bodkin," *Notes & Queries* 226 (1981): 129, which traces the use of that term.

21. Eleanor Prosser, *Hamlet and Revenge* (Stanford, Calif.: Stanford University Press, 1967), 91, dismisses the importance of Macduff's speech on the grounds that it contradicts his earlier declaration that he aims to kill Macbeth in order to liberate Scotland. But that earlier instance occurred before Macduff knew of the murder of his wife and children. His aim in the final scene is indeed to avenge the latter crime.

22. Thomas Aquinas, *De Regimine Principium*, in *St. Thomas Aquinas: Political Writings*, ed. and trans. R. W. Dyson (Cambridge: Cambridge University Press, 2002), 48.

23. See also Geoffrey Aggeler, *Nobler in the Mind: The Stoic-*

Skeptic Dialectic in English Renaissance Tragedy (Newark: University of Delaware Press, 1998), 145, 159. Monsarrat, *Light from the Porch*, refers only to the Stoicism of Horatio, never noting the centrality of the creed in this speech, while Peter Mercer, *Hamlet and the Acting of Revenge* (Basingstoke: Macmillan, 1987), 201–02, focuses primarily on the Senecan and Stoic aspects of the play, confessing that he is puzzled at the reference in this speech and concluding that Hamlet "is not really thinking logically."

24. Ben Jonson owned a heavily annotated a copy of the 1623 edition of Lipsius's *Politica*, as noted in Robert C. Evans, *Jonson, Lipsius, and the Politics of Renaissance Stoicism* (Durango, Colo.: Longwood Academic Press, 1992).

25. See Justus Lipsius, *Manuductio* (Antwerp, 1604), 3.22–23. Details of Lipsius's influence can be found in Mark Morford, *Stoics and Neostoics* (Princeton, N.J.: Princeton University Press, 1991), esp. 168–72.

26. John Dolman's translation of Cicero's *Tusculean Disputations* (London, 1561).

27. Robert N. Watson, *The Rest Is Silence: Death as Annihilation in the English Renaissance* (Berkeley and Los Angeles: University of California Press, 1994), 10, which includes a chapter on *Hamlet* that focuses not on suicide but on the concept of revenge as a means of "resurrecting" the dead. See also James L. Calderwood, *Shakespeare and the Denial of Death* (Amherst: University of Massachusetts Press, 1987).

28. Michael Dalton, *The Country Justice* (London, 1626), 254.

29. Michael MacDonald and Terence R. Murphy, *Sleepless Souls: Suicide in Early Modern England* (Oxford: Oxford University Press, 1990), 1; Georges Minois, *History of Suicide: Voluntary Death in Western Culture*, trans. Lydia G. Cochrane (Baltimore: Johns Hopkins University Press, 1995).

30. John Donne, *Biathanatos* (London, 1644), 18, 200, 216.

31. Augustine, *The City of God*, ed. Vernon J. Bourke (New York: Doubleday, 1958), 1.xv–xxvi. Roland M. Frye, *Shakespeare and Christian Doctrine* (Princeton, N.J.: Princeton University Press, 1963), 25, cites the relevant sources for the Elizabethan condemnation of suicide.

32. Michel de Montaigne, "A Custom of the Isle of Cea," and "Of Cruelty," in *The Essaies*, trans. John Florio (London, 1904).

33. Sir Thomas Browne, *Religio Medici*, in *Major Works*, ed. C. A. Patrides (Harmondsworth: Penguin Books, 1977), 115.

34. Anthony Stafford, *Niobe Dissolv'd into a Nilus* (London, 1611) 94–95.

35. Roland M. Frye, *The Renaissance Hamlet: Issues and Responses in 1600* (Princeton, N.J.: Princeton University Press, 1984), 150, 297–309.

36. Stephen J. Greenblatt, *Hamlet in Purgatory* (Princeton, N.J.: Princeton University Press, 2001), 313.

37. The term "conscience" was often used in the Elizabethan era in the sense of "consciousness" or knowledge, as the entry in *OED* confirms.

38. Gertrude has been defined in feminist terms as a victim unfairly castigated for her "blatant sexuality." See Jacqueline Rose, "Sexuality in the Reading of Shakespeare," in *Alternative Shakespeares*, ed. John Drakakis (London: Methuen, 1986), 95.

39. Knight, *The Wheel of Fire*, esp. 23.

40. Donne, *Sermons*, ed. E. M. Simpson and G. R. Potter (Berkeley and Los Angeles: University of California Press, 1962–), 10:239–40.

41. Ernest Jones, *Hamlet and Oedipus* (New York: Doubleday, 1949), 128.

42. Quoted in G. I. Duthie, *The "Bad" Quarto of Hamlet* (Cambridge: Cambridge University Press, 1969), 78.

43. For a brilliant discussion of the scene in terms of Bakhtin's theory of carnivalesque, see Michael D. Bristol, *Carnival and Theatre: Plebeian Culture and the Structure of Authority in Renaissance England* (New York: Methuen, 1985).

44. Donne, *Sermons*, 4:53.

45. Knight, *The Wheel of Fire*, 38.

46. Stephen Greenblatt, *Sir Walter Ralegh: The Renaissance Man and His Roles* (New Haven: Yale University Press, 1973), 7.

47. Harry Levin, *The Question of Hamlet* (New York: Compass Books, 1961), 111.

48. Bradley, *Shakespearean Tragedy*, 101.

49. Marjorie Garber, *Shakespeare's Ghost Writers: Literature as Uncanny Causality* (London: Methuen, 1986), referring to Paul De Man, "Sign and Symbol in Hegel's *Aesthetics*," in *Critical Inquiry* 8 (1982): 761, and Jacques Derrida, *Mémoires for Paul De Man* (New York: Columbia University Press, 1986), 56.

50. On the nature of the apparition, see Arthur F. Kinney's editorial introduction to *Hamlet: New Critical Essays* (New York: Routledge, 2002), 15. For earlier accounts, see Wilson, *What Happens in "Hamlet,"* 52–86; Roy Battenhouse, "The Ghost in Hamlet: A Catholic 'Linchpin'?" *Studies in Philology* 68 (1951): 161–62; Miriam Joseph, "Discerning the Ghost in *Hamlet*," *PMLA* 76 (1961): 302; Robert F. Fleissner, "Subjectivity as an Occupational Hazard of 'Hamlet Ghost' Critics," *Hamlet Studies* 1

(1979): 23–33; and Reuben Sanchez, "Thou Com'st in Such a Questionable Shape," *Hamlet Studies* 18 (1996): 65. Calderwood, *To Be or Not to Be*, 206, takes a similar view of Hamlet's initial conviction of the Ghost's actuality, and his fastening upon the possibility of its being a devil as an excuse for postponing action.

51. Geoffrey Hartman, "The Interpreter's Freud," reprinted in *Easy Pieces* (New York: Columbia University Press, 1985).

52. Samuel Johnson, *Preface to Shakespeare* (London, 1765).

53. Virginia Woolf, *Moments of Being: Unpublished Autobiographical Writings*, ed. Jeanne Schulkind (London: Hogarth, 1985), 108, and I. A. Richards, *The Philosophy of Rhetoric* (New York: Oxford University Press, 1936), 40. I discuss Lawrence's debt to Freud in *The Search for Selfhood in Modern Literature* (Basingstoke: Palgrave, 2002).

NOTES TO CHAPTER 3, "SPENSER AND THE PAGAN GODS"

1. From the introduction to Spenser's *Poetical Works*, ed. J. C. Smith and E. de Selincourt (Oxford: Oxford University Press, 1975), lvi. All quotations are from this edition.

2. Ibid., 470.

3. Angus Fletcher, *The Prophetic Moment: An Essay on Spenser* (Chicago: University of Chicago Press, 1971), 70.

4. Quoted without source by J. Isaacs, "The Sixteenth-Century English Versions," in *The Bible in Its Ancient and English Versions*, ed. H. Wheeler Robinson (Oxford: Clarendon Press, 1940), 176.

5. See Grace Landrum, "Spenser's Use of the Bible and His Alleged Puritanism," *PMLA* 41 (1926), which includes as her assumption that Spenser's mention of the "Cedar proud and tall" is based on "Thus saith the Lord: I will take of the highest branch of the high cedar and will crop off the top of its young twigs" (Ezek. 17:22).

6. Ibid., 517, and Naseeb Shaheen, *Biblical References in "The Faerie Queene"* (Memphis: Memphis State University Press, 1978). Carol V. Kaske, *Spenser and Biblical Poetics* (Ithaca, N.Y.: Cornell University Press, 1999), is concerned not with biblical references but with Spenser's indebtedness to the literary forms of the Bible and with identifying the versions he used, while John N. King, *Spenser's Poetry and the Reformation Tradition* (Princeton, N.J.: Princeton University Press, 1990), aims at tracing the poet's indebtedness to such Protestant traditions as the attitude to marriage or the satirical portrayal of monks.

7. Shaheen, *Biblical References in "The Faerie Queene,"* 105.
8. Nicholas of Cusa, *De pace fidei*, sec. 6.
9. For a study of the philosophical relations between Plato and Christianity, especially in the earlier phase, see Elizabeth Bieman, *Plato Baptized* (Toronto: University of Toronto Press, 1988), and for more general aspects of Spenser's use of Plato, Jon A. Quitslund, *Spenser's Supreme Fiction: Platonic Natural Philosophy and "The Faerie Queene* (Toronto: University of Toronto Press, 2001).
10. Boccaccio, *Genealogica of the Pagan Gods*, trans. and ed. C. G. Osgood (Princeton, N.J.: Princeton University Press, 1956), xx.
11. Leonard Barkan, *The Gods Made Flesh: Metamorphosis and the Pursuit of Paganism* (New Haven: Yale University Press, 1986), esp. 202–03 and 222–23.
12. John Donne, *Holy Sonnet X*, "Batter my heart," in *The Divine Poems*, ed. Helen Gardner (Oxford: Clarendon Press, 1952).
13. The same cannot be said of the reference in *FQ* 3.11.30. The narrator there is merely describing a scene depicted on a tapestry hanging in Mulciber's castle, and offers no authorial corroboration.
14. Ms. Pal. Lat. 1726 fol. 43n.
15. From the drinking song beginning, "*Aestuans intrinsecus . . .*," reprinted in *The Oxford Book of Medieval Verse*, ed. Stephen Gaselee (Oxford: Clarendon Press, 1937), 124.
16. See Rashi's comment on Exod. 25:18.
17. Panofsky, *Renaissance and Renascences in Western Art*, 199, notes that *Venus coelestis* is represented here as opposed to *Venus vulgaris*, but he makes no connection with the promulgation of the papal bull concerning the Immaculate Conception. I have offered a fuller discussion of the painting in my *Renaissance Perspectives: In Literature and the Visual Arts* (Princeton: Princeton University Press, 1987), 157–60.
18. Robert Ellrodt, *Neoplatonism in the Poetry of Spenser* (Geneva: Darby Books, 1960), 48, discusses the significance of Venus in the epic. Kathleen Williams, S*penser's Faerie Queene: The World of Glass* (London: Routledge & Kegan Paul, 1966), 100, notes the ambiguous relationship between Spenser's Venus representing Love's consummations and his Diana representing Chastity, that ambiguity rooted in pagan tradition.
19. Harry Berger Jr., *Revisionary Play: Studies in the Spenserian Dynamics* (Berkeley and Los Angeles: University of California Press, 1988), 84.

20. William Empson, *Seven Types of Ambiguity* (London: Meridian Books, 1930), 43.
21. Darryl J. Gless, *Interpretation and Theology in Spenser* (Cambridge: Cambridge University Press, 1994), 3, 136.
22. Sir Thomas More, *English Works* (London, 1557), 1:136.
23. Helen C. White, *English Devotional Literature [Prose], 1600–1640* (Madison: University of Wisconsin Press, 1931), 190.
24. Michael Zell, *Reframing Rembrandt* (Berkeley and Los Angeles: University of California Press, 2002), 166.
25. John Calvin, *Institutes*, trans. Henry Beveridge (London, 1599), sec. 20.
26. Achsah Guibbory, *Ceremony and Community from Herbert to Milton* (Cambridge: Cambridge University Press, 1998), 48–50.
27. William Perkins, *Works* (London, 1612–13), 3:102–03. The phrase is from the Gospels, but the context there is very different: "If ye then, being evil, know how to give good gifts unto your children: how much more shall your heavenly Father give the Holy Spirit to them that ask him?" (Luke 11:13).
28. *State Papers, Domestic* (1635), 111, 122, and 132.
29. The movement, developing during the latter part of the sixteenth century, was formulated in William Ames's influential *Medulla Theologiae* ("The Marrow of Theology") of 1623.
30. Jonathan Mitchell, *Nehemiah on the Wall in Troublesome Times* (Cambridge, 1671), a sermon delivered in 1667. Reprinted in *The Puritans*, ed. P. Miller and T. H. Johnson (Evanston, Ill.: Harper & Row, 1963), 1:237–42.
31. W. W. Greg, *Materialen zur kunde des alteren Englischen Dramas* (Louvain, 1904), vol. 5. The reference to the Egyptians relies on the interpretation that the rebellion was instigated by a rabble of camp followers who had joined the Hebrews on leaving Egypt.
32. The attribution of this play to Udall, now generally accepted, was first suggested by Leicester Bradner, "A Test for Udall's Authorship," *Modern Language Notes* 42 (1927): 278.
33. Lady Cary was drawn to the Roman Catholic Church—a tendency in part responsible for the friction with her husband—but she was, of course, Protestant in background and upbringing.
34. See Ellrodt, *Neoplatonism*, 195.
35. Lilian Winstanley, "Spenser and Puritanism," *Modern Language Quarterly* 3 (1900): 6; F. M. Padelford, "Spenser and the Theology of Calvin," *Modern Philology* 12 (1914): 1; James J. Higginson, *Spenser's "Shepherd's Calendar"* (London: Columbia University Press, 1932); and Virgil Whitaker, *The Religious Basis*

of Spenser's Thought (Stanford: Stanford University Press, 1950). There is also an unpublished thesis at New York University by Thomas P. Nelan, *Catholic Doctrines in Spenser's Poetry* (1943), that argues for an allegiance diametrically opposed to Puritanism.

36. Anthea Hume, *Edmund Spenser: Protestant Poet* (Cambridge: Cambridge University Press, 1984).

37. L. T. Golding, *An Elizabethan Puritan: Arthur Golding* (New York: R. R. Smith, 1937), 194–95.

38. See Raphael Lyne, *Ovid's Changing Worlds: English Metamorphoses, 1567–1632* (Oxford: Oxford University Press, 2001), 62, 66.

39. I am indebted for certain details within this account to Jon Whitman, "The Body and the Struggle for the Soul of Romance: *La Queste del Saint Graal,*" in *The Body and the Soul in Medieval Literature,* ed. Piero Boitani and Anna Torti (Cambridge: Cambridge University Press, 1999), and to his helpful comments on this passage. Elements of the legend differ in the various versions, but the account here follows the main outline.

40. The difficulties in the process of establishing this lineage, of distinguishing ancient Rome from Catholic Rome is discussed in Linda Gregerson, *The Reformation of the Subject: Spenser, Milton, and the English Protestant Epic* (Cambridge: Cambridge University Press, 1995).

41. John Cotton, *The Way of Life* (London, 1641), 104–05, a collection of sermons probably delivered in England.

42. C. K. Zacher, *Curiosity and Pilgrimage: The Literature of Discovery in Fourteenth-Century England* (Baltimore: Johns Hopkins University Press, 1976), examines the emergent sense of exploration in this period.

43. Spenser's use of metamorphosis is discussed in terms of metaphor in Rufus Wood, *Metaphor and Belief in "The Faerie Queene"* (Basingstoke: Macmillan, 1997).

44. *Epistolae obscurorum virorum,* ed. and trans. F. G. Stokes (New Haven: Yale University Press, 1925), 343–44.

45. John Calvin, *A Commentarie on the Whole Epistle to the Hebrewes,* trans. C. Cotton (London, 1605), 200.

46. Luther, *Reply to Esmer,* and William Tyndale, *The Obedience of a Christian Man* (London: W. Hill, 1548).

47. Margaret Ashton, *England's Iconoclasts* (Oxford: Oxford University Press, 1988), 1:270.

48. Lancelot Andrewes, *The Pattern of Catechistical Doctrine,* delivered as a sermon at Pembroke College, Cambridge, during his Puritan phase in the 1580s. It was first printed in 1640 but is reported as having circulated widely before then.

49. Stephen Gosson, *An Apologie for the Schoole of Abuse*, ed. Edward Arber (Birmingham, Ala.: n.p., 1868), 65–68.
50. William Prynne, *Histriomastix* (London, 1633), 28, 79–80.
51. George Sandys, *Ovid's Metamorphosis*, ed. Karl K. Hulley and Stanley T. Vandersall (Lincoln: University of Nebraska Press, 1970), 123–24. D. C. Feeney, *The Gods in Epic: Poets and Critics of the Classical Tradition* (Oxford: Oxford University Press, 1991), devotes his opening chapter to instances of hostility to the tradition, such as Xenophanes's charge that Homer and Hesiod attribute to the gods everything in mankind that is disgraceful, including deceit, theft, and adultery. Feeney, however, is concerned only with epics and critics dating from the classical period, not from the Renaissance.
52. Geoffrey Hartman, preface to *Deconstruction and Criticism* (New York: Seabury Press, 1979), viii.
53. Jacques Derrida, "Living On—Border Lines," in ibid., 84 and 137.

Notes to Chapter 4, "*Volpone*, Comedy or Mordant Satire?"

1. Samuel Pepys, *Diary*, ed. H. B. Wheatley (London: G. Bell, 1928–35), 4:309; Brian Parker's introduction to the new Revels edition of *Volpone* (Manchester: Manchester University Press, 1999), 44; R. B. Parker, "*Volpone* in Performance, 1921–1972," *Renaissance Drama*, n.s. 9 (1978): 147; Ejner J. Jensen, *Ben Jonson's Comedies on the Modern Stage* (Ann Arbor: University of Michigan Press, 1985), 52–78; and *Ben Jonson and Theatre: Performance, Practice, and Theory*, ed. Richard Cave, Elizabeth Schafer, and Brian Woolland (London: Routledge, 1999).
2. Jonas A. Barish, introduction to *Jonson's "Volpone": A Casebook* (Basingstoke: Macmillan Press, 1972).
3. Una Ellis-Fermor, *The Jacobean Drama* (1936; reprint, London: Methuen, 1965), 113–14; Jonas A. Barish, "The Double Plot in *Volpone*," *Modern Philology* 1 (1955): 83; L. A. Beaurline, *Jonson and Elizabethan Comedy* (San Marino, Calif.: Huntington Library, 1978), 170; C. H. Herford and Percy Simpson, eds., *Ben Jonson* (Oxford: Oxford University Press, 1925–50), 2:55; Rainer Pineas, "The Morality Vice in *Volpone*," *Discourses* 5 (1962): 451; Alan C. Dessen, *Jonson's Moral Comedy* (Evanston, Ill.: Northwestern University Press, 1971), 76; John J. Enck, *Jonson and the Comic Truth* (Madison: University of Wisconsin Press, 1966), 114; and Gabriele B. Jackson, *Vision and Judgment*

in *Ben Jonson's Drama* (New Haven: Yale University Press, 1968), 85. See also Harold Bloom, ed., *Ben Jonson's "Volpone": Modern Critical Interpretations* (New York: Chelsea House, 1988), 8.

4. *Sunday Times*, July 20, 1952.

5. William Empson, "Volpone," *Hudson Review* 21 (1968): 651. In a similar vein, Richard Andrews, *Scripts and Scenarios: The Performance of Comedy in Renaissance Italy* (Cambridge: Cambridge University Press, 1993), 214, notes that a large part of Renaissance comedy was based on an unwritten contract, whereby the fictional status of the play entitled audiences to hold their normal ethical criteria in abeyance. Renaissance theorists, straitjacketed by the classical precept that art is imitative of reality, were unable to incorporate that dichotomy into their dramatic formulations; but the playwrights themselves demonstrated constantly that they understood on an instinctive level the separation of the fictive from the actual.

6. Foster Watson, *The English Grammar Schools to 1660* (Cambridge: Cambridge University Press, 1908), 322.

7. Marvin T. Herrick, *Italian Comedy in the Renaissance* (Urbana: University of Illinois Press, 1960), 223–25, discusses the influence of Italian comedy on Elizabethan and Jacobean drama. See also Eleanor P. Lumley, *The Influence of Plautus on the Comedies of Jonson* (New York: Knickerbocker Press, 1901).

8. Jonson, *Timber, or Discoveries*, in Herford and Simpson, *Ben Jonson*, 8:638.

9. Henry Parratt, *Springes for Woodcocks* (1613), cited in Joseph Loewenstein, *Ben Jonson and Possessive Authorship* (Cambridge: Cambridge University Press, 2002), 119n.

10. Daniel C. Boughner, *The Devil's Disciple: Ben Jonson's Debt to Machiavelli* (New York: Philosophical Library, 1968), devotes an entire chapter to *Volpone* but makes none of the points suggested here. Robert Watson, *Ben Jonson's Parodic Strategy* (Cambridge: Harvard University Press, 1987), 87, mentions *La Mandragola* but only to note Volpone's "miscasting" of himself in the role of the lover as part of his general "corruption" and inability to read the characters of people around him.

11. Northrop Frye, *Anatomy of Criticism* (Princeton, N.J.: Princeton University Press, 1971), 163.

12. Quotations are from the edition of *La Mandragola*, trans. Anne and Henry Paolocci (New York: Liberal Arts, 1957).

13. Rocco Coronato, *Jonson versus Bakhtin* (Amsterdam: Rodopi, 2003), is concerned with Bakhtin's theory of the carnivalesque, not his dialogic theory.

14. All *Volpone* quotations are from the Herford and Simpson edition of *Ben Jonson*, vol. 5, unless otherwise noted. David Bevington, "Why Re-edit Herford and Simpson," in *Re-presenting Ben Jonson*, ed. Martin Butler (Basingstoke: Macmillan Press, 1999), 20–30, presents a strong case for producing a modernized text, but meanwhile this remains the most reliable version.

15. W. Daniel Kay, *Ben Jonson: A Literary Life* (Basingstoke: Macmillan Press, 1995), 91; Helena W. Baum, *The Satire and the Didactic in Ben Jonson's Comedy* (Chapel Hill: University of North Carolina Press, 1947), 98.

16. F. S. Boas, *An Introduction to Stuart Drama* (London: Oxford University Press, 1946), 108; and Beaurline, *Jonson and Elizabethan Comedy*, 179.

17. Christopher Marlowe, *Works*, ed. Fredson Bowers (Cambridge: Cambridge University Press, 1973), 1:88.

18. Douglas Duncan, *Ben Jonson and the Lucianic Tradition* (Cambridge: Cambridge University Press, 1979), 148; S. L. Goldberg, "Folly into Crime: The Catastrophe of *Volpone*," *Modern Language Quarterly* 20 (1959): 223; and Robert E. Knoll, *Ben Jonson's Plays* (Lincoln: University of Nebraska Press, 1964), 104. See also Alexander Leggatt, *Ben Jonson: His Vision and His Art* (London: Methuen, 1981), 24.

19. The entry in *OED* also cites the Coverdale Bible's reference to the "connynge craftesmen" who built the Temple.

20. Richard Ehrenberg, *Capital and Finance in the Age of the Renaissance* (New York: Harcourt Brace, 1928), 333.

21. Alvin Kernan, *The Plot of Satire* (New Haven: Yale University Press, 1965), 123.

22. See L. C. Knights, *Drama and Society in the Age of Jonson* (London: Chatto and Windus, 1937), and Don E. Wayne's alternative view in *Renaissance Drama*, n.s. 13 (1982): 103. Jonathan Haynes, *The Social Relations of Jonson's Theater* (Cambridge: Cambridge University Press, 1992), provides a lively study of the dramatist's response to the economic and social changes of his time, but disappointingly makes almost no mention of *Volpone*.

23. Donne, *The Relique*, 12–18, in Gardner, *Elegies*, 89.

24. Barish, "The Double Plot in *Volpone*," 84.

25. D. A. Scheve, "Jonson's *Volpone* and Traditional Fox Lore," *Review of English Studies*, n.s. 1 (1950): 242. See also R. B. Parker, "*Volpone* and Reynard the Fox," *Renaissance Drama*, n.s. 7 (1976): 3.

26. Stephen Greenblatt, "The False Ending in *Volpone*," *Journal of English and Germanic Philology* 75 (1976): 90.

27. J. C. Trewin, *Birmingham Post*, December 5, 1962.
28. For details, I am indebted to Parker, "*Volpone* and Reynard the Fox."
29. David Riggs, *Ben Jonson: A Life* (Cambridge: Harvard University Press, 1987), 137.
30. George A. E. Parfitt, "Ethics and Christianity in Ben Jonson," *New Perspectives on Ben Jonson*, ed. James E. Hirsh (London: Fairleigh Dickinson Press, 1997), 77–89.
31. Jonson, *Poems*, ed. Ian Donaldson (London: Oxford University Press, 1975), 197.
32. Herford and Simpson, *Ben Jonson*, 8:595
33. Deborah Burks, "I'll Want my Will Else," *Journal of English Literary History* 62 (1995): 759.
34. Kathleen McLuskie, *Renaissance Dramatists* (New York: Harvester Press, 1989), 175. Although Karen Newman, *Fashioning Femininity and English Renaissance Drama* (Chicago: University of Chicago Press, 1991), does not deal directly with *Volpone*, she examines the attitude toward women, often as sex objects, in this period. For a gender reading of this scene, see Grace Tiffany, *Erotic Beasts and Social Monsters: Shakespeare, Jonson, and Comic Androgyny* (Newark: University of Delaware Press, 1995), 108–09.
35. *Hali Maidenhead*, ed. F. J. Furnivall (New York: Greenwood Press, 1969), 63. There is a full account in Karen Bamford, *Sexual Violence on the Jacobean Stage* (New York: St. Martin's Press, 2000), 25–28.
36. F. S. Boas, *Shakespeare at the Universities* (Oxford: Oxford University Press, 1923), 261. For Jonson's personal connections with the two chancellors, see Richard Dutton, "The Lone Wolf: Jonson's Epistle to *Volpone*," in *Refashioning Ben Jonson*, ed. Julie Sanders, Kate Chedgzoy, and Susan Wiseman (New York: St. Martin's Press, 1998), 122.
37. Only John Marston had preceded him in the practice, and then only in embryonic fashion. Marston's *Antonio and Mellida* of 1602 was ironically dedicated to "Nobody" and his later *Malcontent* of 1604 to Jonson himself. See Loewenstein, *Ben Jonson and Possessive Authorship*, 164n.
38. E. N. S. Thompson, *The Controversy between the Puritans and the Stage* (New York: Henry Holt, 1908), 100; Thomas Nashe, *Pierce Pennilesse*, in his *Works*, ed. Ronald B. McKerrow (London, 1883–84), 2:92; and John Selden, *Works*, ed. David Wilkins (London, 1726) 2:1690.
39. *The History of the University of Oxford* (Oxford: Oxford University Press, 1997), 4:180.

40. Edward Partridge, *The Broken Compass* (New York: Columbia University Press, 1958), 70; Northrop Frye, *Anatomy of Criticism* (Princeton, N.J.: Princeton University Press, 1971), 165.
41. Robert Watson, *Ben Jonson's Parodic Strategy* (Cambridge, Mass.: Harvard University Press, 1987), 83, terms Celia's return to her husband an instance of "genre displacement."
42. Brian Parker, in his introduction to the Revels edition of *Volpone*, notes the audience's pleasure in the Fox's final appearance.

NOTES TO CHAPTER 5, "DONNE AND THE MEDITATIVE TRADITION"

1. Louis L. Martz, *The Poetry of Meditation* (New Haven: Yale University Press, 1962), 4.
2. *The English Poems of George Herbert*, ed. C. A. Patrides (London: J. M. Dent, 1974), 179.
3. Martz, *The Poetry of Meditation*, 6–13. Barbara K. Lewalski's argument was presented first in *Donne's "Anniversaries" and the Poetry of Praise: The Creation of a Symbolic Mode* (Princeton, N.J.: Princeton University Press, 1973), and then more fully in *Protestant Poetics and the Seventeenth-Century Religious Lyric* (Princeton, N.J.: Princeton University Press, 1979).
4. Saint John of the Cross quoted from R. V. Young, *Doctrine and Devotion in Seventeenth-Century Poetry* (Suffolk: Boydell and Brewer, 2000), 5. For an examination of the genre in its broadest form, see David H. Radcliffe, *Forms of Reflection: Genre and Culture in Meditational Writing* (Baltimore: Johns Hopkins University Press, 1993). See also Jeffrey Johnson, *The Theology of John Donne* (Cambridge: D. S. Brewer, 1999).
5. *Holy Sonnet III*. Quotations from Donne's poems are from *The Elegies and the Songs and Sonnets* (Oxford: Clarendon Press, 1966); and *The Divine Poems* (Oxford: Clarendon Press, 1978)—both edited by Helen Gardner—and from *The Satires, Epigrams, and Verse Letters* (Oxford: Clarendon Press, 1967).
6. John Stachniewski, "John Donne: The Despair of the Holy Sonnets," *Journal of English Literary History* 48 (1981): 690.
7. Frank L. Huntley, *Bishop J. Hall and Protestant Meditation in Seventeenth-Century England* (Binghamton, N.Y.: Center for Medieval and Early Renaissance Studies, 1981), 4–5.
8. G. R. Potter and Evelyn Simpson, eds., *The Sermons of John Donne* (Berkeley and Los Angeles: University of California Press,

1953–62), 9:201; hereafter cited as *Sermons* by volume and page number.

9. Young, *Doctrine and Devotion*, 5, 99. For an examination of the genre in its broadest form, see Radcliffe, *Forms of Reflection*.

10. In *John Donne and the Protestant Reformation: New Perspectives*, ed. Mary A. Papazian (Detroit: Wayne State University Press, 2003).

11. See Paul R. Sellin, *John Donne and the "Calvinist" Views of Grace* (Amsterdam: VU Boekhandel, 1983), 1.

12. Jeanne Shami, *John Donne and Conformity in Crisis in the Late Jacobean Pulpit* (Cambridge: D. S. Brewer, 2003).

13. See George Klawitter, "John Donne's Attitude toward the Virgin Mary," in *John Donne's Religious Imagination*, ed. R. J. Frontain and F. M. Malpezzi (Conway: University of Central Arkansas Press, 1995), 122.

14. See William R. Mueller, *John Donne, Preacher* (Princeton, N.J.: Princeton University Press, 1962), 152.

15. Gardner, *The Divine Poems*, liv; N. J. C. Andreasen, "Donne's *Devotions* and the Psychology of Assent," *Modern Philology* 62 (1965): 207; Thomas F. Van Laan, "John Donne's *Devotions* and the Jesuit Spiritual Exercise," *Studies in Philology* 60 (1963): 191; and Kate G. Frost, *Holy Delight: Typology, Numerology, and Autobiography in Donne's "Devotions Upon Emergent Occasions"* (Princeton, N.J.: Princeton University Press, 1990), esp. 14 and 32.

16. John Carey, *John Donne: Life, Mind, and Art* (New York: Oxford University Press, 1980), 30. P. M. Oliver, *Donne's Religious Writing: A Discourse of Feigned Devotion* (London: Longman, 1997), takes a similar approach, deducing from the inclusion in Donne's legacies of pictures of saints and of a medal commemorating the Council of Dort that his conversion was never complete.

17. Annabel Patterson, "Misinterpretable Donne: The Testimony of the Letters," *John Donne Journal* 1 (1982): 40; and Dennis Flynn, *John Donne and the Ancient Catholic Nobility* (Bloomington: Indiana University Press, 1995).

18. Preface to John Donne, *Pseudo-Martyr*, ed. Anthony Raspa (Montreal: McGill University Press, 1993), 13.

19. Charles H. George and Katherine George, *The Protestant Mind of the English Reformation, 1570–1640* (Princeton, N.J.: Princeton University Press, 1961), 69.

20. *Ignatius His Conclave*, ed. T. S. Healy (Oxford: Clarendon Press, 1969), 11–13.

21. Luther, *Answer to Goat Emser*, in *Martin Luther's Basic*

Theological Writings, ed. T. F. Lull and W. R. Russell (Minneapolis: Fortress, 2005), 3:10.

22. Donne's *Devotions*, "Expostulation XIX," in Donne's *Devotions on Emergent Occasions*, ed. Anthony Raspa (Oxford: Oxford University Press, 1987), 99. On Donne's sense of the figurative nature of the biblical text, see John R. Knott Jr., *The Sword of the Spirit: Puritan Responses to the Bible* (Chicago: Chicago University Press, 1980), 52.

23. *Sermons* 10:238.

24. Described in Samuel Clarke, *Lives of Thirty-Two English Divines* (London, 1677), 144.

25. Richard Sibbes, *The Spiritual Jubilee*; available at http://www.puritansermons.com/sermons/sibbes5.htm, p. 9.

26. See A. C. Southern, *Elizabethan Recusant Prose, 1559–1582* (London: Sands, 1950); and Helen C. White, *English Devotional Literature, 1600–1640* (Madison: University of Wisconsin Press, 1931).

27. Saint Ignatius Loyola, *The Spiritual Exercises*, trans. A. Mottola (New York: Doubleday, 1964), 132.

28. Donne, *Pseudo-Martyr*, 13.

29. William Perkins, *Workes* (London, 1612–13), 3:102–03.

30. From a letter by Guilio Clovio, quoted in Peter and Linda Murray, *A Dictionary of Art and Artists* (Baltimore: Johns Hopkins University Press, 1963), 139–40.

31. *A short and pretie Treatise touching the perpetuall Reioyce of the godly, euen in this lyfe* (London, 1568), sig. Ca.

32. Richard Rogers, *Seaven Treatises* (London, 1604), 247, and Richard Baxter, *The Saints' Everlasting Rest* (Philadelphia 1914), 291, referring to Genesis 24:63. See also Joseph Hall, *Art of Meditation*, in *Bishop Joseph Hall and Protestant Meditation in Seventeenth-Century England*, ed. Frank L. Huntley (New York, 1981), ix, which includes an edition of the text. For access to most of the manuals, I am indebted to the microfilmed versions in the Early English Text series, graciously made available to me by the library of the University of Virginia.

33. *The Collected Works of St. John of the Cross*, trans. Kieran Kavanaugh and Otilio Rodriguez (Washington, D.C.: ICS Publications, 1964), 295.

34. Teresa of Avila, *Vida*, book 11, section 13.

35. The quotation from Luis de Granada is from the translation by Richard Hopkins (Douai, 1612), 203. See also Thomas B. Kempis, *Imitatio Christi*, chap. 23. The quotation from Puente is from *Meditations on the Mysteries of our Holie Faith*, trans. John Heigham (St. Omer, 1619), 1:77.

36. Sir Thomas Browne, *Religio Medici*, in *Major Works*, ed. C. A. Patrides (Harmondsworth: Penguin Books, 1977), 78–79.
37. Joseph Hall, *Works*, 6:204; Baxter, *Saints' Everlasting Rest*, 135.
38. Herbert, "The Flower," in Patrides, *The English Poems of George Herbert*, 171.
39. Marvell, "On a Drop of Dew," 33–36, in *Poems*, ed. Hugh MacDonald (London: Routledge & Kegan Paul, 1956), 6.
40. Delivered at the funeral of Sir William Cokayne, 1626, in *Sermons* 7:264–65.
41. *Meditation IV*.
42. *Holy Sonnet X*, 7–8.
43. *Satire III*, 79–82, in *Satires, Epigrams and Verse: Letters of John Donne*, ed. W. Milgate (Oxford: Clarendon, 1967), 13.
44. M. A. Symson, *Heptameron, the Seven Dayes: that is, Meditations and Prayers Upon the Worke of the Lord's Creation* (St. Andrews, 1621), 20.
45. John Donne, *Works*, ed. Henry Alford (London: J. W. Parker, 1839), 2:265
46. Sermon delivered at Hanworth, 1622, in *Sermons* 4:171.
47. James Ussher, *Eighteen Sermons Preached in Oxford* (London 1659), 34.
48. Roland H. Bainton, *Here I Stand: A Life of Martin Luther* (New York: New American Library, 1959), 49–50.
49. Arthur Dent, *The Plaine Man's Pathway to Heaven* (London, 1601), 261.
50. Thomas Morton, *A Treatise of the Threefolde State of Man* (London, 1596), 266–67; Perkins, *Workes*.
51. *Calvin's New Testament Commentaries*, trans. T. H. L. Parker (London: SCM Press, 1959), 162.
52. John Conway, *Meditations and Praiers . . . Wherein are added comfortable Consolations* (London, 1570?), sigs. T1–T2.
53. Rogers, *Seaven Treatises*, 44.
54. Joseph Hall, *The Soul's Farewell to Earth* (London, 1651), 359.
55. Baxter, *Saints' Everlasting Rest*, 5.
56. Loyola, *The Spiritual Exercises*, 61.
57. François de Sales, *Introduction to the Devout Life*, trans. Michael Day (London: J. M. Dent, 1961), 33–35.
58. *A History of the Conferences*, ed. E. Cardwell (Oxford: Oxford University Press, 1840), 181.
59. Dent, *The Plaine Man's Pathway*, 85.
60. Richard Sibbes, *The Soules Conflict* (London, 1635), 258.
61. Symson, "Meditation of Death," in *Heptameron*, 197.
62. John Donne, *Hymne to God my God*, 24–27, in Gardner, *The Divine Poems*.

63. Henry Bull, *Christian Prayers and Meditations*, in the Parker Society reprint (Cambridge: Cambridge University Press, 1842), 60, 76.
64. Loyola, *The Spiritual Exercises*, 36.
65. See Terence C. Cave, *Devotional Poetry in France, 1570–1613* (Cambridge: Cambridge University Press, 1969), 22.
66. Gardner, *Divine Poems*, 31.
67. Brent Nelson, "*Pathopoeia* and the Protestant Form of Donne's *Devotions*," in Papazian, *John Donne and the Protestant Reformation*, 248. See also Andreasen, "Donne's *Devotions*, 207.
68. See Lewalski, Donne's "*Anniversaries*," 94.
69. Joseph Hall, *Upon the Tolling of a Passing-bell*, in *Works*, ed. Josiah Pratt (London: Wittingham, 1808), 6:173.
70. Huntley, *Bishop Joseph Hall*, 9.
71. Lancelot Andrewes, *Works*, ed. J. H. Parker (New York: AMS Press, 1967), 5:393.
72. Mario Praz, *The Flaming Heart* (New York: Norton Library, 1973), 205–07.
73. Donne, *Devotions*, 86.
74. Jacques Derrida, *Aporias*, trans. Thomas Dutoit (Stanford: Stanford University Press, 1993), 12, 22.
75. J. Hillis Miller, "The Critic as Host," *Deconstruction and Criticism* (New York: Seabury Press, 1979).

Notes to Epilogue

1. *Midrash and Literature*, ed. Geoffrey H. Hartman and Sanford Budick (New Haven: Yale University Press, 1956).
2. Susan Handelman, "Freud's Midrash: The Exile of Interpretation," in *Intertextuality: New Perspectives in Criticism*, ed. Jeanine P. Plottel and Hanna Charney (New York: New York Literary Forum, 1978), 102. See also Daniel Boyarin, *Intertextuality and the Reading of Midrash* (Indianapolis: Indiana University Press, 1994).
3. Max Kadushin quoted in Harold Fisch, "The Hermeneutic Quest," in Hartman and Budick, *Midrash and Literature*, 251.
4. Maimonides, *Guide for the Perplexed*, trans. M. Friedländer (London: Routledge, 1942), 354.
5. Barry Geween, "State of the Art," *New York Times Book Review*, December 11, 2005.
6. J. Hillis Miller, "The Critic as Host," *Deconstruction and Criticism* (New York: Seabury Press, 1979).
7. Simon Glendenning, ed., *Arguing with Derrida* (Oxford: Blackwell, 2001).

Selected Bibliography

Adelman, Janet. *Suffocating Mothers: Fantasies of Maternal Origin in Shakespeare's Plays.* New York: Routledge, 1992.

Aggeler, Geoffrey. *Nobler in the Mind: The Stoic-Skeptic Dialectic in English Renaissance Tragedy.* Newark: University of Delaware Press, 1998.

Anderson, Douglas. "The Old Testament Presence in *The Merchant of Venice.*" *Journal of English Literary History* 52 (1989): 119.

Andreasen, N. J. C. "Donne's *Devotions* and the Psychology of Assent." *Modern Philology* 62 (1965): 207.

Andrews, Richard. *Scripts and Scenarios: The Performance of Comedy in Renaissance Italy.* Cambridge: Cambridge University Press, 1993.

Ashton, Margaret. *England's Iconoclasts.* Oxford: Clarendon Press, 1988.

Bakhtin, M. M. *The Dialogic Imagination.* Edited by Michael Holquist. Austin: University of Texas Press, 1981.

Bamford, Karen. *Sexual Violence on the Jacobean Stage.* New York: St. Martin's Press, 2000.

Barish, Jonas A. "The Double Plot in *Volpone.*" *Modern Philology* 1 (1955): 83.

———. *Jonson's "Volpone": A Casebook.* Basingstoke: Macmillan Press, 1972.

Barkan, Leonard. *The Gods Made Flesh: Metamorphosis and the Pursuit of Paganism.* New Haven: Yale University Press, 1986.

Barthes, Roland. *Image—Music—Text.* Edited and translated by Stephen Heath. New York: Hill & Wang, 1977.

———. *S/Z.* Translated by Richard Miller. New York: Hill & Wang, 1975.

Baum, Helena W. *The Satire and the Didactic in Ben Jonson's Comedy.* Chapel Hill: University of North Carolina Press, 1947.
Beaurline, L. A. *Jonson and Elizabethan Comedy.* San Marino, Calif.: Huntington Library, 1978.
Berger, Harry, Jr. *Revisionary Play: Studies in the Spenserian Dynamics.* Berkeley and Los Angeles: University of California Press, 1988.
Bloom, Harold, ed. *Ben Jonson's "Volpone": Modern Critical Interpretations.* New York: Chelsea House Publishers, 1988.
———. *"The Merchant of Venice": Modern Critical Interpretations.* New York: Chelsea House, 1986.
Bloom, Harold, et al. *Deconstruction and Criticism.* New York: Seabury Press, 1979.
Boughner, Daniel C. *The Devil's Disciple: Ben Jonson's Debt to Machiavelli.* New York: Philosophical Library, 1968.
Boyarin, Daniel. *Intertextuality and the Reading of Midrash.* Indianapolis: Indiana University Press, 1994.
Braden, Gordon. *Renaissance Tragedy and the Senecan Tradition.* New Haven: Yale University Press, 1985.
Bradley, A. C. *Shakespearean Tragedy.* New York: Meridian Books, 1955.
Bristol, Michael D. *Carnival and Theater: Plebeian Culture and the Structure of Authority in Renaissance England.* New York: Methuen, 1985.
Bush, Douglas. *Mythology and the Renaissance Tradition in English Poetry.* New York: Pageant Book Company, 1957.
Butler, Martin, ed. *Re-presenting Ben Jonson.* Basingstoke: Macmillan Press, 1999.
Calderwood, James L. *Shakespeare and the Denial of Death.* Amherst: University of Massachusetts Press, 1987.
———. *To Be or Not to Be: Negation and Metadrama in "Hamlet."* New York: Columbia University Press, 1983.
Carey, John. *John Donne: Life, Mind, and Art.* New York: Oxford University Press, 1980.
Cave, Richard, et al., eds. *Ben Jonson and Theatre: Performance, Practice, and Theory.* London: Routledge, 1999.
Coghill, Nevill. "The Governing Idea." *Shakespeare Quarterly* 1 (1948): 9.
Cohen, D. M. "The Jew and Shylock." *Shakespeare Quarterly* 31 (1980): 53.
Colley, John S. "Launcelot, Jacob, and Esau: Old and New Law in *The Merchant of Venice.*" *Yearbook of English Studies* 10 (1980): 181.
Cunliffe, J. A. *The Influence of Seneca on Elizabethan Tragedy.* New York: G. E. Stechert, 1925.
Danson, Lawrence. *The Harmonies of "The Merchant of Venice."* New Haven: Yale University Press, 1978.

Selected Bibliography 243

De Man, Paul. *Allegories of Reading.* New Haven: Yale University Press, 1979.
———. *Blindness and Insight.* Minneapolis: University of Minnesota Press, 1983.
Derrida, Jacques. *Aporias.* Translated by Thomas Dutoit. Stanford, Calif.: Stanford University Press, 1993.
———. "Before the Law." Translated by A. Runnell and C. Roulston. In *Acts of Literature,* ed. Derek Attridge. New York: Routledge, 1992.
———. *Writing and Difference.* Translated by Alan Bass. Chicago: University of Chicago Press, 1978.
Dessen, Alan C. *Jonson's Moral Comedy.* Evanston, Ill.: Northwestern University Press, 1971.
Drakakis, John, ed. *Alternative Shakespeares.* London: Methuen, 1986.
Duncan, Douglas. *Ben Jonson and the Lucianic Tradition.* Cambridge: Cambridge University Press, 1979.
Eddins, Dwight, ed. *The Emperor Redressed: Critiquing Critical Theory.* Tuscaloosa: University of Alabama Press, 1995.
Ehrlich, Avi. *Hamlet's Absent Father.* Princeton, N.J.: Princeton University Press, 1977.
Eissler, K. R. *Discourse on Hamlet and "Hamlet."* New York: International Universities Press, 1971.
Ellis-Fermor, Una. *The Jacobean Drama.* London: Methuen, 1965.
Ellrodt, Robert. *Neoplatonism in the Poetry of Spenser.* Geneva: Darby Books, 1960.
Empson, William. *Seven Types of Ambiguity.* London: Meridian Books, 1930.
———. "Volpone." *Hudson Review* 21 (1968): 651.
Evans, Robert C. *Jonson, Lipsius, and the Politics of Renaissance Stoicism.* Durango, Colo.: Longwood Academic Press, 1992.
Feeney, D. C. *The Gods in Epic: Poets and Critics of the Classical Tradition.* Oxford: Oxford University Press, 1991.
Fergusson, Francis. *The Idea of a Theater.* Princeton, N.J.: Princeton University Press, 1949.
Fisch, Harold. *Hamlet and the Word: The Covenant Pattern in Shakespeare.* New York: Ungar Press, 1971.
Fletcher, Angus. *The Prophetic Moment: An Essay on Spenser.* Chicago: University of Chicago Press, 1971.
Flynn, Dennis. *John Donne and the Ancient Catholic Nobility.* Bloomington: Indiana University Press, 1995.
Frontain, R. J., and F. M. Malzeppi, eds. *John Donne's Religious Imagination.* Conway: University of Central Arkansas Press, 1995.
Frost, Kate G. *Holy Delight: Typology, Numerology, and Autobiography in Donne's "Devotions Upon Emergent Occasions."* Princeton, N.J.: Princeton University Press, 1990.

Frye, Roland M. *The Renaissance Hamlet: Issues and Responses in 1600*. Princeton, N.J.: Princeton University Press, 1984.

———. *Shakespeare and Christian Doctrine*. Princeton, N.J.: Princeton University Press, 1963.

Garber, Marjorie. *Shakespeare's Ghost Writers: Literature as Uncanny Causality*. London: Methuen, 1986.

George, Charles H., and Katherine George. *The Protestant Mind of the English Reformation, 1570–1640*. Princeton, N.J.: Princeton University Press, 1961.

Glendinning, Simon, ed. *Arguing with Derrida*. Oxford: Blackwell, 2001.

Gless, Darryl J. *Interpretation and Theology in Spenser*. Cambridge: Cambridge University Press, 1994.

Goldberg, S. L. "Folly into Crime: The Catastrophe of *Volpone*." *Modern Language Quarterly* 20 (1959): 223.

Greenblatt, Stephen J. "The False Ending in *Volpone*." *Journal of English and Germanic Philology* 75 (1976): 90.

———. *Hamlet in Purgatory*. Princeton, N.J.: Princeton University Press, 2001.

Gregerson, Linda. *The Reformation of the Subject: Spenser, Milton, and the English Protestant Epic*. Cambridge: Cambridge University Press, 1995.

Guibbory, Achsah. *Ceremony and Community from Herbert to Milton*. Cambridge: Cambridge University Press, 1998.

Halpern, Richard. *The Poetics of Primitive Accumulation: English Renaissance Culture and the Genealogy of Capital*. Ithaca, N.Y.: Cornell University Press, 1991.

Hartman, Geoffrey H. "The Interpreter's Freud." Reprinted in Hartman, *Easy Pieces*. New York: Columbia University Press, 1985.

Hartman, Geoffrey H., and Sanford Budick, eds. *Midrash and Literature*. New Haven: Yale University Press, 1986.

Haydn, Hiram. *The Counter-Renaissance*. New York: Grove Press, 1960.

Haynes, Jonathan. *The Social Relations of Jonson's Theatre*. Cambridge: Cambridge University Press, 1992.

Herrick, Marvin T. *Italian Comedy in the Renaissance*. Urbana: University of Illinois Press, 1960.

Higginson, James J. *Spenser's Shepherd's Calendar*. New York: Columbia University Press, 1912.

Holmer, Joan O. *"The Merchant of Venice": Choice, Hazard, and Consequence*. Basingstoke: Macmillan Press, 1995.

———. "When Jacob Graz'd his Uncle Laban's Sheep: A New Source for *The Merchant of Venice*." *Shakespeare Quarterly* 36 (1985): 64–65.

Hume, Anthea. *Edmund Spenser: Protestant Poet*. Cambridge: Cambridge University Press, 1984.

Huntley, Frank L. *Bishop J. Hall and Protestant Meditation in Seventeenth-*

Century England. Binghamton, N.Y.: Center for Medieval and Early Renaissance Studies, 1981.
Jackson, Gabriele B. *Vision and Judgment in Ben Jonson's Drama.* New Haven: Yale University Press, 1968.
Jensen, Eijner J. *Ben Jonson's Comedies on the Modern Stage.* Ann Arbor: University of Michigan Press, 1985.
Johnson, Jeffrey. *The Theology of John Donne.* Cambridge: D. S. Brewer, 1999.
Jones, Ernest. *Hamlet and Oedipus.* New York: Methuen, 1949.
Jones, Norman. *God and the Moneylenders.* Oxford: Basil Blackwell, 1989.
Kaske, Carol V. *Spenser and Biblical Poetics.* Ithaca, N.Y.: Cornell University Press, 1999.
Kay, W. Daniel. *Ben Jonson: A Literary Life.* Basingstoke: Macmillan Press, 1995.
Kernan, Alvin. *The Plot of Satire.* New Haven: Yale University Press, 1965.
King, John N. *Spenser's Poetry and the Reformation Tradition.* Princeton, N.J.: Princeton University Press, 1990.
Knight, G. Wilson. *The Wheel of Fire: Interpretations of Shakespearean Tragedy.* New York: Meridian Books, 1957.
Knoll, Robert E. *Ben Jonson's Plays.* Lincoln: University of Nebraska Press, 1964.
Kott, Jan. *Shakespeare, Our Contemporary.* Translated by B. Taborski. London: Methuen, 1964.
Landrum, Grace. "Spenser's Use of the Bible and His Alleged Puritanism." *PMLA* 41 (1926): 517.
Leggatt, Alexander. *Ben Jonson: His Vision and His Art.* London: Methuen, 1981.
Levin, Harry. *The Question of Hamlet.* New York: Compass Books, 1961.
Lewalski, Barbara K. "Biblical Allusion and Allegory in *The Merchant of Venice.*" *Shakespeare Quarterly* 13 (1962): 327.
———. *Donne's "Anniversaries" and the Poetry of Praise: The Creation of a Symbolic Mode.* Princeton, N.J.: Princeton University Press, 1973.
———. *Protestant Poetics and the Seventeenth-Century Religious Lyric.* Princeton, N.J.: Princeton University Press, 1979.
Lewis, C. S. *The Allegory of Love: A Study in Medieval Tradition.* Oxford: Oxford University Press, 1958.
Loewenstein, Joseph. *Ben Jonson and Possessive Authorship.* Cambridge: Cambridge University Press, 2002.
Lyne, Raphael. *Ovid's Changing Worlds: English Metamorphoses, 1567–1632.* Oxford: Oxford University Press, 2001.
MacDonald, Michael, and Terence R. Murphy. *Sleepless Souls: Suicide in Early Modern England.* Oxford: Oxford University Press, 1990.

Martz, Louis L. *The Poetry of Meditation*. New Haven: Yale University Press, 1962.
McLuskie, Kathleen. *Renaissance Dramatists*. New York: Harvester Press, 1989.
Michelson, Hijman. *The Jew in Early English Literature*. Amsterdam: H. J. Paris, 1926.
Minois, Georges. *History of Suicide: Voluntary Death in Western Culture*. Translated by Lydia G. Cochrane. Baltimore: Johns Hopkins University Press, 1995.
Monsarrat, Gilles D. *Light from the Porch: Stoicism and English Renaissance Literature*. Paris: Didier-Erudition, 1984.
Mueller, William R. *John Donne, Preacher*. Princeton, N.J.: Princeton University Press, 1962.
Nelson, Benjamin. *The Idea of Usury*. Princeton, N.J.: Princeton University Press, 1949.
Newman, Karen. *Fashioning Femininity and English Renaissance Drama*. Chicago: University of Chicago Press, 1991.
Oliver, P. M. *Donne's Religious Writing: A Discourse of Feigned Devotion*. London: Longman, 1997.
Padelford, F. M. "Spenser and the Theology of Calvin." *Modern Philology* 12 (1914): 1.
Panofsky, E. *Renaissance and Renascences in Western Art*. New York: Harper & Row, 1972.
Papazian, Mary A., ed. *John Donne and the Protestant Reformation: New Perspectives*. Detroit: Wayne State University Press, 2003.
Parker, R. B. "*Volpone* in Performance, 1921–1972." *Renaissance Drama*, n.s. 9 (1978): 147.
———. "*Volpone* and Reynard the Fox." *Renaissance Drama*, n.s. 7 (1976): 3.
Partridge, Edward. *The Broken Compass*. New York: Columbia University Press, 1958.
Pettet, E. C. "*The Merchant of Venice* and the Problem of Usury." *Essays and Studies* 31 (1945): 19.
Plottel, J. P., and H. Charney, eds. *Intertextuality: New Perspectives in Criticism*. New York: New York Literary Forum, 1978.
Praz, Mario. *The Flaming Heart*. New York: Norton Library, 1973.
Prosser, Eleanor. *Hamlet and Revenge*. Stanford, Calif.: Stanford University Press, 1967.
Radcliffe, David H. *Forms of Reflection: Genre and Culture in Meditational Writing*. Baltimore: Johns Hopkins University Press, 1993.
Riggs, David. *Ben Jonson: A Life*. Cambridge, Mass.: Harvard University Press, 1987.
Rist, J. M. *Stoic Philosophy*. Cambridge: Cambridge University Press, 1969.

Sandbach, H. F. *The Stoics.* Bristol: Bristol Press, 1989.
Sanders, Julie, Kate Chedgzoy, and Susan Wiseman, eds. *Refashioning Ben Jonson.* New York: St. Martin's Press, 1998.
Scheve, D. A. "Jonson's *Volpone* and Traditional Fox Lore." *Review of English Studies,* n.s. 1 (1950): 242.
Sellin, Paul R. *John Donne and the "Calvinist" Views of Grace.* Amsterdam: VU Boekhandel, 1983.
Seznec, Jean. *The Survival of the Pagan Gods.* Princeton, N.J.: Princeton University Press, 1972.
Shaheen, Naseeb. *Biblical References in "The Faerie Queene."* Memphis: Memphis State University Press, 1978.
Shami, Jeanne. *John Donne and Conformity in Crisis in the Late Jacobean Pulpit.* Cambridge: D. S. Brewer, 2003.
Shapiro, James. *Shakespeare and the Jews.* New York: Columbia University Press, 1996.
Sinsheimer, Hermann. *Shylock: The History of a Character.* New York: Citadel Press, 1964.
Southern, A. C. *Elizabethan Recusant Prose, 1559–1582.* London: Sands, 1950.
Stachniewski, John. "John Donne: The Despair of the Holy Sonnets." *Journal of English Literary History* 48 (1981): 690.
Stevenson, Laura. *Praise and Paradox: Merchants and Craftsmen in Elizabethan Popular Literature.* Cambridge: Cambridge University Press, 1984.
Stone, Lawrence. *The Crisis of the Aristocracy, 1558–1641.* Oxford: Oxford University Press, 1967.
Tawney, R. H. *Religion and the Rise of Capitalism.* Harmondsworth: Penguin, 1948. Originally published 1922.
Tiffany, Grace. *Erotic Beasts and Social Monsters: Shakespeare, Jonson, and Comic Androgyny.* Newark: University of Delaware Press, 1995.
Van Laan, Thomas F. "John Donne's *Devotions* and the Jesuit Spiritual Exercise." *Studies in Philology* 60 (1963): 191.
Watson, Robert N. *Ben Jonson's Parodic Strategy.* Cambridge, Mass.: Harvard University Press, 1987.
———. *The Rest Is Silence: Death as Annihilation in the English Renaissance.* Berkeley and Los Angeles: University of California Press, 1994.
Wheeler, Thomas, ed. *The Merchant of Venice: Critical Essays.* New York: Garland Press, 1991.
Whitaker, Virgil. *The Religious Basis of Spenser's Thought.* Stanford, Calif.: Stanford University Press, 1950.
White, Helen C. *English Devotional Literature [Prose] 1600–1640.* Madison: University of Wisconsin Press, 1931.

———. *Social Criticism in Popular Religious Literature of the Sixteenth Century.* New York: Octagon Press, 1973.

Whitman, Jon. "The Body and the Struggle for the Soul of Romance." In *The Body and the Soul in Medieval Literature,* ed. Piero Boitani and Anna Torti. Cambridge: Cambridge University Press, 1999.

Williams, Kathleen. *Spenser's "Faerie Queene": The World of Glass.* London: Routledge & Kegan Paul, 1966.

Wilson, J. Dover. *What Happens in "Hamlet."* Cambridge: Cambridge University Press, 1960.

Wind, Edgar. *Pagan Mysteries in the Renaissance.* New York: W. W. Norton, 1967.

Winstanley, Lilian. "Spenser and Puritanism." *Modern Language Quarterly* 3 (1900): 6.

Wood, Rufus. *Metaphor and Belief in "The Faerie Quene."* Basingstoke: Macmillan, 1997.

Young, R. V. *Doctrine and Devotion in Seventeenth-Century Poetry.* Suffolk: Boydell and Brewer, 2000.

Zacher, C. K. *Curiosity and Pilgrimage: The Literature of Discovery in Fourteenth-Century England.* Baltimore: Johns Hopkins University Press, 1976.

Index

Aaron (Herbert), 172–73
Abraham, 108–10, 115
Abraham Sacrifiant (Bèze), 115
Acolastus (Gnaphaeus), 139
Adelman, Janet, 42
Aeneas, 119
afterlife: Donne and, 67–70; in *Hamlet*, 55–56, 63–64, 68–70, 77, 79
Agass, Edward, 48–49
Albricus, 95
Alchemist, The (Jonson), 151
allegory: Protestantism and, 127–31; scriptural interpretation and, 127–29; in Spenser's *Faerie Queene*, 127, 131
Ambassadors, The (Holbein), 67
ambivalence, 82–84
Amphitryon (Plautus), 140
Andreasen, N. J. C., 177
Andrewes, Lancelot, 129, 204, 230n48
angels, 100
Anglican church, 116, 160, 209. See also Church of England
Annals (Tacitus), 50
Antony and Cleopatra (Shakespeare), 60
Apologie for the Schoole of Abuse (Gosson), 129–31
aporia: deconstruction and, ix, xii, 213, 217; in *Hamlet*, 41, 81–85
Aquinas, Thomas, 53, 174

Arguing with Derrida (Glendenning), 217
Aristotle, 45
Arnolfini Marriage, The (Van Eyck), 66
Arraignment and Conviction of Usury (Mosse), 21, 31
Ars Moriendi, 189
art, 216–17
Arthur, King, 118, 120–21
Art of Meditation (Rogers), 197
Ascham, Roger, 139
ataraxia, 44, 52
atheism, 56
audience: of *Hamlet*, 79–80; of *Volpone*, 135, 144–45, 149, 153–54, 156. See also Elizabethan audience; Jacobean audience
August (Limbourg brothers), 40
Augustine, Saint, 45, 58, 108, 177

"Bad Quarto," 55
Bakhtin, Mikhail M., x–xii, 138, 169, 219n3
Bale, John, 114, 154
Barber of Seville (Rossini), 144
Barish, Jonas, 136, 154
Barkan, Leonard, 97
Barthes, Roland, x
"Batter my heart" (Donne), 182
Baum, Helena, 146
Baxter, Richard, 190, 197

249

Beaurline, Lester, 136, 146
Beecher, William, 15
Berger, Harry, 103
Bernard, Richard, 26
Bernard of Clairvaux, 122
Bertram, Master, 9
Betrayal scenes, 9
Bèze, Theodore de, 115
Biathanatos (Donne), 57–58
Bible: allegorical interpretation of, 127–29; *The Faerie Queene* and, 87–93, 98–99; *The Merchant of Venice* and, 1–2; midrashic interpretation of, 213–15; suicide prohibited in, 51; in vernacular usage, 92
bigamy, 111
Birth of Venus, The (Botticelli), 100–101
Boas, F. S., 146, 165
Boccaccio, Giovanni, 94–95
Boethius, Anicius Manlius Severinus, 45
Booke of Honor and Armes (Segar), 53
Book of Prayer and Meditation (Granada), 188–89
Boron, Robert de, 119–20
Botticelli, Sandro, 100–101
Bourne, Immanuel, 23
Braden, Gordon, 51, 224n18
Bradley, A. C., 42–43, 72
Brome, "Sacrifice of Isaac," 108
Brooks, Cleanth, 83
Brown, J. R., 31
Browne, Thomas, 59, 189
Brutus, Marcus Junius, 49
Brutus of Troy, 119
Bucer, Martin, 19
Buckhurst, Lord, 166
Bull, Henry, 202
Burden, Chris, 216
Burghley, Lord, 15
Burks, Deborah, 162

Calderwood, James, 41, 81
Calidore, 118
"Calling," 195
Calvin, John, 19, 49–50, 110–11, 127–28, 195–96
Cambridge University, 164–66
Campbell, Douglas, 158–59
Canterbury Tales (Chaucer), 40
capitalism, 152
Carey, John, 178

Cary, Elizabeth, 115, 229n33
Case of Conscience, A, the Greatest that ever was (Perkins), 195
casuistry, 180–82, 205–07
casus, 19
Catholic Church: and *concetto* (dazzling wit), 206; death's significance for, 199–200; devotional manuals of, 171, 173, 178, 182–89, 193, 197–98, 202–03, 205, 208–09; Donne and, 174–211; and fame, 66; Jonson and, 160; legitimacy of, 125–26; and salvation, 194, 197–200; Spenser's hostility toward, 116; suicide prohibited by, 59; and trade and banking, 18–19; and vocation, 121
Cato, Publius Valerius, 23–24, 45, 46, 49, 58–59
Catullus, Gaius Valerius, 147
Cave, Terence, 203
Caxton, William, 155
Cecchi, Giovan Maria, 143
Cecil, Robert, 166
centrifugal factors, x–xi, xiii, 145, 209
centripetal factors, x–xiii, 145, 209
Charon, Pierre, 59
Chaucer, Geoffrey, 40, 122, 125
Chester, Mary, 112
Christ, 5–6, 12, 27, 35
Christianity: conversion of Jews to, 7; devil in, 5; devotional practice in, 171–72; versus Hebraic legalism, 2–3, 10–14; paganism and, 93–101, 117–18, 129–31; in Shakespeare's works, 2; and Stoicism, 48, 54; and suffering, 51–54, 203; suicide prohibited by, 54–58, 61–64; theater and, 165–66; trade and, 27, 29–35; and usury, 16–18; in *Volpone*, 162–63, 168. *See also* Catholic Church; Protestantism
Christians Watch, The (Leigh), 56
Christian-Terence plays, 139
Chrysippus, 47
Church of England, 61. *See also* Anglican church
Cicero, Marcus Tullius, 46, 49, 50, 55
Cimabue, 100
class, xi
classical mythology: Christianity and, 93–101, 117–18, 129–31; in Spenser's *Faerie Queene*, 89–92, 98–99, 101–07, 120–21, 133

Cleanthes, 49
Coeur, Jacques, 18
Coleridge, Samuel Taylor, 39, 44
comedy: as fertility rite, 141–42; Jonson on, 160; morality and, 137–39, 232n5; Renaissance, 232n5; Roman, 139–40. See also Italian comedy
Comedy of Errors, The (Shakespeare), 140
Commedia dell'Arte. See Italian comedy
commerce. See trade
Complaints (Spenser), 88
concetto (dazzling wit), 206
Concordia Discordantium Canonum, 16–17
Consolation of Philosophy (Boethius), 45
Constitutions, Anglican, 61
Conway, John, 196
Corona, La (Donne), 176
Correggio, 97
Cotton, John, 121
Council of Trent, 174
Council of Vienne, 17
Cromwell, Oliver, 92
cuckolded husband, 141–43, 144–48
Cupid, 100, 102

Danaë (Titian), 97
da Vinci, Leonardo. See Leonardo da Vinci
death: Catholic view of, 199–200; deconstruction and, 209–10; Donne and, 67–70, 84, 184, 201, 210; in *Hamlet*, 43, 68–71, 73–74, 79–80, 85; Mannerist attitude toward, 66–68; Protestant view of, 199–200; Renaissance attitude toward, 65–71; Stoicism and, 47–49, 55
De Clementia (Seneca), 50
De constantia (Lipsius), 54
deconstruction: and *aporia*, ix, xii, 36, 41, 213, 217; and death, 209–10; and *Hamlet*, 73; and indeterminacy, 214–16; and intertextuality, 132–33, 169; and Midrash, 213–15; vs. univocal interpretations, 82–84, 213; and *Volpone*, 169
Deconstruction and Criticism (Hartman), 132

Defence of Death, The (Du Plessis-Mornay), 49
De finibus (Cicero), 49
De la Sagesse (Charon), 59
De Man, Paul, 36, 73
Dent, Arthur, 195, 199
De pace fidei (Nicholas of Cusa), 94
Derrida, Jacques, 36, 73, 132–33, 209–10, 216
Dessen, Alan, 136
devil: in Christianity, 5; Hamlet's ghost as, 77–79; Judas Iscariot as, 9; Shylock as, 5, 7–9, 35; usury and, 27
devotional literature, 109
devotional manuals: Catholic, 171, 173, 178, 182–89, 193, 197–98, 202–03, 205, 208–09; Protestant, 171, 173, 187, 192–93, 195–96, 199–203, 207–09
Devotions (Donne), 177
dialogic imagination, x–xii
Dialogues of the Dead (Lucian), 151
Discourse on Usury, A (Wilson), 21
Disobedient Child (Ingelend), 139
Dod, John, 111
Doerksen, Daniel W., 175
Dollenkopf, Conrad, 127
Dolman, John, 49, 55
Donizetti, Gaetano, 144
Donne, John: "Batter my heart," 182; *Biathanatos*, 57–58; and casuistry, 180–82, 205–07; Catholic Church attacked by, 179; Catholic sources for, 174–211; conflicting religious elements in, 180, 184, 209–11; conversion of, 178–79; *La Corona*, 176; and death, 67–70, 84, 184, 201, 210; *Devotions*, 177; *The Flea*, 191; Fourth Prebend Sermon, 175; *Goodfriday 1613, Riding Westward*, 203; and hell, 202–03; *Holy Sonnet III*, 174; *Holy Sonnet VII*, 186–87; *Hymne to God my God, in my Sicknesse*, 201; *Ignatius His Conclave*, 179; and logic, 191–93; *Meditations*, 181–82, 191, 206–07; and nature, 190–93; passing-bell meditation of, 204, 206–07; Protestant sources for, 174–77; *Pseudo-Martyr*, 178–79; on relics, 154; and religious controversy, 176–77; and religious ecstasy, 97–98; and salvation, 199,

208; sermons of, 176, 181, 205–08; and sex, 84; structure of works of, 177; and suicide, 57–58; and theology, 179; "unsettled conscience" theory about, 178–79, 236n16
Don Pasquale (Donizetti), 144
double entendres, 83
Drake, Francis, 25
drama, xi–xii, 43
Duncan, Douglas, 149
Du Plessis-Mornay, Philippe, 48–49
Dutch painting, 109–10

East India Company, 24
Edward, King, 20
Ehrenberg, Richard, 150
El Greco, 185–86
Eliot, T. S., 39, 171
Elizabeth, Queen, 24, 107, 129
Elizabethan audience, 7–8, 48–51
Ellis-Fermor, Una, 136
Empson, William, 83, 103, 126, 137–38, 232n5
Enck, John, 137
England, trade in, 24–25
English Gentleman (Hogenberg), 67
epic poetry, xi–xii
Epictetus, 46–47
Erasmus, Desiderius, 22, 49
Essex, Earl of, 50
Eunuchus (Plautus), 139
Excellent Discours de la vie et de la mort (Du Plessis-Mornay), 48–49
Eyck, Jan van, *The Arnolfini Marriage*, 66

Faerie Queene, The (Spenser): allegory in, 127; Bible and, 87–93, 98–99, 103–07; British ancestry in, 118–19; Christian theme of, 103, 131–33; classical allusions in, 89–92, 98–99, 101–07, 120–21, 133; classical form of, 103; classical virtues in, 120–21, 132; comic theme in, 144; and contemporary world, 121–26; disguise as theme in, 122–26; intertextuality in, 132–33; and suicide, 51, 58; syncretism of, 87, 133; and truth, 125–26
faith, 194–97, 201
fame, 65–66, 69–74, 80–81
fate, 46, 48
felicity, 80

Fergusson, Francis, 42
Ficino, Marsilio, 95
Fiedler, Leslie, 6
Fisch, Harold, 7
Flea, The (Donne), 191
Fletcher, Angus, 90–91
Flynn, Dennis, 178
Fourth Prebend Sermon (Donne), 175
fox, 155
Foxe, John, 117
Freud, Sigmund, 5, 42, 82–84
Fried, Michael, 216
Frobisher, Martin, 25
Frost, Kate, 177
Frye, Northrop, 141, 167
Frye, Roland, 62–63

Gager, William, 165–66
Galahad, 120
Garber, Marjorie, 73–74
Gardner, Helen, 177
Garnet, Father, 180, 206
Gascoigne, George, 139
Genealogica of the Pagan Gods (Boccaccio), 94–95
Geoffrey of Monmouth, 119
George, Charles, 27, 179
George, Katherine, 27, 179
Gesner, Conrad, 154
Gesta Romanorum, 11
Geween, Barry, 216
Ghiberti, Lorenzo, 66
Gilby, Anthony, 117
Giorgio, Francesco di, 97
Glass of Government (Gascoigne), 139
Gless, Darryl, 105–06
Gnaphaeus, 139
God, 3, 96, 98–99, 129
Godly Mans Guide, The (Bourne), 23
gods, 94–101, 130–31
Gods Made Flesh, The (Barkan), 97
Goethe, Johann Wolfgang von, 39
Goldberg, S. L., 149
Golding, Arthur, 117–18, 127
Goodfriday 1613, Riding Westward (Donne), 203
Gorboduc (Sackville and Norton), 40
Gosson, Stephen, 129–31
Gozzoli, Benozzo, 122
Granada, Luis de, 188–89
Granville-Barker, Harley, 40
Gratian (Benedictine monk), 16–17
Graves, Robert, 83

Great Lakes Shakespeare Festival, 159
Greenberg, Clement, 216
Greenblatt, Stephen, 63, 70, 157
Gresham, Thomas, 24, 67, 150
Grierson, Herbert, 171
Groto, Luigi, 143
Guinevere, Queen, 120
Guthrie, Tyrone, 135–36, 158

halakhah, 215
Hali Maidenhead, 163
Hall, Joseph, 177, 189–90, 196, 204
Hall, Peter, 136, 159
hamartia, 45
Hamlet (Shakespeare), 39–85; afterlife in, 77, 79; audience of, 79–80; death in, 43, 68–71, 73–74, 79–80, 85; fame in, 69–74, 80–81; Ghost in, 75, 77–79; Hamlet's character in, 45, 65; Hamlet's madness in, 71–72; Hamlet's monologue in, 51–56, 64; Horatio in, 43–45; humanism of, 39–41; human nature in, 68–69, 85; memory in, 73–76; mother's remarriage in, 42–43, 72–73; mystery of, 39–42, 81, 84; Ophelia in, 61–63; resolution of, 81, 84; Stoicism in, 44–45, 51–55, 80; and suicide, 51–57, 61–64
Handelman, Susan, 214
Harrison, William, 27
Hartman, Geoffrey, 82, 132, 213
Harvey, Gabriel, 68, 117
Hawkins, John, 24
Haydn, Hiram, 52
Hebrew language and culture, 108–11
Hegel, G. W. F., 73
Heidegger, Martin, 209
hell, 199–200, 202–03
Henry II, King, 120
Henry V (Shakespeare), 40, 66
Henry VIII, King, 20, 92, 111, 114
Heptameron (Symson), 192
Herbert, George, 172–73, 190
Herford, C. H., 136, 151, 152
heteroglossia, x, xi–xii, 169
Heywood, Jasper, 50
Higginson, J. J., 116
Historia Animalium (Gesner), 154
Historie of Jacob and Esau, The (Udall), 114
History of Reynard the Fox, The, 155
Histriomastix (Prynne), 131
Hobson, Harold, 137

Hogenberg, Remigius, 67
Holbein, Hans, 67
Holmer, Joan, 31
Holy Grail, 119–20
Holy Sonnet III (Donne), 174
Holy Sonnet VII (Donne), 186–87
Holy Trinity (Masaccio), 66, 101
humanism, 39–41, 65
Hume, Anthea, 116–17
Humphrey, Laurence, 117
Huntley, Frank, 175, 204
Hymne to God my God, in my Sicknesse (Donne), 201

iconoclasm, 129
Ignatius His Conclave (Donne), 179
Imitatio Christi, 189
immortality, 65–66
Ingelend, Thomas, 139
Institutes (Calvin), 50
Integumenta super Ovidium Metamorphoseos (John of Garland), 127
interpretation: ambivalence in, 82–84; indeterminacy of, 214–16; Midrash and, 213–15; multiplicity in, 84, 214; univocal, 82–84, 213. *See also* deconstruction
Interpretation of Dreams, The (Freud), 82
intertextuality, 132–33, 169
Italian comedy, 138, 140–41, 143, 145, 147, 163, 167

Jackson, Gabriele B., 137
Jacob (biblical), 31–32
Jacobean audience, 139–40, 153–54
James I, King, 175, 198–99
Jerome, Saint, 17, 22, 45
Jesuit College, 188
Jesuit devotional practice, 177–79, 182–89. *See also* Loyola, Ignatius
Jesus. *See* Christ
Jew of Malta, The (Marlowe), 7, 35
Job, 59
John of the Cross, Saint, 174, 187–88
John of Garland, 127
Johnson, Samuel, 83
Jonson, Ben: academic aspirations of, 164–67; *The Alchemist*, 151; capitalism in works of, 152; character of, 159; Christianity of, 160; on comedy, 160; imitation by, of predecessors, 140–41; on

254 Index

morality of drama, 160–61; and Tacitus's *Annals*, 50; *Volpone*, 25, 125, 135–70
Joseph d'Arimathie (Boron), 119–20
Joseph of Arimathea, 119–20
Jove, 98–99, 102
Judas Iscariot, 9–10
Julius Caesar (Shakespeare), 49, 50
Julius II, Pope, 66
Jupiter, 96, 98–99, 102, 129

Kadushin, Max, 214
Kaske, Carol V., 227n6
Kay, Daniel, 145–46
Kernan, Alvin, 151–52
King, John N., 227n6
King Lear (Shakespeare), xii, 60–61
Knight, Wilson, 43, 65, 70
Knights, L. C., 152
Knights of the Round Table, 119–20
Knoll, Robert E., 149
Kott, Jan, 44
Kyd, Thomas, 71
Kyng John, 114, 154

Laban, 31–32
Lacan, Jacques, 42
Lancelot, 120
Landrum, Grace, 92–93
"Language of Paradox, The" (Brooks), 83
Last Supper, The (Bertram), 9
Law, New versus Old, 2–4, 10–14, 36
Lawrence, D. H., 83
Leicester, Earl of, 117, 118
Leigh, William, 56
Leonardo da Vinci, 39–41, 100, 101
Leo X, Pope, 18
Levant Company, 24
Levin, Harry, 71
Lewalski, Barbara, 2–5, 173–75
Lewis, C. S., 43
Life (Suso), 177
light, 185–86
Limbourg brothers, 40
Lipsius, Justus, 50, 54
literary analysis. *See* interpretation
Littlewood, Joan, 136
Lodge, Thomas, 49
logic, 191–93
London Company of Merchants, 22
Lorenzo the Magnificent, 18
love-hate relationships, 83
Loyola, Ignatius, *Spiritual Exercises*, 171, 182–83, 185, 188, 198, 202,

205, 208. *See also* Jesuit devotional practice
Lucian, 151
Luther, Martin, 19, 25, 111, 128, 180, 194

Macbeth (Shakespeare), 53, 60
Machiavelli, Niccolò, 141–43, 167
Maimonides, 215
Mandragola, La (Machiavelli), 141–43
Mannerism, 66–68, 185–86
manuals, devotional. *See* devotional manuals
Manuductio (Lipsius), 54
Marcus Aurelius, 46, 48
Mariology, 176
Marlowe, Christopher: *The Jew of Malta*, 7, 35; *Tamburlaine the Great*, 66, 147; *The Tragicall History of the Life and Death of Doctor Faustus*, 58
Martial, 131
Martz, Louis, 171–73, 177, 208
Marvell, Andrew, 190
Marx, Groucho, 159
Mary. *See* Virgin Mary
Mary Queen of Scots, 70–71
Masaccio, 66, 101
material world. *See* nature; temporal world
Mather, Cotton, 113–14
Measure for Measure (Shakespeare), 140
Medici family, 18
meditation. *See* devotional manuals
Meditation of Death (Symson), 200
Meditations (Donne), 181–82, 191, 206–07
Meditations (Marcus Aurelius), 48
Meditations (Sales), 198
Meditations on the Mysteries of our Holie Faith (Puente), 189
Meditations and Praiers (Conway), 196
Melancthon, Philipp, 19
Meliboeus, 118
memory, 172
Menaechmi (Plautus), 140
Mendieta, Ana, 216
Mercer, Peter, 225n23
Merchant Adventurers, 222n35
Merchant of Venice, The (Shakespeare), 1–37; Antonio in, 4–6, 31–32; Bassanio in, 33–35;

biblical allusions in, 1–2;
Christians as villains in, 7;
crucifixion theme in, 5, 9–10;
opposites conflated in, 35–37;
Shylock in, 2–13, 31–35;
subversive aspects of, 14–37;
theme of, 2–4, 13–14, 36–37; title
of, 35, 222n37; trade in, 27–37;
traditional aspects of, 1–14; usury
in, 16, 27–37
Metamorphoses (Ovid), 117–18, 124,
131
metaphysical poetry, 171–72, 173–74
Michelangelo, 66
Midrash, 213–15
Midrash and Literature
(Hartman and Budick), 213
Midrash Rabbah, 214–15
Midsummer Night's Dream, A
(Shakespeare), 57, 140
Miller, J. Hillis, ix, 210–11, 213, 217
Milligan, John, 159
Milton, John, 106–07
Mitchell, Jonathan, 113
Mona Lisa (Leonardo da Vinci), 39–41
monotheism, 94
Monsarrat, Gilles D., 224n18, 225n23
Montaigne, Michel de, 58–59
morality: comedy and, 137–39,
232n5; Jonson on drama and,
160–62; in Roman comedy, 139;
in *Volpone*, 136–38, 149–50
More, Thomas, 108
mortal existence. *See* temporal world
Morton, Thomas, 195
Moses (Michelangelo), 66
Mosse, Miles, 21, 31
Mulcaster, Richard, 109, 139
Muscovy Company, 24
mystery cycles, 7–8
Mythographus III (Albricus), 95

nature, 189–93. *See also* temporal
world
Nelson, Brent, 203–04
Neoplatonism, 94–96, 98–100, 117,
130–31
Neo-Stoicism, 54
Nero, 46, 49, 50
New Criticism, 82–84
New Historicism, 220n7
Nice Wanton, 139
Nicholas, Pope, 94
Nicholas of Cusa, 94–95
Nicholas V, Pope, 18

Niobe Dissolv'd into a Nilus
(Stafford), 59–60
Nitsch, Herman, 216
Norton, Thomas, 40
novel, x–xi

Old Testament, 107–16, 112–13,
127–28, 200–201
Oliver, P. M., 236n16
Ophelia, 61–63
Ordo de Ysaac et Rebecca, 114
Ortiz, Rafael, 216
Othello (Shakespeare), 60, 125
*Overthrow of Stage-Playes, The, By
the way of controversie betwixt
D. Gager and D. Rainoldes*
(Rainoldes), 166
Ovid, 95, 117–18, 124, 131
Ovide Moralisé, 96, 127
Owl, The (L'assiuolo) (Cecchi), 143
Oxford University, 164–67

Padelford, F. M., 116
paganism. *See* classical
mythology
Pallavicino, Horatio, 15
Papazian, Mary, 175
Paradise Lost (Milton), 106–07
Parfitt, George, 160
Parratt, Henry, 141
Partridge, Edward, 167
Pastorella, 119
Patterson, Annabel, 178
Paul, Saint, 52, 87, 177, 180
Paul III, Pope, 188
Pecorone, Il, 11
Pepys, Samuel, 135
Perkins, William, 24, 111, 166, 184,
195
Perugino, 100
Petronius, 151
Pharisees, 3, 10–13, 109
physical world. *See* nature; temporal
world
Pico della Mirandola, Giovanni, 54,
65, 95
Pineas, Rainer, 136
*Plaine Man's Pathway to Heaven,
The* (Dent), 195
plain style, of preaching, 180, 181
Plato, 95, 129, 161
Plautus, 138–40, 150
pneuma, 47–48
Poel, William, 135
poetry, xi–xii, 171–211

Poetry of Meditation, The (Martz), 171–73
Politica (Lipsius), 54
postfigurations, 112–14, 200–201
postmodernist criticism, ix–x, 216–17
Praz, Mario, 206
predestination, 173–74, 193–94, 197–99
Price, Daniel, 22
Prosser, Eleanor, 52, 224n21
Protestantism: and allegory, 127–31; death's significance for, 199–200; devotional manuals of, 171, 173, 187, 192–93, 195–96, 199–203, 207–09; Donne and, 174–77; metaphysical poetry and, 173–74; and Old Testament, 107–16, 200–201; and salvation, 194–97, 199–201; Spenser and, 115–16; and temporal world, 187, 189–90; trade and, 18–20, 25–27; and vocation, 121; and wealth, 25–27, 111
Protestant Poetics and the Seventeenth-Century Religious Lyric (Lewalski), 173–75
Prynne, William, 131
Pseudo-Martyr (Donne), 178–79
psyche, 47–48. *See also* soul
psychoanalysis, 82
Puente, Luis de la, 189
Punch and Judy, 137
Puritans, 111–14, 116–17, 129, 166
putti, 100

Quakers, 26
Quiney, Richard, 16

Rainoldes, John, 165–66
Ralegh, Walter, 70–71, 120, 132
rape: allegorical interpretation of, 97–98; Elizabethan/Jacobean view of, 162; in *The Faerie Queene*, 98; in *Volpone*, 138, 144–48, 159, 162–63
Rape of Europa paintings, 97
Raphael, 100
rapture, 97–98
Rashi, 215
reason, 191–93
Regulus, Marcus Atilius, 58
relics, 154
Religio Medici (Browne), 59
religion. *See* Catholic Church; Christianity; classical mythology; Protestantism
Rembrandt van Rijn, 109–10
Removal of the Body of St. Mark (Tintoretto), 186
Renaissance: comedy in, 232n5; and death, 65–71; humanism in, 39–41, 65; and immortality through fame, 65–66; Stoicism in, 45–46; trade in, 18–27, 35
Reni, Guido, 97
rent contracts, 18–19
reputation. *See* fame
Resurrection (El Greco), 186
retreats, 185
Reuchlin, Johann, 108–09
revenge, 52–53
Richard III (Shakespeare), 8–9
Richards, I. A., 83
Richardson, Ralph, 135, 137
Riding, Laura, 83
Ridley, Bishop, 129
Riggs, David, 159–60
Rivers, W. H., 83
Robin Hood, 151
Rogers, Richard, 187, 196–97
Roman comedy, 139–40
Romeo and Juliet (Shakespeare), 53, 60
Rosenberg, Harold, 216
Rossini, Gioacchino Antonio, 144
Royal Exchange, 150
Royal Maids of Honor, The (Las Meninas) (Velasquez), 152
Ruth's Recompense (Bernard), 26

Sackville, Thomas, 40
Sacrifice of Abraham (Rembrandt), 109–10
Saints Everlasting Rest (Baxter), 197
Sales, François de, 198
salvation: Catholic view of, 194, 197–200; Donne's view of, 199, 208; Protestant view of, 194–97, 199–201
Sampson, Thomas, 117
Sandys, George, 131
Savile, Henry, 50
Scheve, D. A., 154
Schonaeus, Cornelius, 139–40
Schoole of Abuse (Gosson), 129
Schücking, L. L., 6
scientia, 122

Scofield, Paul, 135, 159
Second Lateran Council, 18
Segar, William, 53
Seneca, Lucius Annaeus, the Younger, 46–52, 59
senex, 141, 144. *See also* cuckolded husband
Seven Sacraments Altarpiece (Van der Weyden), 100
Seven Treatises (Rogers), 187
Seven Types of Ambiguity (Empson), 83
sex, 84, 97. *See also* rape
sfumato, 39
Shaheen, Naseeb, 93
Shakespeare, William: *Antony and Cleopatra*, 60; and characterization, 40; *The Comedy of Errors*, 140; and drama's function, 43; father's death, 68; finances of, 16, 29; *Hamlet*, 39–85; *Henry V*, 40, 66; *Julius Caesar*, 49, 50; *King Lear*, xii, 60–61; *Macbeth*, 53, 60; *Measure for Measure*, 140; *The Merchant of Venice*, 1–37; *A Midsummer Night's Dream*, 57, 140; *Othello*, 60, 125; punning of, 83; religion in works of, 2; *Richard III*, 8–9; *Romeo and Juliet*, 53, 60; suicide in works of, 60–61; and usury, 15–16; *The Winter's Tale*, 137–38
Shakespeare and the Jews (Shapiro), 220n7
Shami, Jeanne, 175–76
Shapiro, James, 220n7
Shepheardes Calendar, The (Spenser), 101, 117
short and pretie Treatise touching the perpetuall Reioyce of the godly, euen in this lyfe, A, 187
Shrewsbury, Lord, 15
Shylock: as devil figure, 5, 7–9, 35; as Judas Iscariot, 9–10, and legalism, 10–13; as Pharisee, 2–3; sympathetic interpretations of, 6–9, 220n7
Sibbes, Richard, 26, 181, 200
Sidney, Lady, 118
Sidney, Philip, 50, 117, 118, 161
Sinsheimer, Hermann, 13
Sixtus IV, Pope, 100
Socrates, 46, 49, 95

soul, 172. *See also* psyche
Soules Conflict (Sibbes), 200
Southern, A. C., 182
Spanish Armada, 24
Spanish Tragedy (Kyd), 71
Speght, Thomas, 68
Spenser, Edmund: and Bible, 88; *Complaints*, 88; *The Faerie Queene*, 51, 58, 87–133, 144; Hebrew studied by, 109; language usage by, 101, 103; and Protestantism, 115–16; and Puritanism, 116–17; *The Shepheardes Calendar*, 101, 117; and suicide, 51, 58
Spiritual Exercises. See Loyola, Ignatius
Stachniewski, John, 174
Stafford, Anthony, *Niobe Dissolv'd into a Nilus*, 59–60
Stevenson, Laura, 23
Stoicism: appeal of, 45–46; Christianity and, 48, 54; and death, 47–49, 55; early, 46; Elizabethan knowledge of, 48–51; and fate, 46, 48; in *Hamlet*, 44–45, 51–55, 80; in Renaissance, 45–46; Roman, 46–48; and suicide, 46–47, 49–52, 54, 58–59
Strauss, Jakob, 19
Stubbes, Philip, 23–24
suffering, 51–54, 203
suicide: biblical prohibition of, 51; Christian prohibition of, 54–58, 61–64; in *Hamlet*, 51–57, 61–64; by mentally deranged, 61–63; official reaction to, 57; in Shakespeare's works, 60–61; Stoicism and, 46–47, 49–52, 54, 58–59
Supper of Trimalchio (Petronius), 151
Suso, Henry, 177
Symson, M. A., 192, 200
Szatek, Karoline, 28, 29

Tacitus, Cornelius, 50
tactile world. *See* temporal world
Tailleped, Noel, 77–78
Tamburlaine the Great (Marlowe), 66, 147
Tawney, R. H., 15, 25, 27
temporal world: Catholic embrace of, 187–88; *The Faerie Queene* and, 121–26; Jesuit withdrawal from,

185–86, 188–89; Protestantism and, 184, 187, 189–90. *See also* nature; wealth
Terence, 138–40
Terentius Christianus (Schonaeus), 140
Teresa of Avila, 188
Thrasea, Paetus, 50
Thraseas (Lipsius), 54
Tintoretto, 185, 186
Titian, 40, 97
trade: Christianity and, 27, 29–35; defense of, 22–23; medieval attitudes toward, 16–17; in *The Merchant of Venice*, 27–37; Protestantism and, 18–20, 25–27; Renaissance, 18–27, 35; usury and, 16, 19–24, 31
tragedy, xi–xii
Tragedy of Mariam, The (Cary), 115
Tragicall History of the Life and Death of Doctor Faustus, The (Marlowe), 58
Traske, John, 112
Treasure, The (Il Thesuro) (Groto), 143
Treatise of Commerce (Wheeler), 23
Treatise of Ghosts (Tailleped), 77–78
Treatise of the Threefolde State of Man, A (Morton), 195
Trent, Council of, 174
Trewin, J. C., 159
truth, 125–26, 192–93
Tusculean Disputations (Cicero), 49
Tyndale, William, 128

Udall, Nicholas, 114
understanding, 172
univocal interpretations, 82–84, 213
Upon the Tolling of a Passing-bell (Hall), 204
Ussher, James, 194
usury: medieval attitudes toward, 16–18; in *The Merchant of Venice*, 16, 27–37; Protestantism and, 19; Shakespeare and, 15–16; sixteenth century context for, 15, 20–27; trade and, 16, 19–24, 31

Van Laan, Thomas F., 177
Velasquez, Diego, 152
vengeance, 52–53
Venus, 99–103
Veronese, 97

Vienne, Council of, 17
Virgin Mary, 99–102, 176
vocation, 121
Volpone (Jonson), 135–70; and academic expectations, 164–65; audience response to, 135, 144–45, 149, 153–54, 156, 158; Christian setting in, 162–63, 168; comic elements in, 144–49, 161–62; conclusion of, 167–69; conflicting elements in, 138, 160–62, 169–70; critics' responses to, 136–38, 145–46, 149, 152, 169; disguise in, 125; entertainers in, 152–53; Mosca in, 155–57; productions of, 135–36, 158–59; rape in, 138, 144–48, 159, 162–63; theatrical sources of, 138–39; on trade, 25; turning point in, 157–64; Volpone's character in, 136–37, 149–55, 169; wealth in, 149–52

Walsingham, Francis, 118
Walton, Izaak, 179
Watson, Robert, 56
wealth: in *The Merchant of Venice*, 27–29; Protestant attitudes toward, 25–27, 111; sixteenth and seventeenth century attitudes toward, 25–27, 150–51; in *Volpone*, 149–52. *See also* trade; usury
Weber Max, 25
Weyden, Rogier van der, 100
Wheeler, John, *Treatise of Commerce*, 23
Whitaker, Virgil, 116
White, Helen C., 109
will, 172
Wilson, J. Dover, 42, 43
Wilson, Thomas, 21
Winstanley, Lilian, 116
Winter's Tale, The (Shakespeare), 137–38
Winthrop, John, 114
Wolfit, Donald, 135, 158
Woolf, Virginia, 83
works, covenant of, 112–13, 194
worldly existence. *See* temporal world

Young, R. V., 174–75
Young Englishman (Titian), 40

Zell, Michael, 110
Zeno, 49